D0088203

Exploring Corpus Linguistics

Routledge Introductions to Applied Linguistics is a series of introductory level textbooks covering the core topics in Applied Linguistics, primarily designed for those entering postgraduate studies and language professionals returning to academic study. The books take an innovative 'practice to theory' approach, with a 'back-to-front' structure. This leads the reader from real-world problems and issues, through a discussion of intervention and how to engage with these concerns, before finally relating these practical issues to theoretical foundations. Additional features include tasks with commentaries, a glossary of key terms, and an annotated further reading section.

Corpus linguistics is a key area of applied linguistics and one of the most rapidly developing. Winnie Cheng's practical approach guides readers in acquiring the relevant knowledge and theories to enable the analysis, explanation and interpretation of language using corpus methods.

Throughout the book practical classroom examples, concordance based analyses and tasks such as designing and conducting mini-projects are used to connect and explain the conceptual and practical aspects of corpus linguistics.

Exploring Corpus Linguistics is an essential textbook for postgraduate/graduate students new to the field and for advanced undergraduates studying English Language and Applied Linguistics.

Winnie Cheng is Professor of English in the Department of English, The Hong Kong Polytechnic University. Her publications include *Intercultural Conversation* (2003), *A Corpus-driven Analysis of Discourse Intonation* (2008), *Professional Communication: Collaboration between academics and practitioners* (2009), and *Language for Professional Communication: Research, practice & training* (2009).

Routledge Introductions to Applied Linguistics

Series editors:

Ronald Carter, *Professor of Modern English Language,*
University of Nottingham, UK

Guy Cook, *Professor of Language and Education*
Open University, UK

Routledge Introductions to Applied Linguistics is a series of introductory level textbooks covering the core topics in Applied Linguistics, primarily designed for those entering postgraduate studies and language professionals returning to academic study. The books take an innovative 'practice to theory' approach, with a 'back-to-front' structure. This leads the reader from real-world problems and issues, through a discussion of intervention and how to engage with these concerns, before finally relating these practical issues to theoretical foundations. Additinal features include tasks with commentaries, a glossary of key terms and an annotated further reading section.

Exploring English Language Teaching
Language in Action
Graham Hall

Exploring Classroom Discourse
Language in Action
Steve Walsh

Exploring Corpus Linguistics
Language in Action
Winnie Cheng

'The innovative approach devised by the series editors will make this series very attractive to students, teacher educators, and even to a general readership, wanting to explore and understand the field of applied linguistics. The volumes in this series take as their starting point the everyday professional problems and issues that applied linguists seek to illuminate. The volumes are authoritatively written, using an engaging 'back-to-front' structure that moves from practical interests to the conceptual bases and theories that underpin applications of practice.'

Anne Burns, *Aston University, UK,*
University of New South Wales, Australia

Exploring Corpus Linguistics

Language in Action

Winnie Cheng

Routledge
Taylor & Francis Group

LONDON AND NEW YORK

First published 2012
by Routledge
2 Park Square, Milton Park, Abingdon, Oxon OX14 4RN

Simultaneously published in the USA and Canada
by Routledge
711 Third Avenue, New York, NY 10017

Routledge is an imprint of the Taylor & Francis Group, an informa business

© 2012 Winnie Cheng

The right of Winnie Cheng to be identified as author of this work has been
asserted by her in accordance with sections 77 and 78 of the Copyright,
Designs and Patents Act 1988.

All rights reserved. No part of this book may be reprinted or reproduced
or utilised in any form or by any electronic, mechanical, or other means,
now known or hereafter invented, including photocopying and recording,
or in any information storage or retrieval system, without permission in
writing from the publishers.

Trademark notice: Product or corporate names may be trademarks or
registered trademarks, and are used only for identification and explanation
without intent to infringe.

British Library Cataloguing in Publication Data
A catalogue record for this book is available from the British Library

Library of Congress Cataloging in Publication Data
Cheng, Winnie.
  Exploring corpus linguistics: language in action/Winnie Cheng.
  p. cm. – (Routledge Introductions to Applied Linguistics)
  Includes bibliographical references and index.
  1. Corpus linguistics.   2. Language and languages – Study and teaching.
  3. Applied linguistics.
  I. Title.
  P126.C68.C54 2011
  410.1'88 – dc22   2011014235

ISBN 13: 978–0–415–58546–0 (hbk)
ISBN 13: 978–0–415–58547–7 (pbk)
ISBN 13: 978–0–203–80263–2 (ebk)

Typeset in Sabon
by Florence Production Ltd, Stoodleigh, Devon

Contents

Series editors' introduction

The *Introducing Applied Linguistics* series

This series provides clear, authoritative, up-to-date overviews of the major areas of applied linguistics. The books are designed particularly for students embarking on masters-level or teacher-education courses, as well as students in the closing stages of undergraduate study. The practical focus will make the books particularly useful and relevant to those returning to academic study after a period of professional practice, and also to those about to leave the academic world for the challenges of language-related work. For students who have not previously studied applied linguistics, including those who are unfamiliar with current academic study in English speaking universities, the books can act as one-step introductions. For those with more academic experience, they can also provide a way of surveying, updating and organising existing knowledge.

The view of applied linguistics in this series follows a famous definition of the field by Christopher Brumfit as:

> The theoretical and empirical investigation of real-world problems in which language is a central issue.
>
> (Brumfit 1995: 27)

In keeping with this broad problem-oriented view, the series will cover a range of topics of relevance to a variety of language related professions. While language teaching and learning rightly remain prominent and will be the central preoccupation of many readers, our conception of the discipline is by no means limited to these areas. Our view is that while each reader of the series will have their own needs, specialities and interests, there is also much to be gained from a broader view of the discipline as a whole. We believe there is much in common between all enquiries into language related problems in the real world, and much to be gained from a comparison of the insights from one area of applied linguistics with another. Our hope therefore is that readers and course designers will not choose only those volumes relating to their own particular interests, but use this series to construct a wider knowledge and understanding of the field, and the many cross-overs and resonances between its various areas. Thus the topics to be covered are wide in range, embracing an exciting mixture of established and new areas of applied linguistic enquiry.

The perspective on applied linguistics in this series

In line with this problem-oriented definition of the field, and to address the concerns of readers who are interested in how academic study can inform their own professional practice, each book follows a structure in marked contrast to the usual movement *from* theory *to* practice. In this series, this usual progression is presented back to front. The argument moves *from* Problems, *through* Intervention, and *only* finally to Theory. Thus each topic begins with a survey of everyday professional problems in the area under consideration, ones which the reader is likely to have encountered. From there it proceeds to a discussion of intervention and engagement with these problems. Only in a final section (either of the chapter or the book as a whole) does the author reflect upon the implications of this engagement for a general understanding of language, drawing out the theoretical implications. We believe this to be a truly *applied* linguistics perspective, in line with definition given above, and one in which engagement with real-world problems is the distinctive feature, and in which professional practice can both inform and draw upon academic understanding.

Support to the reader

Although it is not the intention that the text should be in anyway activity-driven, the pedagogic process is supported by measured guidance to the reader in the form of suggested activities and tasks that raise questions, prompt reflection and seek to integrate theory and practice. Each book also contains a helpful glossary of key terms.

The series complements and reflects the *Routledge Handbook of Applied Linguistics* edited by James Simpson, which conceives and categorises the scope of applied linguistics in a broadly similar way.

Ronald Carter
Guy Cook

Reference

Brumfit, C.J. (1995) 'Teacher professionalism and research' in G. Cook and B. Seidlhofer (eds) *Principle and Practice in Applied Linguistics*. Oxford: Oxford University Press, pp. 27–42.

Note

There is a section of commentaries on a number of the tasks, at the back of the book from p. 199. The (TC) symbol in the margin indicates that there is a commentary on that task.

Acknowledgement

Some of the work described in this book is substantially supported by a grant from the Research Grants Council of the Hong Kong Special Administrative Region (Project No.: G-YG10).

Part I

Problems and practices

1 Introduction

This chapter briefly introduces the reader to corpus linguistics by answering two basic questions and explaining related concepts. The questions addressed are:

- What is a corpus?
- What is corpus linguistics?

What is a corpus?

A corpus is a collection of texts that has been compiled for a particular reason. In other words, a corpus is not a collection of texts regardless of the types of texts collected or, if a variety of text types (i.e., genres) are in the corpus, the relative weightings assigned to each text type. A corpus, then, is a collection of texts based on a set of design criteria, one of which is that the corpus aims to be representative. These design criteria are discussed in detail in Chapter 4, and so here we examine some of the wider issues that have to be thought about and decided upon when building a corpus. In this book, we are interested in how corpus linguists use a corpus, or more than one corpus (i.e., 'corpora'), in their research. This is not to say that only corpus linguists have corpora, or only corpus linguists use corpora in their research. Corpora have been around for a long time, but in the past they could only be searched manually, and so the fact that corpora are now machine-readable has had a tremendous impact on the field.

Corpora are becoming ever larger thanks to the ready availability of electronic texts and more powerful computing resources. For example, the Corpus of Contemporary American English (COCA) contains 410 million words (see http://corpus.byu.edu/coca/) and the British National Corpus (BNC) over 100 million words (see www.natcorp.ox.ac.uk/ or http://corpus.byu.edu.bnc/). Corpora are usually studied by means of computers, although some corpora are designed to allow users to also access individual texts for more qualitative analyses. It would be impossible to search today's large corpora manually, and so the development of fast and reliable corpus linguistic software has gone hand in hand with the growth in corpora. The software can do many things, such as generate word and phrase frequencies lists, identify words that tend to be selected with each other such as *brother* + *sister* and *black* + *white* (termed 'collocates'), and provide a variety of statistical functions that assist the user in deciphering the results of searches. You do not have to compile your own corpus. A number of corpora are available online, or commercially, with built-in software and user-friendly instructions.

Corpus linguists are researchers who derive their theories of language from, or base their theories of language on, corpus studies. As a result, one basic consideration when collecting spoken or written texts for a corpus is whether or not the texts should be naturally occurring. Most corpus linguists are only interested in corpora containing texts that have been spoken or written in real-world contexts. This, therefore, excludes contrived or fabricated texts, and texts spoken or written under experimental conditions. The reason for this preference is that corpus linguists want to describe language use and/or propose language theories that are grounded in actual language use. They see no benefit in examining invented texts or texts that have been manipulated by the researcher. Another consideration when collecting texts for a corpus is whether only complete texts should be included or if it is acceptable to include parts of texts. This can become an issue if, for example, the corpus compiler wants each text to be of equal length, which almost certainly means that some texts in the corpus are incomplete. Some argue that there are advantages when comparing texts to have them all of the same size, while others argue that cutting texts to fit a size requirement impairs their authenticity and possibly removes important elements, such as how a particular text type ends. The consensus, therefore, is to try to collect naturally occurring texts in their entirety. Another reason for carefully planning what goes into a corpus is to maintain a detailed record of each text and its context of use – when it happened, what kind of text it is, who the participants are, what the communicative purposes are and so on. This information is then available to users of the corpus, and is very useful in helping to interpret and explain the findings.

There are many different kinds of corpora. Some attempt to be representative of a language as a whole and are termed 'general corpora' or 'reference corpora', while others attempt to represent a particular kind of language use and are termed 'specialised corpora'. For example, the 100 million-word British National Corpus (BNC, see http://corpus.byu.edu/bnc/) contains a wide range of texts which the compilers took to be representative of British English generally, whereas the Michigan Corpus of Academic Spoken English (MICASE, see http://micase.elicorpora.info/) is a specialised corpus representing a particular register (spoken academic English) that can also be searched based on more specific text types (genres) such as lectures or seminars. The latter corpus is also special in the sense that it is comprised only of spoken language. Spoken language is generally massively underrepresented in corpora, a problem for those corpora that aim to represent general language use, for example. The logistics and costs of collecting and transcribing naturally occurring spoken data are the reasons for this, whereas the sheer ease and convenience of the collection of electronic written texts has led to the compilation of numerous written corpora. This imbalance needs to be borne in mind by users of corpora because what one finds in spoken and written corpora may differ in all kinds of ways.

Corpora are typically described in terms of the number of words that they contain and this raises another set of considerations because of the basic question: what is a word? When you count the number of words you have typed on your computer, the number of words is not based on the number of words, but on the number of spaces in the text and this is also how some corpus linguistic software packages arrive at the number of words in a corpus. However, what about something such as *haven't*? Should this be counted as one word or two (*have* + *n't*)? Or what about *PC* (as in 'personal computer')? Is this a word or two words or something else? All of these issues, of course, have to be resolved and made clear to the users of the corpus. The words in a corpus are often further categorised into 'types' and 'tokens'. The former comprise all of the unique word types in a corpus, excluding repetitions of the same word, and the latter are made up of all the words in a corpus, including all repetitions.

The 'type' category raises yet another issue. What constitutes a type? For example, *do*, *does*, *doing* and *did*. Each of these words share the same 'lemma' (i.e., they are all derived from the same root form: *DO*), but should they be counted as four different words (i.e., four 'types') in a word frequency list, or as one word based on the lemma and not listed separately? Most corpus linguistic software lists them as separate types. Similarly, if you search for one of these four words, do you want the search to include all the other forms as well? Some software packages allow the user to choose. Again, these are things to think about for corpus compilers, corpus linguistic software writers and corpus users. Counting words, categorising words and searching for words in a corpus all raise issues that corpus linguists have to address. An option for corpus compilers is to add additional information to the corpus, such as identifying clauses or word classes (e.g., nouns and verbs) by means of annotation (i.e., the insertion of additional information into a corpus), which enables the corpus linguistic software to find particular language features.

To summarise, a corpus is a collection of texts that has been compiled to represent a particular use of a language and it is made accessible by means of corpus linguistic software that allows the user to search for a variety of language features. The role of corpora means that corpus linguistics is evidence-based and computer-mediated. While not unique to corpus linguistics, these attributes are central to this field of study. Corpus linguistics is concerned not just with describing patterns of form, but also with how form and meaning are inseparable, and this notion is returned to throughout this book. The centrality of corpora-derived evidence is perhaps best encapsulated in the phrase 'trust the text' (see, for example, Sinclair 2004), which underscores the empirical nature of this field of language study.

What is corpus linguistics?

Corpus linguists compile and investigate corpora, and so corpus linguistics is the compilation and analysis of corpora. This all seems reasonably straightforward, but not everyone engaged in corpus linguistics would agree on whether corpus linguistics is a methodology for enhancing research into linguistic disciplines such as lexicography, lexicology, grammar, discourse and pragmatics, or whether it is more than that and is, in effect, a discipline in its own right. This debate is explored later in this book, and is covered elsewhere by, for example, Tognini-Bonelli (2001) and McEnery *et al.* (2006). The distinction is not unimportant because, as we shall see, the position one takes is likely to influence the approach adopted in a corpus linguistic study. Simply put, those who see corpus linguistics as a methodology (e.g., McEnery *et al.*, 2006, 7–11) use what is termed the 'corpus-based approach' whereby they use corpus linguistics to test existing theories or frameworks against evidence in the corpus. Those who view corpus linguistics as a discipline (e.g., Tognini-Bonelli, 2001; Biber, 2009) use the corpus as the starting point for developing theories about language, and they describe their approach as 'corpus-driven'. These approaches and their differences are examined in detail later in this book. For now, it is sufficient to understand that there is not one shared view of exactly what corpus linguistics is and what its aims are. In other words, even though the two main groupings both compile and investigate corpora, they adopt very different approaches in their studies because one sees corpus linguistics as a tool and the other as a theory of language. The author, it should be noted, subscribes to the latter view, and this will be foregrounded as the book unfolds.

As mentioned above, the fact that corpora are machine-readable opens up the possibility for users to search them for a multitude of features. The frequencies of types and tokens can be generated all but instantly, along with lists of key words. Key words are those that are either unique to, or have a higher frequency in, one corpus or text compared with a reference corpus. Lists of key words can tell us about what is termed the 'keyness' of texts and corpora (see Bondi and Scott, 2010). Also, how a word or phrase is distributed through a corpus, or each text in a corpus, can be displayed (see Scott, 2008) to enable the user to see if it is found throughout the text or corpus, or confined to a particular section. Another type of search can find sequences of words, such as *a lot of* and *there is*, which make up a sizeable amount of the language patterning, or phraseology, found in language. These sequences are variously termed 'lexical bundles', 'clusters', 'chunks' and 'n-grams'. More recently, the investigation of the extent of phraseological variation has received increased attention (see Cheng *et al.*, 2006 and Cheng *et al.*, 2009), in addition to the study of the fixed phraseologies found in n-gram searches. The ways in which words tend to collocate (form patterns of association) are a major focus of corpus linguistics, and associations based on structure and grammatical categories (termed 'colligation') are another important focus. The extent of patterning in the language is termed its phraseo-logical tendency by Sinclair (1987), and corpus linguistics has shown how meaning is created not by meaning residing in single words, but by patterns of word co-selections. This process of meaning creation and the retrieval of the resultant phraseologies is discussed at length in this book.

In order to view the results of searches, corpus linguists have devised ways of displaying the results of searches, and the concordance is probably the best known of these. Below, a concordance for the search item *services* in a corpus of political speeches (see http://rcpce.engl. polyu.edu.hk/policy_addresses/default.htm) is shown (Figure 1.1).

A concordance is a display of all of the search items in a corpus and is usually presented on the computer screen in the KWIC format (i.e., Key Word in Context), which centres the search item and provides its immediate co-text to the left and right. Figure 1.1 is not the full concordance, but is a sample to illustrate what a concordance looks like. Each concordance line has been sorted based on the first word to the left of *services*, which means that the concordance is displayed based on the alphabetical order of the first word to the left. In the case illustrated here, such a search option allows the user to easily identify the words that are used to modify the search item *services* (the software used here is ConcGram 1.0, written by Greaves, 2009). It is also possible to sort to the right of the search item and to sort based on the second, third, fourth word and so on. Thus, the ways in which search outputs can be configured and displayed play an important role in helping the user to investigate the corpus. The inclusion in most corpus linguistic software packages of statistical

```
1   re on medical and health services from the present 15% to
2   r upgrade our healthcare services to benefit the community
3   nd efficient immigration services are essential. Hong Kong
4   e, a hub for information services and logistics and a prem
5    provision of integrated services will also strengthen Hong
6    and comprehensive legal services for dispute resolution ar
7  to support school library services and the Chinese and Engl
8   development of mediation services. On many occasions, inter
9   ct to strengthen medical services for residents. We expect
10   e delivery of municipal services. More importantly, it wil
```

Figure 1.1 Sample concordance lines for *services* sorted one word to the left

measures is another example of how the functionality available to the user can extend the kinds of study undertaken, and these measures are summarised later in the book.

At its core, language is all about creating meaning, and so un-covering how this is realised through the co-selections of words and structures by speakers and writers is of central interest in corpus linguistics. The evidence coming out of corpus linguistics has con-tributed hugely to a better understanding of both the extent of language patterning and the ways in which these patterns are the product of the co-selections made to create meanings. The forms of patterning, and the kinds of co-selections to be found by means of corpus linguistics, are a major focus in this book, along with lots of opportunities for the reader to practise finding these and other language features across a wide range of corpora in the many activities provided in each chapter.

Aims and structure of the book

This book concentrates on aspects of corpus linguistics deemed to be both important and valuable to learners, teachers and researchers who wish to become competent and reflective language users and researchers. It discusses, with many illustrative examples, a wide range of questions that corpus linguistics is able to answer more accurately and effectively, and other questions that only corpus linguistics can answer. Findings from corpus linguistics have challenged many established assumptions in linguistic research. Examples of such findings are that different word forms of a lemma often have different patterns of meaning, that collocation is a good guide to meaning and that combinations of words generate context-specific meanings.

The book adopts an inductive approach in both design and structure. It is organised into three parts: it begins by identifying some major issues and problems in the study of language structure and use in various contexts of communication (Part I), followed by interventions that suggest and exemplify the use of a wide range of language resources and corpus linguistic methods to address the issues and deal with the problems (Part II), and, finally, a systematic description of some major concepts and models of corpus linguistics that underpin research studies in corpus linguistics (Part III). In addition, in both Parts I and II in Chapters 2–5, a large number of activities are included for readers to consolidate their knowledge of corpus linguistics and to try out for themselves different corpus linguistic search methods and functions.

Part I begins with an overview of corpus linguistics and then outlines a number of linguistic inquiries in both speaking and writing in major fields of linguistics and applied linguistics, including lexis, grammar, register, conversation analysis, genre analysis, pragmatics and discourse intonation, across a number of domains of language use and communicative contexts of situations such as academic, business, social and professional contexts. Part I aims to raise the awareness of the reader by highlighting the wide-ranging inquiries that have examined language structure and use, as well as possible and alternative ways of conducting linguistic inquiries.

Part II describes the rationale for studying corpus linguistics as a discipline and using corpus linguistics as a method of linguistic inquiry. It describes different types of corpora and their specific uses, the mechanics of corpus design and construction, and various corpus applications. It also describes basic corpus search functions, major functions in corpus linguistic software and methods of analysis used in corpus linguistics. Building on Part I, Part II describes and exemplifies a wide range of corpus studies in linguistics in areas that have been introduced in Part I, with specific focuses on major contributions made by corpus linguistics in linguistic inquiries, particularly lexical phraseology and the notion of the lexical item. Part II ends with a description of the rationale, procedure and assessment of a corpus-driven language project for those new to corpus linguistics. The project advocates data-driven learning (Johns, 1991a, 1991b) that encourages the learner to take on the role of the researcher and, at the same time, aims to enhance the learner's problem-solving, critical analysis and independent learning capabilities.

Part III returns to the main questions, features and phenomena relating to various linguistic inquiries raised in Part I, and then addressed by means of corpus linguistic approaches and methods in Part II, by describing some of the main concepts and models that underpin corpus linguistic research and illustrating these concepts and models with some significant research findings from corpus linguistic studies across a range of linguistic fields.

This book, through its innovative three-part 'problems-interventions-theories' inductive structure and the large number of guided practical tasks, coupled with detailed commentaries, hopes to dispel any apprehensions that some students, teachers and researchers might have about corpus linguistics. It is also hoped that the best possible arrangements can be made to introduce corpus linguistics to learners, whether as a subject on its own or incorporated into other linguistics subjects, with due consideration being given to the availability of computer and language resources, teacher training, curriculum space and the computer literacy of the learners.

2   Linguistic inquiries

This chapter will:

- introduce the notions of 'text', 'texts' and 'corpus';
- describe and exemplify selected linguistic inquiries in major fields of linguistics and applied linguistics, ranging from features of spoken versus written language, lexis, grammar and lexical semantics to rhetorical functions, conversation analysis, genre analysis, and pragmatics;
- describe and exemplify selected linguistic inquiries of different genres that fulfill specific communicative purposes, including research articles, conversations, public speeches, pro formas, news reports, and ordinances in a range of domains of communication, such as academic, business, professional, media and public contexts of situation;
- describe and exemplify common methods that are used to make linguistic inquiries; and
- by way of the above, draw the attention of the reader to a range of features and phenomena in linguistic research that can be much more accurately and effectively resolved by using corpus linguistic approaches and methods, and give ideas to readers for their own corpus linguistic projects.

Introducing language structure and use

Studies of language can be broadly divided into structure and use. Language structure is about 'identifying the structural units and classes of a language' (e.g., morphemes, words, phrases, grammatical classes, clausal and discoursal) and 'describing how smaller units can be combined to form larger grammatical units' (Biber *et al.*, 1998: 1). Fromkin *et al.* (2011) view grammar as the 'mental representation of a speaker's linguistic competence; what a speaker knows about a language, including its phonology, morphology, syntax, semantics, and lexicon' (p. 580). Systemic functional grammar, grounded in a different viewpoint on language, does not distinguish between lexis and grammar. It views the lexico-grammar of language as a resource for making meaning, and a tool for both understanding how language works and analysing language in use (Halliday and Matthiessen, 2004).

Language use, generally speaking, is about how speakers and writers use language to communicate meanings in various contexts of situation. Different approaches to the study of language use have different focuses, so, for instance, sociolinguistics is concerned with the relation between socially conditioned factors such as sex and culture and variation in language; pragmatics is about meaning in use or meaning in context; conversation analysis is interested in understanding how language users produce and interpret everyday talk; and critical discourse analysis examines the relationship between language, power and ideology.

Text and texts

Studies of language structure and use are primarily carried out by analysing texts and discourses. Then what is 'text' and what is 'a text'? According to Carter and McCarthy (2006), text is a 'stretch of language, either in speech or writing, that is semantically and pragmatically coherent in its real-world context', and a text 'can range from just one word (e.g., a SLOW sign on the road) to a sequence of utterances or sentences in a speech, a letter, a novel, etc.' (p. 926). A text, from the perspective of systemic functional grammar, contains linguistic clues about its context of situation (Halliday and Hasan, 1989: 11). The context of situation (i.e., the environment in which the meanings within a text are exchanged) consists of three features of context that are realised by three meta-functions of language, namely the field of discourse (what is going on) realised by ideational meanings (transitivity, lexis), the tenor of discourse (who are taking part) realised by interpersonal meanings (mood, modality, person), and mode of discourse (language role, channel, medium) realised by textual meanings (theme/rheme, cohesion) (Halliday and Hasan, 1989: 26).

Language studies go beyond isolated words and sentences to new units of analysis, including texts, discourses, conversations, speech acts or communicative events (van Dijk, 2007; Wodak, 2008). 'Texts', from the perspective of critical discourse analysis, contain properties such as 'vocabulary and metaphors, grammar, presuppositions and implicatures, politeness conventions, speech-exchange (turn-taking) systems, generic structure, and style' that are potentially ideological (Fairclough, 1995: 2). However, texts are not analysed only in terms of vocabulary, grammar and textual structures (Fairclough,

A Text	A Corpus
read whole	read fragmented
read horizontally	read vertically
read for content	read for formal patterning
read as a unique event	read for repeated events
read as an individual act of will	read as a sample of social practice
instance of one individual performance	gives insights into the language system
coherent communicative event	not a coherent communicative event

Figure 2.1 Analysing a text versus a corpus

Source: Adapted from Tognini-Bonelli (2001: 3).

2001: 92), but also the relationship between texts, the process and production and interpretation of texts, and the social conditions of production and interpretation of text (p. 21).

The nature of text versus corpus

From Chapter 1, we understand that a corpus is a collection of natu-rally occurring electronic language text that represents a language, a text type, a region or a group of speakers/writers. Corpus linguistics is a field of study that aims to analyse and describe how textual language is used. Then how does analysing a text compare to analysing a corpus?

Tognini-Bonelli (2001) describes the differences between evaluating a text and evaluating a corpus (Figure 2.1), and these contrasts differentiate 'two sources of evidence that may appear similar' but, in fact, 'entail different analytical steps' (p. 3).

Comparing spoken and written language

When texts and discourses are studied, no matter whether corpus linguistic methods are used or not, there have been attempts to study the differences between spoken and written language (e.g., Biber, 1988; Biber *et al.*, 1999). Halliday (1989: 31), for instance, describes

Task 2.1

Choose any newspaper report, either printed or online, and describe it using the features that distinguish a text from a corpus (Tognini-Bonelli, 2001: 3).

the features of spoken language as variation in speed, loudness or quietness, gestures, intonation, stress, rhythm, pitch range, and pausing and phrasing. Table 2.1 lists some of the characteristics of spoken and written language (e.g., Chafe, 1982; Halliday, 1985, 1987; Biber, 1988).

While Table 2.1 seems to suggest a great divide between spoken and written language, a text can in fact be written intended to be read

Table 2.1 Characteristics of spoken and written language

Spoken language characteristics	Written language characteristics
• Utterances instead of clauses and sentences	• Clauses and sentences instead of utterances
• Usually planned	• Planned
• More interactive	• Monologic organization
• Turn-taking organization	• 'Final draft' (polished) being indications of earlier drafts removed
• Structure based on tone groups	• Longer average word length
• Phonological contractions and assimilations	• Grammatical simplicity
• Frequent occurrence of discourse markers (e.g., *okay, so, now, right*, etc.) at beginning or end of tone groups	• High lexical density
	• Wide range and more specific vocabulary
• Spontaneity phenomena (e.g., repetitions, pauses, verbal fillers [filled pauses], false starts, hesitations, interruptions, overlap, incomplete clauses)	• More frequent use of nominalisations
	• More frequent use of passive voice
• Participants are able to take advantage of non-verbal communication	• Complex relations of coordination and subordination
• Grammatical intricacy	• High incidence of attributive adjectives
• Low lexical density (lexically sparse)	• More detached
• More frequent use of active voice	• Longer information units
• Less frequent use of nominalizations	• Use of punctuation, layout/format
• Frequent occurrence of interrogatives and imperatives	• Formal diction
• High incidence of first-person and second-person pronouns	
• References to the writer's mental process and statements that monitor the flow of information (e.g., *I guess, I think, you know, well*)	
• Use of deixis which is context-dependent (person reference, e.g., *you*; place reference, e.g., *there*; time reference, e.g., *later*)	
• Informal diction (e.g., slang, jargon, colloquial phrases, uncommon abbreviations, humour, sarcasm)	

(e.g., newspaper reports and email messages) or written intended to be spoken (e.g., political speeches and play scripts); a text can be spoken spontaneously (e.g., conversation and meetings) or spoken non-spontaneously (e.g., reciting and television advertisements) (Hillier, 2004).

It would make very interesting linguistic inquiries if you were to select any of the spoken language characteristics listed in Table 2.1 and explore the frequencies of their use in written and spoken corpora, and similarly if you were to select any written language characteristics and explore them in written and spoken corpora in order to confirm what have been presented by others as characteristics of spoken and written English language.

Instead of two texts, if you examine two corpora, one written and one spoken, each of 1 million words by means of a software program, you will be able to test and confirm what you find out in Task 2.2.

In the remaining part of this chapter, you will either read about or be asked to make a number of linguistic inquiries in the study of word, grammar, discourse, genre, pragmatics, discourse intonation and so

---

Task 2.2

Compare the written text extracted from an Ethics Standard and a spoken text which is a hotel check-out encounter with reference to the language features specific to written and spoken language:

A A written text:

Pursuant to section 18A of the Professional Accountants Ordinance, Council may, in relation to the practice of accountancy, issue or specify any statement of professional ethics required to be observed, maintained or otherwise applied by members of the Institute.

B A spoken text:

1. A: how are you sir
2. B: thank you
3. A: do you have the key of the mini-bar
4. B: no no nothing
5. A: okay
   (pause)
6. A: I understand that the main charge will um be done by Japan Airlines that's all no other charges that's all
7. B: thank you so (inaudible) much
8. A: no problem

on, as well as in various communicative contexts. In most cases, the linguistic inquiries are based on single texts and discourses. This chapter asks how they would be different if corpus linguistic inquiries were made instead. In other words, how would corpus linguistic functions and features such as types and tokens, word frequencies, key words, and the co-selections of words and structures (as realised in word sequences (phraseology), collocation, colligation and so on through analysing concordances) produce different findings, compared to investigating single texts and discourses?

Linguistic inquiries in new uses and meanings of words

Language changes over time and this is reflected in how words take on new uses and meanings. The following example shows how the Oxford English Corpus (OEC), containing over 2 billion words of real twenty-first-century English as of Spring 2010, has been used to identify new uses and meanings in the language, which results in changing a dictionary entry.

Until recently *edgy* was a word with a single meaning (*Concise Oxford English Dictionary*, 1999, 10th edition):

> **edgy** adj. tense, nervous, or irritable.

When a sample of concordance lines from the Oxford English Corpus (OEC) (www.oxforddictionaries.com/page/oecdictionaryentry) is examined, it is found that *edgy* has acquired a new meaning in addition to the old one. As a result of the discovery of the new sense of the word *edgy* in the OEC, the dictionary entry was updated to reflect this change (*Concise Oxford English Dictionary*, 2004, 11th edition):

> **edgy** adj. 1 tense, nervous, or irritable. 2 *informal* avant-garde and unconventional.

This is an example of how corpus linguistics has had a huge impact on lexicography (i.e., dictionary writing).

Linguistic inquiries in grammar

Core areas of grammar include description of articles, prepositions, noun phrases, tenses, modals, passives and pseudo-passives, direct and indirect speech, and clausal structures such as *if*-constructions and *why*-constructions (Carter *et al.*, 2000). Based on English used in real-life contexts drawn from the Cambridge International Corpus (CIC) (over one billion words), Carter *et al.* (2000) found that:

It, *this* and *that* can be used to refer to things in a text, but they function in different ways:

- *It* simply continues what we are already talking/writing about, without focusing in any special way.
- *This* is used to focus or highlight new, important topics in the text, making them immediate.
- *That* is used to distance ourselves from aspects of the topic.

(p. 89)

This is another example of how corpus linguistics enables us to go beyond descriptions of single clauses, sentences or texts and so be more confident that our findings are generalisable to a particular genre, register or the language as a whole.

Linguistic inquiries in lexical semantics

Semantics is the 'study of the linguistic meaning of morphemes, words, phrases, and sentences' (Fromkin *et al.*, 2011: 592). Lexical semantics, being a subfield of semantics, is about 'the meanings of words and the meaning relationships among words' (p. 584). Halliday (1993: 55–6) discusses the meaning relationship between word forms and the grammatical contexts in which they occur; for instance, *grow* (verb) and *growth* (noun) construe different realities not due to their different morphology but due to the different environments in which they occur.

Task 2.3

Study the following sentences taken from magazines. What are the meanings expressed by *growing* in the first sentence and *growth* in the second sentence? What are the clues in the words before and after *growing* and *growth* that help to make meaning, and how?

The tiger mother's cubs are being raised to rule the world, the book clearly implies, while the offspring of 'weak-willed,' 'indulgent' Westerners are growing up ill equipped to compete in a fierce global marketplace.

(*Time Magazine*, 20 January 2011, www.time.com/time/ nation/article/0,8599,2043313,00.html#ixzz1CD9w35J8)

This year, growth is forecast at 8.5 per cent. Manmohan Singh, the prime minister, predicts that the economy can stretch upwards of 9 per cent in the coming fiscal year.

(*Financial Times*, 27 January 2011, www.ft.com/cms/s/0/ 37492b46-2827-11e0-8abc-00144feab49a.html#ixzz1CD9NKnB0)

You have just examined the words that are co-selected with *growing* and *growth* in two sentences. If you were to do the same by examining a corpus, you would be able to find out patterns of word co-selections. Figure 2.2 shows a concordance for the search item *growing* and Figure 2.3 the search item *growth* taken from the Corpus of Research Articles (5.6 million words) (http://rcpce.engl.polyu.edu.hk/RACorpus/default.htm).

The word *growing* is a verb (present participle of *grow*) in lines 3 and 6, and an adjective in all other lines. When *growing* is a verb, it is preceded by a verb (*are*) (line 3), an auxiliary verb (*have*) and past participle of *be* (*been*) (line 6). Between *are* and *growing* is an adverb (*not*) (line 3). When *growing* is a verb, it is followed by a noun (*marijuana*) or an adverb (*steadily*). When *growing* is an adjective, it is preceded by articles (*a, the*) and, like the verb *growing*, also followed by a noun (*interest, link, nature, numbers*). Between *the* and *growing* is an adverb (*rapidly*) (line 4).

For the noun *growth*, it forms a noun phrase by co-selecting with another noun either to the right or to the left (*growth rate, organism growth, root growth*). It is preceded by an adjective (*bureaucratic growth*), or co-selects another noun joined together by a conjunction (*and*) (*Jobs and Growth, investment and growth*).

These examples illustrate again the important role that corpus linguistic inquiries play in establishing patterns of language use that not only distinguish the usages of forms of words, but, more importantly, how each form creates different meanings.

```
1 de has been marked by a growing interest in the development
2  been attributed to the growing link between income and edu
3  for people who are not growing marijuana, knowing that pol
4 , not least the rapidly growing nature of longer-haul tour
5 ue to have them in ever-growing numbers. Indeed, for some
6 rism receipts have been growing steadily. As opposed to the
```

Figure 2.2 Sample concordance lines for *growing*

```
1 e and spatial distance, growth rate is another attribute i
2 luenced by the Jobs and Growth Tax Relief Reconciliation A
3 he kind of bureaucratic growth that in turn permitted rule
4  experience of organism growth. The organismic analogy bri
5 lity for investment and growth. The major argument in Dawe
6 arlier portions of root growth this necessarily also holds
```

Figure 2.3 Sample concordance lines for *growth*

Linguistic inquiries in conversation analysis

Conversation analysis (Sacks *et al.*, 1974) is concerned about how participants manage the organisational and social aspects of conversation. The aim of conversation analysis is to study 'small phenomena' that 'may give an enormous understanding of the way humans do things' (Sacks, 1984: 18). An example is McCarthy's (2003) study, which examines short listener response tokens in spoken discourse such as social conversation, telephone calls between friends and social chats among friends. Short listener response tokens are characterised by the features 'of being superfluous to transactional needs, of being focused on the interpersonal plane of discourse and whose social functions seem to overlap with those of phatic and relational episodes in different types of talk' (p. 33).

The following extract is a telephone call between two British friends who were arranging a barbecue (p. 22). The two instances of the response token 'Lovely' not only signal topical boundaries but also indicate the positive relationship that exists between the speakers. In the second instance, 'Lovely' is said even after Speaker B has confirmed the arrangement with 'Yeah' transactionally. The response token 'Lovely', therefore, shows 'both a response function and (simultaneously in its second occurrence) a discourse-marking one' (p. 22):

A: I would love it if you could bring a salad.
B: Yeah.
A: It would be very nice.
B: I will do then. I'll do that this afternoon then yeah.
A: **Lovely.**
B: What time do you want us then?
A: When were you planning?
B: Well you said about fiveish didn't you.
A: Yeah.
B: Yeah.
A: **Lovely.**

The single conversational extract shows two speakers interacting and responding to each other through turn-taking. Large amounts of conversations can be captured and electronically stored in a corpus and then searched for a multitude of features, including the patterning of turn-taking and the patterning in the use of response tokens.

Figure 2.4 shows sample concordance lines for 'lovely' from a conversational corpus in the KWIC format. Speakers are identified by ':', with, for example, 'A' referring to a female native speaker of English, and 'a' a female non-native speaker of English. The lines present linguistic realisations of speaker turn-taking horizontally, and

```
1 ugh))  A: no no  a1: it's  lovely  A: I wouldn't say it's w
2                  ** that's  lovely  A2: okay  a: okay thank
3 happened great good lads  lovely  a3: oh * ((inaudible))
4 rabbits (.) so that was a  lovely  black rabbit and I replac
5 I wouldn't say it's well  lovely  but it's not horrible it
6 light (pause) you've got  lovely  eyes (.) * I've got two t
7 es cheap  B: ** no  B: oh  lovely  for me (.) that's for S__
8 ** yes very interesting  lovely  (.) * I   b: ** oh took
9 ery dynamic  A: he's he's  lovely  I * I really like him he'
10      ** mhm  A: it looks  lovely  I haven't got any plants
```

Figure 2.4 Sample concordance lines for *lovely* (Hong Kong Corpus of Spoken
English, 1 million words)

from examining the immediate co-text to the left and right of 'lovely',
it shows different patterning and uses compared to the example above.
For example, 'it's lovely', 'that's lovely', 'oh lovely for me' 'yes very
interesting lovely' are used as response tokens, and 'lovely' is also found
to be used to qualify nouns and pronouns (e.g., 'a lovely black rabbit',
'he's lovely').

In the above example, we can see that corpus linguistic inquiries
can not only confirm (or refute) the extent and functions of linguistic
features such as short listener response tokens, but can also extend
our understanding by revealing other patterns when speakers respond
with 'lovely'.

Linguistic inquiries in genre analysis

Bhatia (1993) defines a genre as 'a recognizable communicative event
characterized by a set of communicative purpose(s) identified and
understood by the members of the professional or academic community
in which it regularly occurs' and being 'highly structured and conven-
tionalized with constraints on allowable contributions in terms of
their intent, positioning, form and functional value' (p. 13). Askehave
and Swales (2001) examined the genre of response letters to recommendations, which are written by professors to universities in support
of junior academics' job applications. They suggest that the genre of
response letters to recommendations consists of three parts: 'an
opening, a body, and a closing' (p. 202), and that the body can contain
any of the following themes: 'thanking; appreciation of the time and
effort taken; information on the recruitment process; and an indication
of follow-up with the applicant' (p. 202). The example letter (p. 202)
opposite has been analysed, with thanking occurring twice and an
absence of information on the recruitment process:

Dear Dr. Moore,

Thank you very much for your letter of recommendations for Alan Kim for a position on our faculty. (thanking) Recommendations are an important part of our recurring process and we appreciate the time and effort you put into providing thoughtful information. (appreciation of the time and effort taken) We will be getting back in touch with Mr Alan Kim as our recruitment process unfolds. (an indication of follow-up with the applicant) Thanks again for your efforts on Mr Kim's behalf and our recruiting process. (thanking)

Sincerely yours
(signature, name, professional title and positions)

How genres can be examined using corpus linguistic methods will be described and illustrated in Part II.

Linguistic inquiries in pragmatics

There is not one generally accepted definition of pragmatics but pragmatists are all interested in the relationships between language structure and language usage. Those involved in the study of pragmatics come from diverse backgrounds such as discourse and conversation analysis, philosophy, linguistics, psychology, sociology and so on. This makes it difficult to offer one definition because any definition of pragmatics is inevitably influenced by the background and interests of the person concerned, but the definition offered by Thomas (1995) is a useful starting point: pragmatics is '*meaning in interaction*' (p. 22).

Thomas' (1995) definition underlines the fact that meaning in discourse is 'dynamic'. In other words, language in use does not have a fixed meaning or a set of meanings. The meaning of language in use cannot be separated from the context in which it is used. The meanings are negotiated by both speakers/writers and hearers/readers, dependent upon the context (physical, social and linguistic) and the 'meaning potential' of what is said/written (p. 23). The concept of meaning

Task 2.4

As shown above, it is not difficult to identify the themes in one response letter but what would the themes be if 100, 500, or even 1,000 response letters are analysed? Try to think of the difficulties that you might encounter in trying to use such a corpus to identify themes.

potential emphasises the roles of speaker/writer and hearer/reader in the joint construction of meaning through language use.

An important area of study in pragmatics is politeness (Brown and Levinson, 1978, 1987). Politeness in pragmatics describes the relationship between 'how something is said and the addressee's judgment as to how it should be said' (Grundy, 2000: 147). In other words, politeness consists of strategies employed by participants in spoken and written discourse to best achieve their communicative goals in a particular context while attempting to maintain, or even enhance, their relationship with the hearer or reader. One such politeness device is thanking, which is used to express gratitude. With the use of software, a corpus of academic spoken discourse (0.25 million words) was searched with the search item 'thank', and both forms 'thank' and 'thanks' were found. Table 2.2 shows the frequencies and percentages of occurrence of all the phraseologies of expressing gratitude found in the corpus.

The following describes linguistic inquiries in different contexts of situations, namely academic, business, professional, public, media, legal and health care.

Table 2.2 Forms of thanking in academic English

Forms of thanking	Frequency	Percentage (%)
thank you	56	52.33
thank you for	9	8.41
thank you so much	1	0.93
thank you very much	20	18.69
thank you very much for	4	3.77
thanks	12	11.21
thanks a lot	1	0.93
thanks for	3	2.80
thanks very much	1	0.93
Total	107	100

Task 2.5

Corpus linguistic software is a powerful tool that can search a large corpus and show the patterning of language almost instantly, as shown in Table 2.2. With reference to Thomas' (1995: 22) definition of pragmatics as 'meaning in interaction', how would you want to explore the spoken academic corpus further to study how speakers in the corpus thank each other when they interact?

Linguistic inquiries in academic contexts

In the academic context, linguistic inquiries into speaking and writing can include classroom discourse, student discussion and presentations, student writing, research papers, teaching materials and textbooks, and teacher-student supervision. When discussing the strategy of self-promotion in research articles, Harwood (2005) gives examples of the use of the pronouns *I* and *we* at both the start and the close of journal articles in different linguistic fields. At the start of articles, *I* and *we* are used to emphasise the originality of the research work reported in the article and, at the end, the pronouns function to underscore 'the groundbreaking aspects of their work' (p. 1219), and so are equally self-promotional.

Task 2.6

(TC)

Study the following extracts from Harwood (2005). In what sense are the uses of *I* and *we* (in **bold**) self-promotional?

At the start of a journal article in *Business & Marketing* (B&M):

> We do not seem to have [a] theory of how users initially comprehend the capabilities of a technology. The features-based theory of sensemaking triggers (FBST) **I** present here attempts to fill this gap. (B&M 8)

(Harwood, 2005: 1219)

At the close of a journal article in *Physics* (PHYS):

> Here, **we** have achieved, at the very best, an accurate analytic representation of the thermodynamic functions of pu at the temperatures cited.

(PHYS 10)

Harwood (2005) examined 10 journal articles each from the disciplines of Physics, Economics, Computing Science, and Business & Management (40 articles in total). He concluded that, '(w)hile this study has taken a qualitative rather than quantitative approach, I have shown that the pronouns *I* and *we* which help to promote authors and their work are found in both hard and soft disciplines' (p. 1226).

How would some quantitative findings make the study more informative, by asking such questions as 'Is *I* or *we* used more frequently to promote authors and their work?', 'Is *I* or *we* used more frequently for this communicative function in hard disciplines or soft disciplines?', and 'Is *I* or *we* used more frequently for this communicative function at the start of journal articles in hard and soft disciplines?' and so on?

How might you need to prepare your texts in such a corpus to enable you to compare the relative usage of the pronouns at the start and end of the research articles?

Linguistic inquiries in business and professional contexts

In Cheng and Mok's (2008) study, they analysed a commonplace civil engineering genre, Request for Information (RFI) pro forma, from a civil engineering consultancy firm in Hong Kong. After examining some samples of the RFI pro forma (consisting of a Query and a Response), the authors observed similarities in the linguistic features; for example, heavy use of the hedged imperative such as 'Please advise', 'Please be reminded', and 'Please be informed'; modal verbs 'should' and 'will'; passive voice; and expressions that connect previous and current texts (e.g., 'In accordance with', 'Referring to', and 'Further to') (p. 67). They also found heavy use of 'referential intertextual links' (p. 68) in the RFI pro forma. In the 121-word Query section in one pro forma, they found four instances of intertextual links with previous texts (e.g., 'Your response to our previous RFI No. xxx' and 'The above information') and six instances of links with the enclosed texts (e.g., 'The attached Sketch no. xx/xxxxxxx' and 'For your easy reference, sections of the slope is attached') (p. 68).

Linguistic inquiries in public and media contexts

In public and media contexts, an interesting study was reported by Mollin (2009: 370), who investigated a corpus of more than 3 million words that comprised the public statements, speeches and interviews, and parliamentary proceedings of Tony Blair, Prime Minister of the UK between 1997 and 2007. These public discourses were then compared to general English usage captured in the British National Corpus (100 million words). The study found evidence of Blair's 'idiolectal maximiser collocations' (p. 382). Idiolect is 'the form of a language that a particular person speaks' (*Cambridge Dictionaries Online*). Maximisers, according to Quirk *et al.* (1985), express the very highest point on a scale from high to low, and examples of maximiser adverbs are *absolutely*, *completely*, *entirely* and *totally* (Mollin, 2009: 373–4). Mollin found sixteen maximiser collocations typical of Tony Blair: '*utterly absurd, entirely accept, absolutely blunt,*

Task 2.7

Now think of a business or professional context and a genre specific to that particular context. How would you obtain sample texts of the genre? What items might you search for to find out whether or not referential intertextual links are used and their frequencies of use?

Task 2.8

With reference to Mollin's (2009) study of the idiolectal collocations of Tony Blair in the UK, which political figure in your country would you be interested in studying? How easy would it be to collect political speeches? How would you replicate Mollin's study?

absolutely committed, completely committed, fully consistent, thoroughly decent, absolutely frank, wholly innocent, entirely justified, wholly new, perfectly prepared, completely unacceptable, entirely understand, totally understand, completely wrong' (p. 387).

Linguistic inquiries in legal contexts

In legal contexts, typical professional genres include contracts, deeds, jury instructions, orders/judgments/decrees, letters of advice, legal opinions, pleadings, statutes and wills.

Linguistic inquiries in health care contexts

In health care contexts, in a paper that suggests ways to improve the communication skills of health care professionals working in oncology, Schofield *et al.* (2008) give examples of 'inhibitory/blocking verbal behaviours' from a qualitative study of doctor-patient dialogue (p. 7). Inhibitory behaviours are those that reduce and prevent the patient from providing information, and blocking behaviours are those that prevent a patient from becoming emotional by changing the topic (p. 6).

Task 2.9

Study the following text. What kind of text is this? Is there a word that seems to be occurring more frequently here than in general English?

Subject to compliance with applicable laws, any full-time or part-time employee, executive or officer of the Group, executive or non-executive director of the Group, or full-time or part-time employee, executive, officer or director of BOC or any of its subsidiaries serving as a member of any committee of the Group.

The word is 'or'. Is this word more common in legal texts generally? How would corpus linguistics help you to answer this question?

Task 2.10

Study the following examples of inhibitory/blocking verbal behaviours. How are they able to achieve the goals of reducing and preventing disclosure of important patient information and negative emotion expressed by the patient?:

Closed questions: 'Are you having problems sleeping?'
Leading questions: 'I suspect that was alright then, was it?'
Multiple questions: 'How is your appetite – how are you eating and how's your sleep?'
Minimising or normalising comments: 'It is natural for you to feel like that?'
Premature or inappropriate advice: Patient says 'I was worried about the pain'. Doctor/nurse responds 'The pain may be because of . . .' Moves away from the worry.
False or premature reassurance: 'It's nothing to worry about, you will be fine'.
Switching focus: Patient 'I was worried, but not bothered by waiting'. Doctor/nurse 'How long did you have to wait?'
Switching person: Patient 'I thought I was going to die'. Doctor/nurse 'What did your husband think about that?'
Passing the buck: 'You need to talk to the doctor about that – can I make you an appointment?'
Overt blocking: Patient 'I am not worried about death – just the process of dying'. Doctor/nurse 'What do you think of the hospice?'

(adapted from Schofield *et al.*, 2008: 7)

How would it be possible to find out whether or not, or the extent to which, the recommended inhibitory/blocking verbal behaviours are widely used by doctors or nurses in health contexts?

Imagine you had access to a corpus of transcriptions of 200 nurse-patient consultations. How would such a corpus help you to find out whether these behaviours were used, how frequently they were used and other kinds of language patterns used to perform the behaviours?

Concluding remarks

The chapter introduces a range of areas of linguistic inquiries in different linguistic fields and different contexts of situation. Some of the fields are central to corpus linguistics, such as phraseologies and genre analysis (i.e., concerned with conducting a quantitative analysis of words and grammatical categories specific to individual moves) and some are not (e.g., discourse analysis, conversation analysis and pragmatics). Even for areas that are not central to corpus linguistics, this chapter, and in fact the book, argues that there is great value in incorporating corpus methods into these linguistic fields. In later chapters, you are asked to engage in corpus linguistic inquiries of your own. Some of the discussion tasks in this chapter could be returned to as the basis for such inquiries.

Part II

Interventions

3 An introduction to corpus linguistics

This chapter will:

- describe the rationale for studying corpus linguistics as a discipline and using corpus linguistics as a method of linguistic inquiry;

- describe different types of corpora and their specific uses;

- describe the mechanics of corpus design and construction;

- describe corpus applications, including the tracking of variation and change in the English language, the production of dictionaries and other reference materials, and the study of different aspects of linguistics; and

- describe and exemplify a wide range of corpus studies in linguistics, including lexis, grammar, phraseology, lexico-grammar, literal and metaphorical meanings, discourse, pragmatics, discourse intonation, registers (e.g., academic, business, social, scientific and legal) and genres (e.g., university textbooks, financial reports, conversation, plays and contracts).

What is corpus linguistics?

One of the most debated questions about corpus linguistics is: is corpus linguistics a branch of linguistics (such as phonology, grammar, semantics, lexical studies) or a methodology of language studies? For example, in an international conference on corpus linguistics held in the US in 2005, a panel of corpus linguists discussed the topic 'Corpus Linguistics: Methodology or Sub-field?'. Corpus linguistics is viewed by some as an empirical method of linguistic analysis and description, using real-life examples of language data stored in corpora as the starting point (Crystal, 1992; Jackson, 2007). Corpus linguistics is 'maturing methodologically' (McEnery and Wilson, 2001); it is 'an approach or methodology for studying language use' (Bowker and Pearson, 2002: 9). Others view corpus linguistics as theory, and so much more than methodology (Sinclair, 1994, 1996, 2001, 2004). Halliday (1993: 4) asserts that corpus linguistics 're-unites data gathering and theorising and this is leading to a qualitative change in our understanding of language'. This view is echoed by Teubert and Krishnamurthy (2007), who suggest that corpus linguistics is a 'bottom-up' approach that looks at 'the full evidence of the corpus', 'analyses the evidence with the aim of finding probabilities, trends, patterns, co-occurrences of elements, features or groupings of features' (p. 6); and to 'search behind the curtain of language data for an underlying system which would explain those data' (p. 2). Corpus linguistics is regarded as 'a new philosophical approach to linguistic enquiry' (Tognini-Bonelli, 2001: 1). The debate is likely to continue and may never be fully resolved.

Corpus design and construction

A corpus usually refers to a text corpus, defined as 'a collection of pieces of language text in electronic form, selected according to external criteria to represent, as far as possible, a language or language variety as a source of data for linguistic research' (Sinclair, 2005a: 16). It is 'a collection of texts assumed to be representative of a given language put together so that it can be used for linguistic analysis' (Tognini-Bonelli, 2001: 2), or 'collections of texts (or parts of text) that are stored and accessed electronically' (Hunston, 2002: 2) for linguistic study.

A corpus is not just any collection of texts; it is 'a collection of naturally occurring language texts, chosen to characterize a state or variety of a language' (Sinclair, 1991: 171). In other words, a corpus is designed and compiled based on corpus design principles. Sinclair (2005a) details a set of core principles and these are listed below:

1   Corpus contents are selected based on their communicative purpose in the community without regard for the language that they contain.

2   The control of subject matter in the corpus is imposed by the use of external, and not internal, criteria.

3   Only components in the corpus that are designed to be independently contrasted are contrasted (i.e., 'orientation').

4   Criteria determining the structure of the corpus are small in number, separate from each other, and efficient at delineating a corpus that is representative.

5   Samples of language for the corpus, whenever possible, consist of entire texts.

6 Any information about a text, such as part-of-speech tags and the typography and layout of a printed document, should be stored separately from the plain text (i.e., the words and punctuation of the text) and only merged when needed.

7 The design and composition of the corpus are fully documented with full justifications.

8 The corpus design includes, as target notions, representativeness and balance.

9 The corpus aims for consistency in its components while maintaining adequate coverage.

(adapted from Sinclair, 2005a: 2–17)

One of the corpus design principles is 'orientation' (i.e., only those components in the corpus that are designed to be independently contrasted are contrasted) (Sinclair, 2005a: 3). If your purpose is to find out what a standard language is like, you will examine a reference corpus such as British National Corpus (BNC) (100 million words), Bank of English (650 million words as of 2011), or the Corpus of Contemporary American English (COCA) (425 million words, 1990–2011). If you want to find out whether the grammar in different registers is different, you will examine register-based corpora; see, for example, Biber *et al.*'s (1999) corpus-based description of the grammar of four registers of English: conversation, fiction, news and academic texts.

External, rather than internal, criteria need to be used when selecting subject matter for the corpus (Sinclair, 2005a: 11). Common external criteria include: the mode of the text (e.g., speech, writing and electronic mode); the type of text (e.g., in the case of a written corpus, whether books, journals, emails or letters should be chosen); the domain of the text (e.g., academic or popular); the language, languages or language varieties of the corpus (e.g., Australian, Irish or American English); the location of the texts (e.g., the English of the UK or Australia); and the date the texts were spoken or written (e.g., the *Time Magazine* Corpus (100 million words, 1923–2006) compiled by Mark Davies).

Task 3.1

If you are interested in knowing the English that you write and speak at university, what are some useful corpora that you could build? Discuss the 'orientation' to the language that you would select.

Task 3.2

Four predetermined external criteria, except the date, are built into the name of Michigan Corpus of Academic Spoken English at http://micase.elicorpora.info/. Try to work out what each criterion means:

1 Mode:

2 Type:

3 Domain:

4 Language:

5 Date (either side of the millennium):

Types of corpora

In an overview of what corpora are available, Lee (2010) describes three categories of corpora: major English language corpora (Table 3.1), developmental, learner and lingua franca corpora (Table 3.2), and non-English corpora and multilingual corpora (the third category is not summarized in this chapter). You will read about many of the corpora listed in Tables 3.1 and 3.2, as well as many that are not listed, in this and the following chapters.

In corpus linguistics, a corpus is often described as being either 'general' or 'specialised'. General corpora are usually much bigger than specialised corpora. For example, the Bank of English is over 600 million words; COCA is more than 400 million words; and the BNC is 100 million words, and all are general corpora. Specialised corpora, on the other hand, can usually be measured in the thousands or low millions of words, although there are some that are very large. However, size is not the main factor distinguishing the two types of corpora. What distinguishes general corpora from specialised corpora is the purpose for which they are compiled. General corpora aim to examine patterns of language use for a language as a whole, and specialised corpora are compiled to describe language use in a specific variety, register or genre. The selection of the contents of a specialised corpus often requires the corpus linguist to seek advice from experts in the field to ensure its representativeness and balance.

Specialised corpora cover a wide range of registers, genres, language forms and language varieties, and they have grown in recent years. As corpus linguistics has grown, so too has the demand for more specific studies and applications that specialised corpora are often best designed

Table 3.1 Major English language corpora (Lee, 2010: 109–16)

Types of English language corpora	Representative corpora
'General English' corpora (written, spoken and both)	Brown Corpus of written American English, FROWN (Freiburg-Brown Corpus of written American English), Lancaster Oslo-Bergen (LOB) corpus of written British English, FLOB (Freiburg- LOB corpus of written British English, Wellington Corpus of Written New Zealand English, Australian Corpus of English (ACE), Kolhapur Corpus of Indian English, International Corpus of English (ICE), Bank of English, British National Corpus (BNC), American National Corpus (ANC), Corpus of Contemporary American English (COCA)
Speech corpora	Spoken English Corpus (SEC), Machine Readable Spoken English Corpus (MARSEC), London-Lund Corpus of Spoken English, Intonation Variation in English (IViE) Corpus, Freiburg Corpus of English Dialects FRED (FRED), Cambridge and Nottingham Corpus of Discourse in English (CANCODE), Switchboard Corpus, Santa Barbara Corpus of Spoken American English (SBCSAE)
Parsed[1] written corpora	Lancaster Parsed Corpus (LPC), Surface and Underlying Structural Analyses of Naturalistic English (SUSANNE) Corpus, ICB-GB (Great Britain), Penn-Helsinki Parsed Corpus of Middle English, York-Helsinki Parsed Corpus of Old English Poetry
Historical corpora	Helsinki Corpus of English, A Representative Corpus of Historical English Registers (ARCHER), Corpus of Historical American English (COHA), Lampeter Corpus, Newdigate Newsletter Corpus, Corpus of Early English Correspondence (CEEC), Corpus of Late Eighteenth-Century Prose, Corpus of later Modern English Prose, Zurich English Newspaper Corpus, Old Bailey Corpus, Corpus of English Dialogues (CED)
Specialised corpora	Michigan Corpus of Academic Spoken English (MICASE), British Academic Spoken English corpus (BASE), Limerick-Belfast Corpus of Academic Spoken English (LIBEL CASE), City University Corpus of Academic Spoken English (CUCASE), British National Corpus (academic component), LOB (category J texts: 'learned and scientific writings'), Chemnitz Corpus of Specialised and Popular Academic English (SPACE), Reading Academic Text corpus (RAT), Professional English Research Corpus (PERC), Wolverhampton Business English Corpus, Business Letters Corpus (BLC)
Multimedia corpora	Santa Barbara Corpus of Spoken American English (SBCSAE), Scottish Corpus of Texts and Speech (SCOTS), English Language Interview Corpus as a Second-Language Application, Singapore Corpus of Research in Education (SCoRE), multimedia corpus of European teenager talk (SACODEYL project)

Table 3.2 Developmental, learner and lingua franca corpora (Lee, 2010: 116–18)

Types of developmental, learner and lingua franca corpora	Representative corpora
Developmental language corpora	CHILDES database and Polytechnic of Wales (POW) Corpus, Louvian Corpus of Native English Essays (LOCNESS; 324,000 words), British Academic Written English Corpus (BAWE; 6.5 million words), Michigan Corpus of Upper-level Student Papers (MICUSP; 2 million words)
ESL/EFL learner corpora	International Corpus of Learner English (ICLE; 3.7 million written words), Louvian International Database of Spoken English Interlanguage (LINDSEI; 1 million words), Lancaster Corpus of Academic Written English (LANCAWE), Montclair Electronic Language Learners' Database (MELD; 98,000 words), Chinese Academic Written English (CAWE; 408,000 words), International Corpus of Crosslinguistic Interlanguage (ICCI), Japanese EFL Learner Corpus (JEFLL Corpus; 700,000 words), Learner Business Letters Corpus (Learner BLC; 200,000 words), Learning Prosody in a Foreign Language (LeaP corpus; more than twelve hours of recordings)
Lingua franca[2] corpora	Vienna-Oxford International Corpus of English (VOICE Corpus; 1 million words, 120 hours), The Corpus of English as a Lingua Franca in Academic Settings (ELFA Corpus; 1 million words, 131 hours)

to meet. Having a specific focus can also mean that they can be used to inform the learning and teaching of language for specific purposes, especially when the patterns of language use are benchmarked with a general corpus to highlight similarities and differences.

When discussing building small specialised corpora, Koester (2010: 67–8) asks 'How small and how specialized?', and answers the question by quoting Flowerdew (2004: 21):

- Specific purpose for compilation, e.g., to investigate a particular grammatical or lexical item

- Contextualization: particular setting, participants and communicative purposes, e.g., a job interview that involves a candidate and a panel of interviewers

- Genre, e.g., promotional (grant proposals, sales letters)

- Type of text/discourse, e.g., biology textbooks, casual conversation

- Subject matter/topic, e.g., economics

- Variety of English, e.g., Learner English

Increasingly, multi-modal corpora are becoming important. Multi-modal corpora consist of 'video, audio and textual records of interaction (and associated metadata information) extracted from recordings of naturally occurring conversational episodes which are *streamed* in an easy-to-use interface' (Knight *et al.*, 2010: 16). An example is the Nottingham eLanguage Corpus comprising both 'Text-based eLanguage data' (e.g., SMS/MMS messages, emails and blogging entries) and 'Language "in the wild"' that captures the receptive (not productive) linguistic experience of 'specific language individuals on a *day-to-day* basis' (Knight *et al.*, 2010: 16), including texts, video, audio and field notes.

Lee (2010: 115–16) discusses using the web as a corpus, quoting Kilgarriff and Grefenstette's (2003) view about whether the web can be considered a corpus:

> [many linguists] mix the question: 'What is a corpus?' with 'What is a good corpus (for certain kinds of linguistic study)?', muddling the simple question 'Is corpus x good for task y?' with the semantic question, 'Is x a corpus at all?' . . . We define a corpus simply as 'a collection of texts'. If that seems too broad, the one qualification we allow relates to the domains and contexts in which the word is used rather than its denotation: A corpus is a collection of texts when considered as an object of language or literary study. The answer to the question 'is the web a corpus?' is yes.
>
> (Kilgarriff and Grefenstette, 2003: 334)

Task 3.3

(TC)

Study a specialised corpus Hong Kong Engineering Corpus (9,224,384 words) at http://rcpce.engl.polyu.edu.hk/HKEC/. Based on the information on the website, make notes of the following as far as possible:

- Specific purpose for compilation:

- Contextualization:

- Genre:

- Types of text/discourse:

- Subject matter/topic:

- Variety of English:

> **Task 3.4**
>
> Go to WebCorp at www.webcorp.org.uk. Find out about 'Search term → pattern', 'Search engine', 'Concordance Span', 'Case options', and 'Advanced Search Options'. Then type in a search item of your choice and describe the types of WebCorp output for your query term. Try searching for the same search item in different domains. Are the results similar or different?

However, it is useful to point out that when Sinclair's (2005a) corpus design principles are considered, the web cannot be viewed as a corpus.

The web, nonetheless, is viewed as a corpus by others who define a corpus 'simply as "a collection of texts"' (Kilgarriff and Grefenstette, 2003: 334), which can be examined using such web concordance programs as WebCorp, WebKWiC, KWiCFinder, the Linguist's Search Engine, Birmingham University's WebCorpLSE and ukWaC (Lee, 2010: 116).

The microblogging service Twitter has become very popular in recent years for expressing opinions, broadcasting news and communication (Petrovic *et al.*, 2010), and an open-source Twitter dataset with 97 million tweets with information about the users who posted the tweets is available at http://demeter.inf.ed.ac.uk/ (Petrovic *et al.*, 2010).

The Hong Kong Corpus of Spoken Corpus (HKCSE) (2 million words) consists of four sub-corpora: academic, business, conversation and public sub-corpora. It is an intercultural corpus with Chinese Hong Kong non-native speakers of English (NNSE) and native speakers of English (NSE). The Hong Kong speakers are primarily professionals from different industries and business settings, with some university students in the academic sub-corpus. The orthographic transcriptions of half of the HKCSE (about 1 million words) are available at http://rcpce.engl.polyu.edu.hk/. This 1-million HKCSE has been prosodically transcribed and analysed in terms of discourse intonation (Cheng *et al.*, 2008).

Studying corpora

There are many different ways in which a text corpus can be studied with the use of computer software programs; in other words, the corpus is 're-created inside the computer' (Sinclair, 1991: 28) and the computer software 'selects, sorts, matches, counts and calculates' (Hunston and Francis 2000: 15) the corpus examined. Basic methods of corpus investigation are token, type, lemma, word-lists, concordances, collocates, key words, positive and negative keyness, n-grams, skipgrams and concgrams (see Chapter 5). Some of the corpus analysis tools are WordSmith Tools 5.0 (Scott, 2008), AntConC (Anthony, 2006), ParaConc and MonoCono Pro (MP2.2) (Barlow, 2008) and ConcGram 1.0 (Greaves, 2009). Advanced methods of corpus study include using Wmatrix (Rayson, 2009) to perform automatic part-of-speech (POS) and semantic tagging, followed by POS and semantic field analysis, and using the Sketch Engine, which is a 'Corpus Query System incorporating **word sketches, grammatical relations,** and a **distributional thesaurus**', and a word sketch is 'a one-page, automatic, corpus-derived summary of a word's grammatical and collocational behaviour' (Adam Kilgarriff, www.sketchengine.co.uk/).

Corpus applications

Tracking of English language variation and change

The growth of corpus linguistics since the 1980s has led to more accurate studies of language change. Examples are provided by Leech *et al.* (2009) in their study of five corpora spanning 60 years to track language change:

US English	British English
	BLOB (1931)
Brown (1961)	LOB (1961)
Frown (1991)	FLOB (1991)

All of the corpora are based on written texts and have used the same design criteria to allow comparisons to be made across the two varieties of English and across time. One major change is declining use of modals *must, shall* (*shall* has been halved), *should* and *ought to* (*should* and *ought to* have almost disappeared from American English). Another change is the increasing use of semi-modals *have to, want to, need to* (*need to* has increased five-fold), and *supposed to*.

Leech (2007) suggests four main reasons for all the changes he describes:

1 Grammaticalisation explains why lexical words have become grammatical; for example, present progressive has increased by 30 per cent from 1961 to 1991, and semi-modals (e.g., *going to* and *have to*) are most frequent.

2 Colloquialisation explains why written language has become more like spoken language. There has been a decrease in passive, relative clauses, with *which, who*, etc., and 'of' genitive (e.g., *defeat of*

Liverpool), and an increase in relative clauses with *that* or 'zero', contractions, 's'-genitive (e.g., *Liverpool's defeat*), semi-modals and present progressive.

3 Americanisation, meaning new norms have developed in the US, results in an increase in the use of American terms such as *guy(s)* to refer to both men and women and the use of subjunctive mood (words that indicate wishes, demands, not facts) (e.g., *The doctors suggested remain in bed* and *Hence it's important that the process be carried out immediately*), and increased use of *radio* (from *wireless*) and *movies* (from *films*), etc.

4 Democratisation means overtly linguistic inequalities in society have been avoided; for example, a decrease in the use of honorifics (e.g., *Mr, Mrs, Sir, Madam*), an increase in 'camaraderie' that replaces polite distance with more use of first or given names that are often reduced or abbreviated, an increase in the use of familiar vocatives (direct address forms); for example, *man, dude, guy*, etc., an increase in 'disguised imperatives' (e.g., *why don't you . . .*, *do you want to . . .*, *let's . . .*), and an increase in gender neutralisation (especially 1961–91); for example, *Ms, chairperson/chair, his* have become *her/his*, and the use of singular *they* and *them*. In the past, such usage was viewed as grammatically incorrect, but now they have become widely used and accepted (Leech *et al.*, 2009).

Task 3.5

Log on to the *Time Magazine* Corpus of American English at http://corpus.byu.edu/time/ and find out the frequencies of the following words in different periods of time. What do you notice?

Word(s)	1920s	1960s	2000s
must			
ought to			
going to			
guy			
Madam			

Production of dictionaries

Major modern-day English dictionaries are corpus-based. Do you want to find out more about the English dictionary that you are using?

Production of other reference materials

Apart from dictionaries, corpus analysis has resulted in different types of reference materials such as textbooks, grammars and practice books.

Task 3.6

Answer all the questions below to understand more about the dictionary you are using.

- Name of English dictionary:

- Go to the dictionary online – URL:

- Name of the corpus the dictionary is based on:

- Details about the corpus (e.g., size, year(s) of creation, contents of the corpus, different texts in each corpus, how the corpus was used to create the dictionary, types of computer program used to search the corpus, etc.):

Task 3.7

To learn about the Cambridge International Corpus (CIC), go to www.cambridge.org/hk/elt/catalogue/subject/item2701617/Cambridge-International-Corpus/?site_locale=zh_HK.

1 Read the landing page of the CIC and answer the following questions:
   - What is a corpus?
   - What is it used for?

2 Try to answer the questions on the landing page to find out why using a corpus is useful and how.

3 Now click 'Look at a list of all Cambridge titles that are based on or informed by the Corpus'. Which of the titles do you find most useful for you, and in what ways?

4 On the left, click 'What can the corpus do for me?' and click 'if you are a student'.

Using a corpus for language research

In addition to tracking English language changes and production of dictionaries, textbooks and other learning and reference materials, a major application of corpora is to study different aspects of linguistics, including lexis, multi-word units, grammar, discourse, pragmatics, discourse intonation, registers (e.g., academic, business, social, scientific and legal) and genres (e.g., university textbooks, financial reports, conversation, plays and contracts). In the following, you will complete a number of activities to know more about how corpus linguistics can be applied in the study of a range of linguistic phenomena and features. These will be further developed and illustrated in Chapters 5, 6 and 7. Chapter 8 reinforces your knowledge and skills by describing more relevant research findings on the topics presented in this chapter.

Lexis

The basic information that computer software can find in a corpus is the word frequency list – 'All corpora do is reveal which words are used in their constituent texts and how frequent they are' (Moon, 2010: 197). In addition to word frequencies, the general lexicon (i.e., the main words) of a language can be found. Table 3.3 shows the distribution of lemmas (base forms and inflections) in the Bank of English (BoE), a general English reference corpus, and 'their approximate frequencies per million words of corpus text' (Moon, 2010: 197–8).

Searching a corpus can also provide information about word formation: derivation and word compounds (Moon, 2010: 199). Table 3.4 shows frequent derivations from *colour/color*, frequent words formed with the prefix *hyper-*, and frequent compounds (Moon, 2010: 199).

Corpus linguistic studies have found that different word forms of a lemma behave differently, in the kinds of words they are co-selected with and their semantic and pragmatic meanings. As Sinclair (1991) remarks: 'There is a good case for arguing that each distinct form is potentially a unique lexical unit, and that forms should only be conflated into lemmas when their environments show a certain amount and type of similarity' (pp. 44–51). At the basic level of word frequency, for example, 'the base and -ed forms occur more frequently than the -ing and -s forms' (Hunston, 2010: 146).

In addition to word frequency lists, another basic corpus search function and method of analysis used in corpus linguistics is to generate and study the concordances of search items. A concordance is 'a collection of the occurrences of a word form, each in its own textual environment' (Sinclair, 1991: 32), where textual environment equates to the immediate co-text on either side of the search item.

Table 3.3 Distribution of lemmas in the Bank of English (BoE)

Number of items	Percentage of BoE	Approximate rate of occurrence
Top 10	23.5	8,000+ occurrences per million
Top 100	44.9	1,000 per million
Top 1,000	68.5	100+ per million
Top 10,000	88.9	5+ per million
Top 25,000	92.5	1+ per million
Top 1,000,000	94.5	1+ per 20 million

Task 3.8

(TC)

Study the information below (Moon, 2010: 197–8) and describe the characteristics of words in the Bank of English (BoE):

Top ten frequent words in BoE (450 million words)	Lexical words in top 100 words in BoE (450 million words)
the, be, of, and, a, in, to (infinitive particle), have, to (preposition), and it	• year, time, person/people, day, man, way • say, go, make, get, take, know, see, come, think, give • new, good

Moon (2010: 208) examines BoE's 20-million-word sub-corpus of English conversation and local radio broadcasts and finds that the lexicon is 'smaller and more homogenized, with fewer types, just under 47,000' ('types' are distinct words in a corpus). The top 100 include lexical words: 'mean', 'sort', 'thing', 'want', and discourse markers and phatics: 'yeah', 'yes', 'right', 'well', 'okay', 'er', 'erm', 'mm', etc.

Compare the frequent words in the whole BoE with those in the spoken BoE. What do you find about the characteristics of the two corpora?

Table 3.4 Examples of frequent word formation in Bank of English (BoE)

Derivations from colour/color	Words formed with prefix hyper-	Frequent compounds of colour
colourful, colourless, discolour, colourant, clourist, colouration, uncoloured, colourable, colourism, colouristic, recolour, etc.	hypertension, hyperactive, hyperinflation, hypermarket, hypertext, hyperventilate, hypersensitive	watercolour, colourway, colour-fast, colour-washed, colour coded, hair colour (dye), full-colour, two/four colour (of printing), etc.

Task 3.9

Go to BYU-BNC: BRITISH NATIONAL CORPUS at http://corpus. byu.edu/bnc/. Search for any four verbs and find out the relative frequencies of the -ed, -ing, and -s forms. See grid below. The percentages of the first two examples 'fill' and 'disappear' are extracted from Leech *et al.* (2001).

1. fill 35%	filled 47%	filling 14%	fills 5%
2. disappear 25%	disappeared 59%	disappearing 9%	disappears 7%
3.			
4.			
5.			
6.			

Task 3.10

Corpus data shows that the lexical word 'thing' can function as 'a proform or vagueness marker', and in the formula 'the NOUN is', 'thing' can preface a reason, point or new information' (Moon, 2010: 209). Study the concordance lines in Figure 3.1 from the Hong Kong Financial Services Corpus (HKFSC) (7,341,937 words) at http://rcpce. engl.polyu.edu.hk/HKFSC/ and describe the functions of 'thing'.

Task 3.11

Study the sample concordances of 'round' in Figure 3.2 from the Hong Kong Corpus of Construction and Surveying English, http:// rcpce.engl.polyu.edu.hk/HKCSCE/ (5.7 million words). Identify the word class of 'round' (noun, adjective, verb, preposition, adverbial particle) (Granath, 2009: 50) in each line.

1 inions in our discussion. In fact, the most valuable **thing** about Hong Kong is the freedom of everybody to

2 for regional nitiatives to surface. This is no bad **thing** and perhaps the pragmatic way forward, given the

3 standardised product means everybody buying the same **thing** and this gives people assurance and helps break

4 easy task. The key, I believe, is to do the right **thing** at the right time. Had our public finances yielded

5 network for catastrophe insurance. Awareness is one **thing** but where and how to get the right insurance is

6 divulge or communicate to any court any matter or **thing** coming under his notice in the exercise of his

7 sed, in contravention of subsection (3)(b);(b) any **thing** done in reliance on any such resolution, shall be

8 by reason of any error of judgement or any matter or **thing** done or suffered or omitted to be done by it in

9 y reason of any error of judgement or any matter or **thing** done or suffered or omitted to be done by it in

10 diversification and how is it going to do the right **thing** for China so this is a big issue and um Chinas

11 experience will have implication for all of us. One **thing** for sure is that Marsh has helped raise the

12 try to kind of bridge this pension shortfall first **thing** governments always think of of course is taxes

13 e about it. CPD is a pet subject of Mark. The first **thing** he told me was that the old CPD programme had an

14 nada 18 years ago. "At that happy moment, the first **thing** in mind was to take a photo at the HSBC main

15ay have different views on the issues. The important **thing** is for us to work closely together and maintain

16 We believe that everyone has dreams – the important **thing** is how to bring them to reality. Through this

17 est of it but this is actually going on (.) second **thing** is that starting with Shanghai but then also other

18 perience on their tour to Hong Kong. The depressing **thing** is that such instances are definitely not the

19 velop, we will all stand to benefit.?The important **thing** is to ensure that Hong Kong retains its

20 11 the more strength when it is over. The important **thing** is we must notlose heart now. The biggest tragedy

Figure 3.1 Sample HKFSC concondance lines for *thing*

1 house of beauty and creative gardening. A walk **round** its fifteen acres is like taking a trip round
2 and asked if I'd like to go on a `Cezanne tour" **round** Gardanne. I thought it would be quite
3 with Lytham St Ann's at its mouth and Southport **round** the corner. [p] Upstream from Preston is the
4 alias Norman Lumsden, rather than the other way **round**. Those Yellow Pages certainly have
5 blue chickens and men with daggers for lips all **round** the pool table. My heart pants. Two days
6 in modern and traditional kitchens a like a **round** 4.5-pint cocotte casserole costs around &
7 again, of trying to make what water there is go **round** all the industries, farmers and domestic
8 ELECTIONS SECOND ROUND [/h] The second **round** of voting in parliamentary elections in the
9 Open [/h] There was a huge upset in the third **round** of the Austrian Open in Kitzbuhel when the
10 n Golders Green Road. `Sorry to bring you this **round**–about route to Laura's, but she asked me to
11 first part of the chicane as Ayrton was coming **round**. Obviously I spoilt his line, however
12 liffs. They were kneeling on the bank, and all **round** them on the grass like pale flowers clothing
13 nsual family expenses recently. When she gets **round** to looking into her accounts, she'll find
14 it wouldn't surprise me." He spun Angelica **round** with fingers which clawed into her neck. `
15 in Bombay yesterday with a 38-minute first-**round** win over Ahmed Faizy, of Egypt. However,
16 about once a week, both of them will buy a **round**, at a cost of £ 20 a time pound; 1,
17 re emerging to add a competitive edge to early-**round** matches, with Chanda Rubin brightening the
18 ground was evident again in Faldo's opening **round**, a one-under-par 70, in the MCI Classic at
19 Caernarfon Castle. Quite a lot of people came **round** to the house to watch. [p] I have never been
20 [p] Graeme Sharp scored their first, sneaking **round** the back to meet Nick Henry's diagonal ball

Figure 3.2 Sample HKCSCE concordance lines for *round*

Grammar

Grammar is about 'how sentences and utterances are formed' and the two basic principles of grammar are 'the arrangement of items (syntax) and the structure of items (morphology)' (Carter and McCarthy, 2006: 2). Corpus linguists, such as Carter and McCarthy (2006) and Biber *et al.* (1999) have made major contributions to the description of spoken and written English grammar. They describe 'common and uncommon choices' speakers and writers make in large collections of texts, and showing 'the patterns that reveal what is typical and untypical in particular of contexts' (Conrad, 2010: 228). Carter and McCarthy's (2006) *Cambridge Grammar of English* is based on the 700-million-word Cambridge International Corpus (CIC). One of their important findings is that 'the grammar of academic English is closer (in both its spoken and written forms) to the grammar of general written English than to the grammar of general spoken English' (Carter and McCarthy, 2006: 267), and, for example, they find that, in academic style, adjectives are frequently pre-modified by adverbs. Complete Task 3.12.

Phraseology

Corpus linguistics has shown that meaning is not created by isolated words, but rather meaning is created by the co-selection of words. In other words, patterns of co-selection among words have a direct connection with meaning. Corpus linguistics has shown how words were used in texts, particularly the importance of surrounding language (co-text) and the strong recurrent patterns of language. Corpus findings have established that, to different degrees, 'words occur as parts of phraseologies, whether collocational, structural, or both' (Moon, 2010: 199) (see Sinclair, 1987, 2004: 24–48; Stubbs, 2001: 80ff; O'Keeffe *et al.*, 2007: 14–15). Phraseologies range from idioms (e.g., *as red as blood*, *green-eyed monster*, *white lie*), phrasal verbs (e.g., *keep on*,

---

Task 3.12

Carter and McCarthy (2006: 267) note that, in academic English, the demonstrative pronoun 'this' is used as a textual signal to 'signal the structure or organization of the text' and 'guide the reader around the text and point to how the writer/speaker wants the text to be interpreted'. In the 5.6-million-word Corpurs of Research Articles (CRA), http://rcpce.engl.polyu.edu.hk/RACorpus/default.htm, there are 33,467 instances of 'this'. Study the sample concordance lines on p. 46 and find out the functions of 'this' in each line. See Figure 3.3.

1   Pockrass 1986; Weitzer 1985, 1986, 1987 a, b), **this** forms only part of RUC duties, given the
special position of

2   the characteristics of divided societies, the focus of **this** study also has a relevance, of increasing
proportion,

3   the social context in which it operates, but **this** context is both a spur and a hindrance to
research on the RUC.

4   very controversial topic in a sensitive environment, and **this** sensitivity has implications for the
research

5 some of the social processes lying behind and operating upon **this** study. Above all, however, this chapter is

6   (Holdaway 1982, 1983: 12). The only exception to **this** is the discussion of the likely reactive
effect caused by the

7   However, an increasing awareness of **this** omission has led some specialists in the
area of ethnographic

8   that which we ourselves have written (Woolgar 1988b). **This** reflexivity, what Woolgar more accurately
calls

Figure 3.3 Sample CRA concordance lines for *this*

Task 3.13

Study the sample concordance lines 'disposable income' from the Hong Kong Financial Services Corpus, http://rcpce.engl.polyu.edu.hk/HKFSC. The total number of occurrences is thirty-two, and nine lines are extracted. Study the co-text to work out the meaning of the phrase. See Figure 3.4.

---

keep up), jargon expressions (e.g., *Doctor of Philosophy (Ph.D)*, *Initial Public Offering (IPO)*), fixed phrases or semi-preconstructed phrases (e.g., *in due course, in order to, by the way*), flexible phrases (e.g., *on the way, on his way, on my way*), fixed sentences (e.g., *I suppose so, I'm afraid not*), to collocates (including n-grams, skipgrams, and concgrams). Many phraseologies are recurrent adjacent words, called n-grams (e.g., *Thank you*).

Another kind of phraseology involves non-adjacent word co-occurrences (e.g., *the . . . of*, *environmental . . . protection, play . . . role* and *role . . . play*.

Lexico-grammar

Corpus linguistics makes the study of frequencies and patterns of vocabulary-grammar co-occurrences (lexico-grammatical) quick and easy, especially if the corpus is annotated in parts of speech (POS).

In addition to studying the frequencies of occurrence of lexico-grammatical patterns, you can focus on the function of the patterns. For example, in grammar, when an adjective is used with a noun, the adjective can have either a 'selecting' function or a 'focusing' function (Sinclair, 2003). A selecting function means drawing attention to 'the essentially physical nature of the meaning of the noun in the context' (Sinclair 2003: 31), and a focusing function lets us know whether the adjective limits someone's full range of experience of the noun to one particular kind of noun. For example, the adjective

---

Task 3.14

Study the sample concordance lines for 'income/recognised/statement' (Annual Reports, Hong Kong Financial Services Corpus). Find out the different patterns of word co-occurrences. See Figure 3.5.

1   from 2003. The per capita **disposable income** for urban households increased from approximately RMB

2   demand, continued increase in **disposable income** has also stimulated domestic consumption of textile an

3   the increasing trend of per capita **disposable income** in Jiangsu Province, there is a possibility that

4   stronger spending power as their **disposable income** increased steadily. A sturdy trend in retail sales i

5   performance and strong growth in public **disposable income** led to the increase in the balance of deposits.

6 China_s urbanization rate and the increase in **disposable income** levels of the urban population in China for

7   China's economy, strong growth in public **disposable income**, limited alternative investment channels and rising

8   GDP, total population and per capita **disposable income** of urban household respectively among all provinces

9   quality. GDP, per capita GDP and per capita **disposable income** of urban households in Jiangsu Province GDP

Figure 3.4 Sample HKFSC concordance lines for *disposable income*

```
1  cognised in equity are recognised through the income statement and classified as 'Gains less losses
2  recognised in reserves are recognised in the income statement. Provisions Provisions for
3  inputs, is not recognised immediately in the income statement but is recognised over the life of the
4     goodwill is recognised immediately in the income statement as it arises. At the date of disposal
5     properties to be recognised directly in the income statement as they arise. Prior to the
6  llion) was recognised as rental income in the income statement in respect of operating
7  fair value gain or loss is recognised in the income statement. r Pension and other post-retirement
8  nder these circumstances is recognised in the income statement in the period in which it occurs.
```

Figure 3.5 Sample concordance lines for *income/recognised statement* (Annual Reports, HKFSC)

Task 3.15

Go to BYU-BNC: BRITISH NATIONAL CORPUS at http://corpus. byu.edu/bnc/. Then go to 'Query syntax' under 'More information' on the right → Part of Speech [More information] → Click here for a list of these parts of speech tags. You will read 'VVZ The -s form of lexical verbs (e.g., forgets, sends, lives, returns)' and 'VVD The past tense form of lexical verbs (e.g., forgot, sent, lived, returned)'. The table shows the search results of entering '[VVZ]' and '[VVD]' as the search word(s): top ten -s form of lexical verbs and top ten past tense form of lexical verbs. What are the similarities and differences that you find?

[VVZ]	Total	[VVD]	Total
SAYS	39,353	SAID	176,671
SEEMS	20,783	WENT	45,772
MAKES	16,385	CAME	44,735
COMES	15,687	TOOK	37,087
GOES	14,586	MADE	35,466
MEANS	13,613	THOUGHT	34,560
TAKES	11,604	GOT	31,292
GIVES	10,328	LOOKED	28,057
FOLLOWS	9,989	SAW	24,524
LOOKS	9,969	KNEW	23,968

Task 3.16

Study the sample concordance lines for all the twenty instances of 'physical' in the Hong Kong Policy Address Speeches 1997–2009 (153,198 words) (http://rcpce.engl.polyu.edu.hk/policy_addresses/ default.htm) one by one to find out whether 'physical' has a focusing or selecting function. See Figure 3.6.

```
1   ind spiritual food and physical food together, and in our
2   ment contract with the physical works contract. Some of t
3   voices for payment for physical work, and passing these t
4   available? The Q S the physical works The physical works.
5   the physical works The physical works. Yeah. We' re gon na
6    report as well as the physical works is it? Yes. Mm. Yes.
7   ablishing not just the physical link of the chunnel but e
8   m and we' re, we' re not physical people are we? We' re not
9   dison Wesley, with U S physical problems restricting the,
10  nt noise pollution and physical stress to the residents.
11  in terms of those with physical disability or learning dis
12  earning disability and physical disability we' re talking
13   very complex cases on physical disability, erm, where we,
14  s, that have to do the physical assessments er, financial
15  e the people doing the physical assessments, for example i
16   by that I mean abuse, physical and sexual abuse, er, con
17  earning disability and physical disability, there will be
18  r? That is People with physical and sensory disabilities,
19   children who need the physical as well? It' s not always
20  so w Shorter Yeah, not physical length of words. Now in a
```

Figure 3.6 Sample concordance lines for *physical*

physical in *physical appearance*, which refers to the complete class of appearance as there is no *mental appearance*, can be omitted, as *physical* is only highlighting an aspect of the meaning of the noun, and so it has a 'focusing' function; whereas, in *stone house*, the adjective *stone* has a 'selecting' function, as there are *brick houses*, *stone houses*, and *wooden houses* (Sinclair, 2003: 36).

Literal and metaphorical meanings

Corpora provide authentic and situated language resources for the study of literal and metaphorical meanings. The 'discourse dynamics' framework (Cameron, 2010), for example, is useful for metaphorical studies in language as it accounts for what we know about actual discourse. Li and Zhong (2008) examine food metaphors in English financial reports, primarily from the Hong Kong Financial Services Corpus (HKFSC). They found that food is often used to talk about aspects of social and cultural life, and compared to topics, such as sex and gender, family, religion and business (Li and Zhong, 2008). Table 3.5 summarises the results.

Table 3.5 Metaphor use in business English

Category of metaphor	Metaphor	Metaphorical meaning
food	• pie • fruit • food	• profit, interest, money • the results of efforts spent over time • things that provide mental stimulus for thinking
food consumption	• eat • swallow • devour • appetite	• damage or destroy something • forced to take in • merge by force • desire

Task 3.17

Study the sample concordance lines for 'fruit' from the Hong Kong Financial Services Corpus (HKFSC) (7.3 million words) at http://rcpce.engl.polyu.edu.hk/HKFSC/. A total of 38 instances of 'fruit' are found. Which of the instances below are used literally and which are used metaphorically? Describe the metaphorical meanings. See Figure 3.7.

```
1    must now reap this first  fruit  and replant its seeds for
2   sion has eventually borne  fruit,  and we are here today to
3      take some time to bear  fruit.  As you would expect, I rem
4    fore the process can bear  fruit.  Certainly, I would not und
5   not mainly made of milk),  fruit  crystal, drink essence 165
6        had continued to bear  fruit  during 2000, with the HKMA
7     on are starting to bear  fruit.  Enterprises are putting m
8    in previous periods bore  fruit.  Foreign exchange option-
9    ls for exhibition, fresh  fruit,  fresh vegetables, plant
10    rice; raw timber; fresh  fruit;  fresh gardening herb; fre
11  nts are beginning to bear  fruit.  Government's support aside
12   res some of the economic  fruit,  growth would not be sustai
13   eloped markets will bear  fruit.  I am sure that in view of
14  t their efforts may bear  fruit  in the future. And this cut
15  or R&D activities to bear  fruit  it is not just funding that
16   01   13/11/2011   32 beer;  fruit  juice; mineral water (drink)
17  of water, soft drinks and  fruit  juices in Hong Kong and the
18    se measures are bearing  fruit.  Let me cite some examples.
19    ss are beginning to bear  fruit.  More needs to be done but
20  pen new markets also bore  fruit.  Newsline Express, an outdo
```

Figure 3.7 Sample HKFSC concordance lines for *fruit*

Discourse

Compared to lexis, phraseology and grammar, corpus research into discourse has had a slow start. Thornbury (2010) discusses the three senses of discourse, namely discourse as connected text, discourse-as-language-in-context/use (p. 270) and discourse-as-social-practice (p. 283). Most of the corpus studies in discourse are of the first sense (i.e., to examine '"the describable internal relationships" of texts' (Thornbury, 2010: 271) in the corpora. Using a Systemic Functional Linguistic approach and corpus-based approach, Herriman and Aronsson (2009: 101–5) study the usage of objective and subjective interpersonal metaphors as themes in 'argumentative writing by Swedish advanced learners in the International Corpus of Learner English and native speakers in the Louvian Corpus of Native English Essays'. The WordSmith Tools concordance program (Scott, 2004) was used to search for subjective interpersonal metaphors such as *I think*, *I believe*, *I am sure*, *I know* and *I feel*. Their research finds that Swedish learners use more multiple themes containing interpersonal information and more cleft constructions to thematise new information and to express personal opinions, resulting in 'a more emphatic style of persuasion and greater involvement and interaction with the reader' (Herriman and Aronsson, 2009: 101).

Below are three types of cleft constructions (Thornbury, 2010: 110):

1   It-cleft: *It is the people's opinion, not the government itself, that worries me.* (ICLE-SW-ULX-037)

2   Basic pseudo-cleft: *What we should try to understand is that we in fact can learn from change and renewal.* (ICLE-SW-UL-108)

3   Reversed pseudo-cleft: *That is what scares me.* (ICLE-SW-ULX-029)

Pragmatics

Pragmatics is 'meaning in interaction' (Thomas, 1995: 22–3), underlying that meaning in discourse is 'dynamic'. In other words, language

Task 3.18   (TC)

Study the sample concordance lines for 'it is' in the BLC Online KWIC Concordancer at www.someya-net.com/concordancer/index.html. The Search Corpus is 01. Business Letter Corpus (BLC2000), with 505 instances of 'it is'. Find out the functions of 'it is'. See Figure 3.8.

```
 1  my opinion, however,  it is  a mistake not to integrate
 2  e you feel good, but  it is  a most worthwhile " thank
 3  ten to the wireless,  it is  a much greater pleasure st
 4  :00442] I understand  it is  a multimedia program and i
 5  :15:02158] In short,  it is  a pleasure to do business
 6  ccessful meeting and  it is  a pleasure to help you in
 7  as season approaches  it is  a pleasure to think back w
 8  such a young man and  it is  a pleasure to wish you a h
 9  316] (For one thing,  it is  a preview of the future.
10  3] Mr. Hardman feels  it is  a privilege to represent t
11  :03437] For my part,  it is  a real pleasure to reflect
12  inting loyalty, then  it is  a record anyone may be pro
13   number of years and  it is  a source of deep satisfact
14  m as yourselves, and  it is  a source of pride to us th
15  ife's milestones and  it is  a special pleasure for me
16   cash flow — worse,   it is  a strain we had not antici
17  C2:25:04994] We hope  it is  a very happy one for you a
18  all we need to prove  it is  a visit from you and your
19  ] For items 2 and 3,  it is  absolutely necessary to ho
20    [ BLC2:32:01970] If  it is  acceptable, the group woul
```

Figure 3.8 Sample BLC concordance lines for *it is*

in use does not have a fixed meaning, or a set of meanings. The meaning of language in use cannot be separated from the context in which it is used; instead, meanings are negotiated by both speakers/writers and hearers/readers, dependent upon the context (physical, social and linguistic) and the 'meaning potential' of what is said/written, that emphasises the roles of speaker/writer and hearer/reader in the joint construction of meaning through language use. The relation between pragmatics and corpus linguistics is problematic, as 'corpora record text, not meaning' (Rühlemann, 2010: 289). A corpus needs to be annotated pragmatically in order for corpus linguistic methods to be applied to the corpus to search for any patterns of pragmatics.

Pragmatic annotation adds information about the kinds of speech act (or dialogue act) that occur in an utterance; for instance, the utterance *okay* can be tagged as an acknowledgement, a request, an acceptance, an agreement or a pragmatic marker initiating a new exchange (Leech, 2005). However, the number of pragmatically annotated corpora is extremely small, except for the Corpus of Verbal Response Modes (VRM) Annotated Utterances Corpus (Stiles, 1992), the Speech Act Annotated Corpus for Dialogue Systems (Leech and

Weisser, 2003) and some speech acts tagged in a small sub-corpus of the Michigan Corpus of Academic Spoken English (MICASE).

In corpus linguistics, at the level of lexical item, the expression of 'a subtle element of attitudinal, often pragmatic meaning' is called 'semantic prosody' (Sinclair 2004: 145). Semantic prosody is used to express the attitude or evaluation of the writer or speaker. It is more abstract, and the effect often 'extends wider, over a considerable stretch of text' (p. 150), but it can be revealed through the study of corpora.

Task 3.19

Study the sample concordance lines for 'global' from a specialised Corpus of Financial Crisis (CFC) (157,146 words) collected from the website of a newspaper (*South China Morning Post*) in Hong Kong from 1 November 2008 to 12 March 2009, with news reports and comments related to financial crisis. Find out the semantic prosody of 'global'. See Figure 3.9.

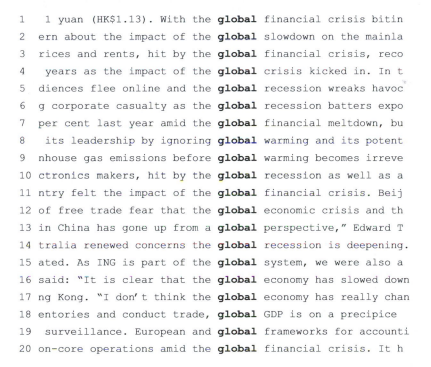

```
1    1 yuan (HK$1.13). With the global financial crisis bitin
2    ern about the impact of the global slowdown on the mainla
3    rices and rents, hit by the global financial crisis, reco
4     years as the impact of the global crisis kicked in. In t
5    diences flee online and the global recession wreaks havoc
6    g corporate casualty as the global recession batters expo
7    per cent last year amid the global financial meltdown, bu
8     its leadership by ignoring global warming and its potent
9    nhouse gas emissions before global warming becomes irreve
10   ctronics makers, hit by the global recession as well as a
11   ntry felt the impact of the global financial crisis. Beij
12   of free trade fear that the global economic crisis and th
13   in China has gone up from a  global perspective," Edward T
14   tralia renewed concerns the  global recession is deepening.
15   ated. As ING is part of the  global system, we were also a
16   said: "It is clear that the  global economy has slowed down
17   ng Kong. "I don't think the  global economy has really chan
18   entories and conduct trade,  global GDP is on a precipice
19    surveillance. European and  global frameworks for accounti
20   on-core operations amid the  global financial crisis. It h
```

Figure 3.9 Sample concordance lines for *global*

Many text corpora, whether or not tagged for parts of speech (POS-tagged), have been studied in the areas of 'conversational organizations, discourse marking and speech act expressions' (Rühlemann, 2010: 292). Cheng (2007), for example, examines the 1-million-word prosodically transcribed Hong Kong Corpus of Spoken English (HKCSE) to study how often intercultural speakers in a variety of communicative contexts and discourses in Hong Kong initiate simultaneous talk (ST), how ST behaviour compares across the four different domains of use of English (academic, business, conversation and public), and what speakers say to initiate ST. Table 3.6 shows that ST is most frequently found in the conversation (58.32 per cent), followed by business (22.44 per cent), public (12.81 per cent), and academic (6.4 per cent) sub-corpora.

Searching for the words taught in school textbooks for interrupting others in the sub-corpora of the HKCSE, Cheng (2007) finds that the most frequently occurring forms are discourse particles which serve as 'complementary acts' (Stenström, 1994: 37), namely *OK/Okay* (394 times), *Well* (132 times), and *Actually* (20 times). Another finding is that, contrary to what the textbooks say, the frequency of politeness markers of apology *Excuse me* (3 times), *Sorry* (5 times) and *I am sorry* (once) is negligible. All of the other language forms suggested by textbooks do not occur at all in the HKCSE (Table 3.7). Based on these findings, Cheng (2007) argues for the value of using corpus findings in textbook writing.

Also based on the HKCSE, speech act studies have been conducted: disagreement (Cheng and Warren, 2005), giving opinions (Cheng and Warren, 2006), and checking understandings (Cheng and Warren, 2007). Adophs (2008) examines speech act expressions (e.g., *why don't you*) that introduce suggestions.

Table 3.6 Number of occurrences of ST initiated by Hong Kong Chinese and native English speakers (NES)

HKCSE sub-corpora	HKC as initiator of ST	NES as initiator of ST	Other speakers as initiator of ST	Total number of occurrences of ST
Academic (26.3%)	600	101	72	773 (6.43%)
Business (16.8%)	2,046	641	9	2,696 (22.44%)
Conversation (29.5%)	3,768	2,865	374	7,007 (58.32%)
Public (27.4%)	1,454	66	20	1,540 (12.81%)
Total (100%)	7,868	3,673	475	12,016 (100%)

Table 3.7 Textbook language forms to interrupt others found in HKCSE

Language form	Academic	Business	Conv.	Public	Total
Excuse me.	0	1	2	0	3
Sorry.	2	3	0	0	5
I'm sorry.	0	1	0	0	1
Just a moment . . .	0	0	0	0	0
Well . . .	3	11	81	37	132
O.K. / Okay	36	188	131	39	394
Well, O.K.	0	0	1	0	1
Actually	2	8	10	1	21
As I was saying . . .	0	0	0	0	0
By the way . . .	0	0	0	0	0
Can I just break in there?	0	0	0	0	0
Can I have a turn?	0	0	0	0	0
Could I just finish my point first?	0	0	0	0	0
If I could just say something . . .	0	0	0	0	0
If I could just come in here . . .	0	0	0	0	0
I want to say something, please.	0	0	0	0	0
I think we are losing balance here.	0	0	0	0	0
To return to my point.	0	0	0	0	0
To get back to what I was just saying.	0	0	0	0	0
Going back to what I was saying.	0	0	0	0	0
Total	43	212	225	77	557

Task 3.20

Cheng and Warren (2006) find 'I think' the most frequent language form used by speakers in the business sub-corpus of the HKCSE when giving opinions. Study the concordance lines on p. 58 from HKCSE to see how 'I think' is used as an opine marker and describe the nature of the opinion given by the speaker, and discuss why 'I think' is used. See Figure 3.10.

Discourse intonation

The Hong Kong Corpus of Spoken English (about 1 million words) is prosodically transcribed and analysed in terms of discourse intonation (Cheng *et al.*, 2008). The prosodically transcribed HKCSE was annotated in such a way that computer keyboard symbols are used to represent the different systems in David Brazil's discourse intonation framework, which consists of prominence, tone, key and termination (Brazil, 1997), and a search engine, iConc, was written for retrieving the discourse intonation systems in the HKCSE (Prosodic). In the iConc

1 ing PhD studies then their fees are paid **I think** ((pause)) B: but I don't know if there's pressure as

2 ask you b1: ** mm questions about so I **I think** that it's really in good order and the only thing

3 something else we can look at that later **I think** that should go (.) * of the second

4 I call on those words B: yeah * **I think** **I think** that that will be useful (.) erm and I don't think

5 a typical financial volatility and third **I think** that trade openness and much of the reforms being

6 stuff a1: yeah they are local people but **I think** (.) that's why B: I see a lot of Chinese girls

7 er as I gave you to you your class rep okay **I think** the first few pages are the appendix what do you

8 n a little bit on er grammar but mostly er **I think** the problem here was organization and not really er

9 you want to add something Raymond b1: yeah **I think** the question also er (.) er your question is whether

10 dgcal b2: I I can't give you a breakdown **I think** there're good reasons for it Edgecal is a listed com

Figure 3.10

prosodic notation system, prominence is represented by 'UPPER CASE letters' (Cheng *et al.*, 2009: 36).

In discourse intonation, 'prominence' is used by speakers as a means of distinguishing those words which are situationally informative (Brazil 1997: 23–5). While selection, or non-selection, of prominence is not fixed, it is possible to observe patterns of recurrent prominence choices by speakers because, while every context of interaction is unique, speaker behaviour is to some extent predictable (Cheng *et al.*, 2009: 85) (e.g., speakers frequently use 'or' in combination with cardinal numbers to represent a vague approximation) (pp. 102–5). Figure 3.11 shows 'one or two' to be understood as having the vague meaning of 'a small number' (Quirk *et al.*, 1985: 963).

Registers and genres

Most modern corpora are organized in terms of text categories (Biber, 2010: 241). The London-Lund Corpus (LLC) of spoken English, for example, is one of the most widely used electronic corpora of English

```
1    } { = through [ < ONE > ] } { \ or [ < TWO > ] } { =
2     { = er after [ < ONE > ] } { \/ or [ < TWO > ] month
3    ATter > } * { \ [ ONE ] or < _ TWO > } b:
4    } { \ we' ll [ DO ] ONE or < TWO > } { = [ EIther ] gr
5    E > ] } { \ par- [ ONE ] or < TWO > } { = particular
6    } { \ [ BEEN ] to one or < TWO > there } { = but i' m
7        < TAKE > ] you one } { = [ < _ OR > ] } { \ maybe tw
8    aBOUT > ] } { \/ [ ONE ] or two ((inaudible)) WARrior
9    { \ [ < WHILE > ] one or two } a1:
10   by [ FOcusing ] on ONE or two < ASpects > } { \ inste
11   < STAY > ] } { \ [ ONE ] or two < DAYS > to } { ? [ <
12   e > of } { = the [ ONE ] or TWO < diSEASE > } (.) * {
13   PEND > ] } { / [ ONE ] or two < MInutes > } { = [ <
14   be just } { \ er [ ONE ] or two < PROjects > } { = it
15   LEAST ] we prePARE ONE or two < SONGS > } { ? you kno
16   E > er } (.) { \ [ ONE ] or TWO < STUdents > } { \ [
17   { \ a period of [ ONE ] or two months at < ^ LEAST >
18   = and [ PERhaps ] one or two Other < _ TOpics > } {
19   Wer > } { \ than [ ONE ] or two Others in the < REgio
20   then [ ^ WE ] find ONE or TWO words < MOST > is the }
21   = in the [ NEXT ] one or two years but < WE > think}
22   may be [ WORK ] in ONE outLET or < TWO > } * { \ for
```

Figure 3.11 Concordance lines for *one or two* in HKCSE (Prosodic)

speech. It contains about half a million words of spoken British English categorised into face-to-face and telephone conversations, discussions, public and prepared speech (Svartvik, 1990). The International Corpus of English (ICE) is a large corpus that contains spoken and written texts from different regional varieties of English all over the world (Greenbaum, 1996). In order to ensure that individual varieties of English in the ICE are compatible, each regional sub-corpus follows a common corpus design. The spoken part of each variety contains 300 texts each of about 2,000 words, amounting to a total of approximately 600,000 words. It is grouped into dialogues and monologues, each containing a range of text categories. Launched in 1991, the Bank of English is one of the largest collections of English texts mainly from Britain, with the inclusion of American and Australian data. There are eleven sub-corpora altogether in the collection and the UK spoken sub-section contains 9.3 million words ('The Bank of English User Guide', n.d.).

Many more corpus studies have focused on the overall description of written registers, such as advertisements, reports, email messages, business letters and academic prose, than spoken register, such as conversation, service encounters, call centre interactions and public speeches, to examine 'a suite of linguistic features that are characteristic of the register' (Biber, 2010: 246). Other corpus studies of register variation focus on a particular linguistic feature, for example, Hyland (1998) studies the use of hedges within the register of scientific research articles, and Swales (2001) studies the discourse functions of *point* and *thing* in university speech in MICASE.

Task 3.21

Go to the Michigan Corpus of Spoken Academic English (MICASE) and browse the 'Transcript Attributes' → 'Speech Event Types'. What are the spoken academic text categories that comprise MICASE?

Task 3.22

Study the sample concordance lines for 'reply' in the BLC Online KWIC Concordancer at www.someya-net.com/concordancer/index. html. The Search Corpus is 01. Business Letter Corpus (BLC2000), with 276 instances of 'reply'. Study the co-text of 'reply' in each line to find out the lexico-grammatical patterns of use and the functions. See Figure 3.12.

```
1    [ BLC2:30:00150] Your kind reply -or perhaps a little le
2    LC2:34:02604] We await your reply and immediate action.
3    n stamped envelope for your reply and thank you in advanc
4    [ BLC2:30:00269] Your prompt reply appreciated.
5    tions of March 27, 1982, we reply as follows:
6    l appreciate receiving your reply as soon as possible, pr
7    k forward to receiving your reply as soon as possible.
8     seem to have received your reply as to the details neces
9    2071] We would appreciate a reply as to whether you can a
10   to receiving your favorable reply at your earliest conven
11   e to receive your favorable reply at your earliest conven
12   74] Would you let me have a reply before < date >?
13    appreciate it if you could reply by August 15.
14   h if you would send me your reply by e-mail (tyamada@jpt.
15   ient as possible for you to reply by enclosing a special
16   t if you would send us your reply by fax at your earliest
17   8271] we'll appreciate your reply by March 2.
18   36:01123] Please screen and reply by or about September
19   to receiving your favorable reply by return.
20       BLC2:18:02075] You may reply by telephone at < teleph
```

Figure 3.12

Concluding remarks

This chapter has discussed the nature of corpus linguistics, highlighted the reasons for undertaking corpus linguistic studies, and explained how corpus linguists design and compile their different corpora. Major categories of corpora were described, along with an overview of the discussion as to whether the language contained on the web can be viewed as a corpus. Those who advocate carefully considered design principles are on one side of this debate and those who view a corpus as simply any collection of texts are on the other. Finally, a cross-section of the many applications of corpus linguistics that covered a diverse collection from lexicography to grammar and pragmatics was exemplified.

Notes

1   Parsing is the analysis of text into constituents, such as phrases and clauses.
2   A 'lingua franca' is 'widely used over a relatively large geographical area as a language of wider communication ... a common language but one which is native only to some of its speakers' (Sebba, 1997).

4 Corpus search and analysis methods

This chapter will:

- describe basic corpus search functions and methods of analysis used in corpus linguistics;

- introduce functions found in corpus linguistic software packages such as the generation of word frequency lists and profiles, keyword lists and keyness, concordances, and text analysis statistics; and

- introduce other functions which are less widely known, e.g., ConcGram (Greaves, 2009), which specialises in finding phraseological variation (see Chapter 6), and those which are dedicated to a particular corpus.

Word frequency lists

Generating a list of the most frequent words in a corpus is easily and quickly done and the results are always interesting. Most programs allow you to view the results either alphabetically or based on frequency of occurrence. Whichever way you choose to view the results, the lists typically display the number of instances for each word form and the percentage of the entire corpus that the word form represents. Corpus linguists tend to speak about 'types' and 'tokens', where the number of types refers to the number of distinct, or unique, words in a corpus and the number of tokens refers to the total number of words in a corpus. Here we immediately get into the whole business of what constitutes a type. For example, some studies, and some software programs, count *isn't* as one type and others as two – *is + n't*. You can see in Table 4.1, which lists the most frequent 100 words in the BNC, that the software not only counts *'s* as a separate type, but it also distinguishes between *'s* (as in *it's* and *she's*) and *'s* (as in *Susan's*). This is because the BNC is part-of-speech tagged, which is discussed elsewhere in this chapter, enabling the software to count them as distinct types. There is also the issue of lemmatisation, discussed elsewhere (see Chapter 6), and whether a word frequency list should list singular and plurals, for instance, or the different inflected forms of a verb together in a word frequency list or separately. Most word frequency lists list word forms separately.

When a word frequency list is generated, the number of types and tokens is also displayed. In addition, sometimes displayed is a ratio – type/token ratio or TTR (i.e., number of types divided by the number of tokens) – which is one way of comparing corpora. The higher the TTR, the greater the variety of types in the corpus, which then means there are fewer repetitions of words, unlike a corpus with a low TTR. The TTR ratio, however, can be problematic in that the larger the corpus, the lower the TTR, which tends to be due to words being more likely to be repeated. The way around this problem is to use a standardised type/token ratio (STTR), which arrives at a ratio by calculating the TTR for sections of the corpus. Once it has done this, the software then generates the average across all of the sections, and this average is the STTR (Baker *et al.*, 2006: 15–151).

Mike Scott's (2008) well-known WordSmith 5.0 provides the TTR and STTR every time it creates a word frequency list. In addition to these ratios, the user is also provided with a lot of other statistics such as mean word length, the frequencies for words of different lengths, as well as the number of sentences, paragraphs, headings, sections and the average number of words contained in each. WordSmith can also provide a visual dispersion plot showing where in the corpus a word occurs. This is useful because there is always the danger that a frequent word might not be found throughout a corpus and its frequency is the result of it being used a lot in one particular text or genre. This function is also useful when applied to a single text as it can reveal patterns of 'textual colligation' (Hoey, 2005), the phenomenon where particular words are found to occur more often in particular parts of a text. For example, a study of *Guardian* newspaper articles (O'Donnell *et al.*, 2008) found that instances of *yesterday* are almost always in the opening paragraph.

In Tables 4.1–4.3, the most frequent words in three different corpora are given to illustrate the information which they contain. Table 4.1 is from the BNC, which is a 100-million-word general corpus of English, while Tables 4.2 and 4.3 are from specialised corpora, the Hong Kong Financial Services Corpus (HKFSC, 7.3 million words) and the Hong Kong Engineering Corpus (HKEC, 9.2 million words).

For those who are new to corpus linguistics, the fact that the most frequent words in all three corpora are function words or grammatical words is notable, and clearly shows the crucial role played by such words in English. It is also the same six words, *the, of, and, to, in* and *a* at the top of each list, although the ranking of the last three varies, and this is true of any corpus made up of written texts, or mostly

Table 4.1 100 most frequent words in the BNC

Rank	Word	Frequency	%	Rank	Word	Frequency	%
1	the	6,184,700	6.29	51	can	235,400	0.24
2	of	2,939,100	2.99	52	her	218,300	0.22
3	and	2,681,700	2.73	53	said	208,700	0.21
4	a	2,162,600	2.20	54	who	205,500	0.21
5	in	1,821,400	1.85	55	one	196,200	0.20
6	to	1,628,400	1.66	56	so	189,300	0.19
7	it	1,087,500	1.11	57	up	179,500	0.18
8	is	998,200	1.01	58	as	177,400	0.18
9	to	934,300	0.95	59	them	173,300	0.18
10	was	923,600	0.94	60	some	171,200	0.17
11	I	887,500	0.90	61	when	171,200	0.17
12	for	841,200	0.86	62	could	168,300	0.17
13	that	730,800	0.74	63	him	164,900	0.17
14	you	695,400	0.71	64	into	163,400	0.17
15	he	681,000	0.69	65	its	163,200	0.17
16	be	664,400	0.68	66	then	159,500	0.16
17	with	657,500	0.67	67	two	156,100	0.16
18	on	647,500	0.66	68	out	154,200	0.16
19	by	509,600	0.52	69	time	154,200	0.16
20	at	479,000	0.49	70	my	152,500	0.16
21	have	473,500	0.48	71	about	152,400	0.15
22	are	470,700	0.48	72	did	143,400	0.15
23	not	462,600	0.47	73	your	138,300	0.14
24	this	462,300	0.47	74	now	138,200	0.14
25	's	459,900	0.47	75	me	136,400	0.14
26	but	457,700	0.47	76	no	134,300	0.14
27	had	445,200	0.45	77	other	133,600	0.14
28	they	433,200	0.44	78	only	129,800	0.13
29	his	428,500	0.44	79	just	127,700	0.13
30	from	413,400	0.42	80	more	127,500	0.13
31	she	380,100	0.39	81	these	125,400	0.13
32	that	379,200	0.39	82	also	124,800	0.13
33	which	371,900	0.38	83	people	124,100	0.13
34	or	370,700	0.38	84	know	123,300	0.13
35	we	357,800	0.36	85	any	122,000	0.12
36	's	349,000	0.35	86	first	119,300	0.12
37	an	343,000	0.35	87	see	118,600	0.12
38	~n't	332,800	0.34	88	very	116,500	0.12
39	were	322,700	0.33	89	new	114,500	0.12
40	as	300,600	0.31	90	may	113,500	0.12
41	do	280,200	0.28	91	well	111,900	0.11
42	been	268,600	0.27	92	should	111,200	0.11
43	their	260,800	0.27	93	her	108,500	0.11
44	has	259,300	0.26	94	like	106,400	0.11
45	would	255,100	0.26	95	than	103,300	0.11
46	there	253,200	0.26	96	how	101,600	0.10
47	what	249,300	0.25	97	get	99,500	0.10
48	will	247,000	0.25	98	way	95,800	0.10
49	all	243,600	0.25	99	one	95,300	0.10
50	if	236,900	0.24	100	our	95,000	0.10

Table 4.2 100 most frequent words in the HKFSC

Rank	Word	Frequency	%	Rank	Word	Frequency	%
1	the	484,439	7.32	51	been	13,205	0.20
2	of	297,781	4.50	52	total	12,790	0.19
3	and	203,418	3.07	53	management	12,743	0.19
4	to	175,283	2.65	54	fund	12,608	0.19
5	in	167,158	2.52	55	all	11,994	0.18
6	a	99,448	1.50	56	exchange	11,968	0.18
7	for	70,878	1.07	57	per	11,953	0.18
8	or	60,299	0.91	58	market	11,450	0.17
9	is	57,610	0.87	59	New	11,438	0.17
10	as	55,712	0.84	60	date	11,416	0.17
11	on	54,750	0.83	61	Net	11,353	0.17
12	by	50,530	0.76	62	directors	11,345	0.17
13	be	41,224	0.62	63	value	11,332	0.17
14	with	38,725	0.58	64	December	10,887	0.16
15	at	38,351	0.58	65	capital	10,861	0.16
16	are	37,198	0.56	66	property	10,656	0.16
17	Hong	37,171	0.56	67	were	10,541	0.16
18	Kong	36,184	0.55	68	I	10,490	0.16
19	that	33,563	0.51	69	US	10,380	0.16
20	from	31,166	0.47	70	services	10,322	0.16
21	company	30,466	0.46	71	period	10,283	0.16
22	which	27,059	0.41	72	income	10,263	0.16
23	any	26,536	0.40	73	no	9,836	0.15
24	HK	26,191	0.40	74	their	9,723	0.15
25	an	25,683	0.39	75	than	9,716	0.15
26	our	25,300	0.38	76	securities	9,700	0.15
27	will	24,050	0.36	77	also	9,629	0.15
28	financial	23,801	0.36	78	bank	9,441	0.14
29	group	23,214	0.35	79	if	9,402	0.14
30	shares	22,314	0.34	80	Mr	9,395	0.14
31	this	21,839	0.33	81	June	8,855	0.13
32	other	21,287	0.32	82	amount	8,815	0.13
33	has	20,508	0.31	83	insurance	8,780	0.13
34	not	20,453	0.31	84	shall	8,648	0.13
35	have	19,859	0.30	85	shareholders	8,527	0.13
36	million	19,477	0.29	86	development	8,525	0.13
37	we	19,181	0.29	87	China	8,390	0.13
38	under	18,190	0.27	88	companies	8,366	0.13
39	its	17,290	0.26	89	RMB	8,347	0.13
40	limited	17,106	0.26	90	these	8,200	0.12
41	may	16,824	0.25	91	information	8,159	0.12
42	was	16,130	0.24	92	offer	8,145	0.12
43	share	16,001	0.24	93	years	8,062	0.12
44	business	15,880	0.24	94	more	8,019	0.12
45	year	15,811	0.24	95	profit	7,985	0.12
46	such	14,643	0.22	96	rate	7,827	0.12
47	it	14,224	0.21	97	time	7,722	0.12
48	assets	13,889	0.21	98	cash	7,506	0.11
49	investment	13,662	0.21	99	equity	7,294	0.11
50	interest	13,256	0.20	100	made	7,273	0.11

Table 4.3 100 most frequent words in the HKEC

Rank	Word	Frequency	%	Rank	Word	Frequency	%
1	the	582,437	6.81	51	control	13,266	0.16
2	of	335,785	3.92	52	power	13,218	0.15
3	and	265,945	3.11	53	new	12,606	0.15
4	to	204,117	2.39	54	C	12,399	0.14
5	in	168,798	1.97	55	used	12,360	0.14
6	a	132,246	1.55	56	been	12,348	0.14
7	for	117,325	1.37	57	if	12,327	0.14
8	be	95,221	1.11	58	under	11,779	0.14
9	is	84,323	0.99	59	use	11,698	0.14
10	on	59,914	0.70	60	were	11,684	0.14
11	with	58,878	0.69	61	services	11,625	0.14
12	by	53,059	0.62	62	site	11,439	0.13
13	or	51,863	0.61	63	management	11,174	0.13
14	as	51,413	0.60	64	our	11,164	0.13
15	are	45,190	0.53	65	development	11,020	0.13
16	at	42,836	0.50	66	their	11,018	0.13
17	that	38,881	0.45	67	its	10,993	0.13
18	from	37,521	0.44	68	m	10,969	0.13
19	Hong	33,999	0.40	69	road	10,939	0.13
20	Kong	32,806	0.38	70	more	10,909	0.13
21	should	27,911	0.33	71	supply	10,855	0.13
22	this	27,797	0.32	72	Mr	10,796	0.13
23	shall	26,990	0.32	73	we	10,766	0.13
24	will	25,730	0.30	74	out	10,647	0.12
25	not	25,356	0.30	75	project	10,613	0.12
26	an	24,907	0.29	76	time	10,435	0.12
27	it	22,546	0.26	77	department	10,089	0.12
28	which	21,855	0.26	78	gas	9,824	0.11
29	system	19,779	0.23	79	section	9,689	0.11
30	water	19,711	0.23	80	quality	9,684	0.11
31	was	18,796	0.22	81	safety	9,641	0.11
32	building	18,655	0.22	82	one	9,622	0.11
33	no	18,221	0.21	83	public	9,549	0.11
34	all	17,871	0.21	84	monitoring	9,454	0.11
35	has	17,766	0.21	85	area	9,444	0.11
36	can	17,526	0.20	86	information	9,444	0.11
37	energy	17,164	0.20	87	these	9,294	0.11
38	have	16,888	0.20	88	waste	9,285	0.11
39	may	16,267	0.19	89	I	9,196	0.11
40	any	15,723	0.18	90	equipment	9,193	0.11
41	construction	15,506	0.18	91	where	9,114	0.11
42	other	15,427	0.18	92	when	8,942	0.10
43	design	15,280	0.18	93	Government	8,684	0.10
44	works	15,111	0.18	94	buildings	8,610	0.10
45	also	14,503	0.17	95	during	8,537	0.10
46	such	14,358	0.17	96	into	8,459	0.10
47	b	14,191	0.17	97	maintenance	8,397	0.10
48	environmental	14,111	0.16	98	engineering	8,337	0.10
49	than	13,772	0.16	99	data	8,208	0.10
50	air	13,593	0.16	100	total	8,158	0.10

written texts (the BNC is 90 per cent comprised of written texts and the two specialised corpora are both made up of more than 90 per cent written texts). Ahmad (2005) has investigated the most frequent words in the BNC and found that these top six words make up about 20 per cent of the entire corpus, and it can be seen that this is also true for the HKFSC and the HKEC. Ahmad also found that the top fifty words in the BNC are all function words and together comprise close to 40 per cent of the corpus. It is here that we find interesting differences between the most frequent words in the BNC and the two specialised corpora. While the BNC has very few lexical words in the top 100, and none in the top fifty, this is not the case for the specialised corpora. In the BNC, it is not until *said* (ranked 53) and *time* (ranked 69) that we find lexically richer words. In the case of the specialised corpora, we find quite a few in the top fifty. The first is in the top twenty in both lists, *Hong Kong* ranked 17 and 19 (here, we conflate *Hong* and *Kong* since it is, in essence, one item in these Hong Kong-based corpora, with fewer instances of *Kong* simply because *Kong's* is counted separately). Just in the top fifty, there are thirteen more lexical words in the HKFSC and nine in the HKEC. In addition, the lexical words themselves readily tell us that we are looking at lists from a financial services corpus (e.g., *company, financial, group, shares, million, limited, business, assets* and *investment*) and an engineering corpus (e.g., *system, water, building, energy, construction, design, works, environmental* and *air*). In fact, it is the very rarity of lexical words in the general corpus, coupled with their lack of specificity (e.g., *said, time, now, just, people, know, very, new* and *way*) that tells us that the list is from a general corpus, whereas the very preponderance of lexical words in the top 100 word list of the two specialised corpora tells us that these are indeed specialised corpora, irrespective of what those words actually are.

What is the reason for this difference? Sinclair (2005a: 16) provides the answer. He makes an interesting observation that, for a specialised corpus, a 'much smaller corpus will be needed for typical studies than is needed for a general view of the language'. This is because the 'number of different word forms, which is a rough estimate of the size of the vocabulary, is far less' in specialised corpora than general

Task 4.1

Table 4.4 shows the top 100 words in a 1-million-word corpus of spoken English. Compare the list with that of the BNC (Table 4.1 above). Discuss what you find in terms of similarities and differences, bearing in mind that 90 per cent of the BNC is comprised of written texts.

Table 4.4 Top 100 most frequent words in the HKCSE

Rank	Word	Frequency	%	Rank	Word	Frequency	%
1	the	45,155	4.74	51	there	2,956	0.31
2	er	24,866	2.61	52	mhm	2,952	0.31
3	to	24,431	2.57	53	from	2,911	0.31
4	and	23,753	2.49	54	don't	2,820	0.30
5	you	21,425	2.25	55	yes	2,812	0.30
6	I	18,922	1.99	56	now	2,806	0.29
7	of	17,474	1.84	57	well	2,707	0.28
8	a	16,020	1.69	58	all	2,704	0.28
9	in	15,046	1.58	59	your	2,656	0.28
10	is	13,999	1.47	60	our	2,641	0.28
11	that	13,118	1.38	61	erm	2,639	0.28
12	it	10,244	1.08	62	oh	2,584	0.27
13	we	9,850	1.03	63	was	2,562	0.27
14	have	8,753	0.92	64	two	2,549	0.27
15	yeah	8,651	0.91	65	that's	2,508	0.26
16	so	8,436	0.89	66	some	2,469	0.26
17	for	7,746	0.81	67	would	2,300	0.24
18	this	7,065	0.74	68	my	2,297	0.24
19	they	6,384	0.67	69	when	2,233	0.23
20	but	6,204	0.65	70	how	2,152	0.23
21	know	5,750	0.60	71	more	2,152	0.23
22	are	5,733	0.60	72	people	2,128	0.22
23	be	5,386	0.57	73	he	2,100	0.22
24	it's	5,299	0.56	74	time	2,074	0.22
25	okay	5,032	0.53	75	also	2,002	0.21
26	not	4,876	0.51	76	by	1,965	0.21
27	um	4,732	0.50	77	say	1,911	0.20
28	one	4,667	0.49	78	see	1,904	0.20
29	mm	4,423	0.46	79	here	1,770	0.19
30	on	4,416	0.46	80	good	1,766	0.19
31	do	4,368	0.46	81	go	1,752	0.18
32	what	4,363	0.46	82	an	1,742	0.18
33	can	4,260	0.45	83	me	1,721	0.18
34	will	4,169	0.44	84	mean	1,695	0.18
35	think	4,067	0.43	85	which	1,661	0.17
36	or	3,966	0.42	86	has	1,641	0.17
37	with	3,841	0.40	87	I'm	1,635	0.17
38	as	3,816	0.40	88	up	1,536	0.16
39	if	3,742	0.39	89	want	1,526	0.16
40	very	3,734	0.39	90	them	1,518	0.16
41	Hong	3,704	0.39	91	going	1,449	0.15
42	Kong	3,497	0.37	92	actually	1,425	0.15
43	because	3,458	0.36	93	get	1,421	0.15
44	like	3,337	0.35	94	three	1,414	0.15
45	at	3,266	0.34	95	these	1,378	0.14
47	right	3,205	0.34	97	really	1,371	0.14
48	about	3,184	0.33	98	other	1,365	0.14
49	no	3,013	0.32	99	got	1,357	0.14
50	just	2,985	0.31	100	out	1,343	0.14

corpora (p. 16). This tendency, Sinclair explains, which is confirmed in Tables 4.2 and 4.3, is due to a specialised corpus highlighting 'a small, probably technical vocabulary' and so the 'characteristic vocabulary of the special area is prominently featured in the frequency lists' (p. 16).

Before we leave word frequency lists, there are two more points to make with regard to function words and lexical words. Most corpus linguistic software packages allow the user to use what is known as a 'stop list' (WordSmith 5.0), also known as an 'exclusion list' (ConcGram 1.0), which excludes the listed words from the search. So a stop list containing the top six function words in English (i.e., *the*, *of*, *and*, *to*, *in* and *a*) would mean that they would not appear in the resulting word frequency list. The use of this kind of list allows the user to focus on the words he or she is interested in by stripping out those which are not being studied. A word of caution is needed here because there is a resurgence of interest in function words, which are generally under-researched, and placing them in a stop list could push them further into the shadows.

Just as the tops of word frequency lists are frequented by function words, so the lower down the list one goes the greater the concentration of lexical words. Most types in a corpus occur only once (usually more than 50 per cent of the total are single instances) and such a word is termed a 'hapax legomenon' (Coulthard and Johnson, 2007) and is almost invariably lexical. Software can exclude these single instances to shorten the length of the list generated by setting a frequency-based cut-off of two or more instances. However, again, a word of caution is needed as any form of exclusion has implications for what you might then find, or not find as the case may be, and in the case of single instances they can be well worth including. For example, in their study of forensic linguistics, Coulthard and Johnson (2007: 165–9) cite cases where the authorship of a text has been, in part, determined by measures aimed at identifying the writer's idiolect. These measures include the choice of particular 'hapax legomena' and also 'hapax dislegomena' (i.e., words used twice in a text or corpus) by the writer (p. 166), as well as measures such as the STTR and average sentence length, all of which amount to a kind of 'linguistic fingerprinting' (p. 161).

Word frequencies are said to follow Zipf's Law (1935) by which the frequencies in a corpus, if plotted on a graph, follow a smooth curve with single instances accounting for about 50 per cent of all the words, two instances 25 per cent, and so on. Sinclair (2005a: 13) demonstrates this interesting aspect of word frequencies by examining the Brown Corpus. He finds that 35,056 of the 69,002 word forms occur only once and the most common word, *the*, has 69,970 instances with the next, *of*, with about half as many at 36,410 (p. 13).

Key words

Above, we compared the word frequency lists of specialised corpora with that of a general corpus and we easily found the words that looked financial services-like and engineering-like simply by looking at the lists. Software can approach this more systematically by allowing the user to generate what Scott terms 'key words' based on the notion of 'keyness' (WordSmith 5.0). Keywords are 'words which are significantly more frequent in one corpus than another' (Hunston, 2002: 68). They are words that are either unique to, or are found more frequently in, a specialised corpus compared with a general reference corpus. In other words, there is a function in a number of available programs that allows the user to find those words that are key in a particular corpus relative to a benchmark corpus. These words can then be described as one of the defining characteristics of the specialised corpus. Others use different terms, 'weirdness' (Ahmad, 2005) and 'specificity' (Greaves, 2009), in place of 'keyness' but the idea is the same: to identify words specific to a particular kind of language use. The formula used for doing this is based on the relative proportional usage of a particular word in the two corpora. Ahmad's (2005) formula for calculating weirdness, which is also used by Greaves (2009), is given below:

$$weirdness(\text{term}) = \frac{f_{special} / N_{special}}{f_{general} / N_{general}}$$

(Ahmad, 2005)

The formula is simply the proportional use of a word in the specialised corpus divided by the proportional use of the word in a general corpus. If weirdness is greater than one, the word is a specialist term; if it is less than one, it is not a specialist term (Ahmad, 2005).

Key word lists are created by first generating the word frequency lists of the two corpora, saving them and then, in the case of WordSmith 5.0, selecting them via the key word list option. The results are then displayed and can be ranked based on frequency or keyness. The identification of key words can indicate what a corpus (or text) is about (i.e., its aboutness). To illustrate this, an example of a keyword list is shown in Table 4.5. In this example, the words from one text are compared with the words in a corpus of texts from the same genre. The genre in question is Hong Kong's annual budget speech[1] and the words in the 2010 budget speech are compared with the words in a corpus of all the budget speeches from 1997–2009 in order to find out the aboutness (Phillips, 1989) of the 2010 budget speech. There are 16,676 words in the 2010 budget speech and 159,779 words in the budget speech corpus.

Table 4.5 Key words and keyness in 2010 budget speech

Rank	Key word	2010 fre-quency	2010 % budgets	Prior budgets fre-quency	Prior budgets %	Keyness
1	tsunami	16	0.09	0	0.00	75.54
2	measures	75	0.44	250	0.15	52.62
3	flats	17	0.10	11	0.01	44.93
4	residential	22	0.13	30	0.02	38.97
5	HA (Housing Authority)	8	0.05	0	0.00	37.77
6	RMB (renminbi – currency in China Mainland)	23	0.14	40	0.02	33.83
7	patients	10	0.06	4	0.002	31.25
8	operation	31	0.18	83	0.05	29.41
9	ETFS (exchange-traded funds)	6	0.04	0	0.00	28.33
10	drug	7	0.04	1	0.001	27.22
11	recovery	23	0.14	52	0.03	26.44
12	research	8	0.05	3	0.002	25.47
13	care	33	0.19	104	0.06	25.16
14	industries	33	0.19	105	0.06	24.81
15	building	21	0.12	47	0.03	24.40
	Non-Key word					
1	our	110	0.65	1,750	1.05	-31.07
2	tax	20	0.12	559	0.34	-31.41

Table 4.5 shows that key words can be words that only occur in the text (or corpus) under investigation such as the key words *tsunami*, *HA* (Housing Authority) and *ETFs* (exchange-traded funds) that appear for the first time in a Hong Kong budget speech in 2010. The remainder are words that are used relatively more frequently in 2010 compared to their use in all of the prior budget speeches. The first 15 words in the table are all key words and, given their specificity relative to prior speeches, they can be said to be indicative of the aboutness of the 2010 budget speech. Conversely, the last two words in the table, *our* and *tax*, are not key words in this text because their relative frequency is lower than in the corpus of prior budget speeches, and this is indicated by the negative keyness value in the final column of the table.

One potential problem with key word lists when applied to a corpus is that a word might be listed as a key word but only occur very frequently in one or two texts in the corpus, and so it is text-specific rather than corpus-specific. To overcome this problem, it is a good idea to examine the visual dispersion plot, such as that available in WordSmith 5.0, to see whether a key word is spread across the corpus

> ### Task 4.2
>
> Create your own corpus based on one genre. Try to identify the aboutness of one of the texts relative to all of the others using word frequency lists and then key word lists. Discuss the problems you encountered and the possible applications of such studies.

or only limited to a few texts. WordSmith 5.0 provides another solution which is the creation of a 'key key word' list based on key words dispersed across multiple texts in a corpus.

N-grams

N-grams (see Chapter 5 for more details) are two or more words that repeatedly occur consecutively in a corpus, such as *in terms of*, *you know*, *I think*, *as soon as*, *it is* and *there are*. These phrases are also known as 'clusters', 'bundles' and 'chunks', among others, and they can be found in a corpus by most corpus linguistic programs. To study the n-grams in a corpus, you can generate a list of all of the two-word, three-word, four-word, etc. n-grams automatically. Table 4.6 shows the top ten three-word n-grams in the BNC. These n-grams were generated using the n-gram search facilities at Fletcher's website, 'Phrases in English' (http://pie.usna.edu/, 27 March 2010), which uses the BNC as its main corpus.

It can be seen that the software developed by Fletcher treats *don't*, for example, as two words, *do* and *n't*. In addition to listing the n-grams and their frequencies, the part-of-speech (POS) annotation

Table 4.6 Top ten three-word n-grams in the BNC

N-gram	Frequency	Part-of-speech
I do n't	36,863	PNP VDB XX0
one of the	35,273	CRD PRF AT0
the end of	20,998	AT0 NN1 PRF
part of the	16,444	NN1 PRF AT0
do n't know	15,779	VDB XX0 VVI
some of the	15,149	DT0 PRF AT0
a number of	15,126	AT0 NN1 PRF
there is a	15,008	EX0 VBZ AT0
a lot of	14,561	AT0 NN1 PRF
# and #	14,451	CRD CJC CRD

Note: # stands for any numeral in the corpus.

that is embedded in the BNC allows this additional information about the words in the n-grams to be listed in the last column of the table (see below for more on POS tagging).

Another way to view n-grams using WordSmith 5.0 is to list the n-grams based around a particular word that the user might be interested in. This is done by first searching for the concordance of the word and then using the 'cluster' function which allows the user to set the word length of the n-gram and the search span (i.e., the number of words to the left and right of the search word to be included). These settings can also be tailored to the user's requirements in WordSmith's automated n-gram search, which is similar to the one developed by Fletcher described above. In Table 4.7, the five most frequent three-word n-grams containing the word *expenditure* extracted from the HKFSC are shown.

Concordances

Entering a search item, displaying its concordance and examining the patterns of co-selection can tell you a lot. Sinclair (1991: 32) describes a concordance as 'a collection of the occurrences of a word form, each in its own textual environment', where textual environment equates to the immediate co-text on either side of the search item. How a concordance is displayed on the computer screen can impact the user's

Table 4.7 Top five three-word n-grams containing *expenditure* in the HKFSC

	N-gram	Frequency
1	and capital expenditure	42
2	capital expenditure and	34
3	the capital expenditure	25
4	capital expenditure incurred	21
5	capital expenditure of	20

Task 4.3

Generate a list of three-word n-grams from your corpus and study the top twenty. Try to group them together using your own classification systems. If you are unable to come up with your own classification systems, see the n-gram section in Chapter 5 for more input. What functions do these n-grams perform and should they be taught to language learners?

ability to identify patterns and construe their meanings. The free online *Time Magazine* Corpus (100 million words, 1920s–2000s) at http://corpus.byu.edu/time/, for instance, is a good example of a KWIC (Key Word in Context) display. This website allows the user to access a 100-million-word sample of the *Time Magazine* Corpus, and by default the number of "hits" (i.e. concordance lines) shown is 100. A search for *computer* in the 1940s shows 10 instances (Figure 4.1).

Another well-known online resource, at www.natcorp.ox.ac.uk, allows the user to conduct simple searches of the entire British National Corpus. If there are more than 50 instances, a random selection of 50 will be displayed. The display differs from the KWIC format illustrated above because the concordance is sentence-based, which means that the lines are not neatly aligned with the search item centred. Instead, each complete sentence containing the search item is displayed. This has the advantage of giving the user more co-text than KWIC and is sometimes preferred by newcomers to corpus linguistics, although it makes the identification of patterns more difficult. In fact, the user can usually access more of the on-screen co-text in a KWIC display. Selecting one instance of the node word allows the user to view it with considerably more of the original text displayed on the screen. To illustrate the difference between the two displays, a sample of sentence-based concordance lines for *storm* is shown in Figure 4.2 opposite. Note that each instance of the word *storm* is in bold to assist the reader, but this is not the case with the actual online version.

Software that uses the KWIC display typically allows the user to choose to sort the concordance lines to the left or right. This means that the lines will be sorted alphabetically based on the first word to the right or to the left. If the concordance is unsorted, the lines displayed will be in the order that they were retrieved from the corpus.

```
1   elements in motion. The computer also makes correction for
2   d during the flight, the computer calculates the plane's latitu
3   navigator," a mechanical computer for quick solution of complex
4   of a milk bottle, with a computer hooked up to the plane's comp
5   peed, range and angle. A computer of complex and secret design
6   lso needed an electronic computer that would allow its statist
7   ectronic brain (analogue computer) which can solve complicated
8   a machine: the Mark III Computer, built by Harvard for the Navy
9   device, the course-line computer, will do the worrying for him.
10  umerical integrator and computer. "Its inventors-Dr. John W. Mau
```

Figure 4.1 Ten concordance lines for *computer* in the online *Time Magazine* Corpus, 1940s

ABH 2426 With those blunt words about the fate of Iraq's
narmy, General Colin Powell, America's top soldier,
briefly revived the faith of Americans in Operation Desert
Storm.

ADD 26 There was a feeling that something was in the air,
that it was the lull before the **storm**.

BM6 641 He then set out in a violent **storm** and heavy
snow for Fort William, where he hoped to take the oath in the
presence of the local commander of government troops.

CH3 770 Inspirational Richards helped Leicester **storm** back
from 18-3 down to 18-11 - and they could have snatched victory
in the dying stages.

GT4 1094 Knowledge of his locality was to be a great boon in
1749 when, as master of The American (owned by Christopher
Scott, a Hull merchant), he was able to recognize the
coastline at Nantucket after a severe **storm** had blown the
vessel off course.

HB6 163 There is no cover for **storm** damage to gates, hedges
or fences.

HHA 18 Storm clouds outside had made even the stained glass
windows a uniform grey.

J13 712 Under strobe lights flickering like a tropical
storm across the deck, the kids dance closepacked, sweating,
eyes glazed against the lights.

K1B 1489 Engineers at HR Wallingford have built a scale
model of part of the threatened coast, they can reproduce
the effects of the **storm** surge floods which can overwhelm
the present defences.

K5D 12488 The rioters, followers of the warlord, Mohamed
Farah Aideed, blockaded streets with barricades of blazing
tyres, fought running battles with the troops and tried
to **storm** the US, French and Egyptian embassies.

Figure 4.2 Sample concordance lines for *storm* in sentence-based format

Sometimes, as is the case with ConcGram (Greaves, 2009), the lines can be sorted based on the second or third word to the left or right. The sort word is then underlined in the display for ease of identification. An example is shown in Figure 4.3 where a search for *system* has been sorted based on the second word to the left. The search was performed using the HKEC and shows that *system* is often preceded by multiple modifiers, one of which is *air*.

There are various other ways of selecting a search item and some of the most common ones are available on the searchable online corpora created by Mark Davies. It is possible to search for combinations of words and to include the number of intervening words you wish to allow between the search words. The search for a lemma is made possible by inserting a specific symbol next to one inflected form in the search dialog box in order to include every form of inflection in the concordance. What is known as a 'wild card' is a symbol which can be entered to stand for any number of letters ('*') or one letter ('?'); for example, searching for 'un*ly' may generate 'unlikely' or 'unusually' and searching for 's?ing*' may generate 'song', 'singer' or 'songbirds'.

```
1   ly over the air monitoring system established in the regio
2   lity, and air purification system that removes odour and k
3   Supply of air purification system escensorb odor neutraliz
4    RGF PHI? Air Purification System can provide effective pr
5   es, etc.] New air purifying system with Flash streamer  The
6   as generator, air sampling system * Scientific software *W
7   oning of the air scrubbing system to remove hydrogen chlor
8   oning of the air scrubbing system to remove hydrogen chlor
9   eration A Type of air side system - FCU FCU B Outdoor air
10  eration A Type of air side system - FCU VAV B Outdoor air
11  s Yes Yes 3. HVAC Air Side System * System load design [ Ai
12  e humidity 40% 5. AIR SIDE SYSTEM DESIGN CRITERIA 5.1 Air
13   Note 11: Type of air side system Fan coil unit system is
14  ve an independent air side system or control, such that th
15  on system and the air side system should be sufficient (or
16  ? Case 5 - change air side system to VAV ?? Case 6 - use e
17   electric system Air start system Hydraulic Lift platform
18  dividual forced-air supply system, adequate fresh air shal
19  n 21  Clean Dry Air Supply System  T-Get II  TSCI (Super C
20  hanical outside air supply system (and other related Mecha
```

Figure 4.3 Sample concordance lines for *system* sorted two words to the left

Task 4.4

Search for different words from different word classes in your corpus and display them first sorting left and then sorting right. What difference, if any, does the sort function make in terms of the patterns of co-selection you are able to identify?

Collocation

The notion of collocation supports the idiom principle (see Chapter 8). If words collocate, this means that they are co-selected by the speaker or writer and they are not a chance co-occurrence. When looking for collocates, how far either side of the node do you look? Sinclair (1991) states that a node word and its collocates are to be found within a span of five words to the left and right, although he says this is a provisional definition.

Figure 4.4 shows a concordance line, *to encourage development of health care in the private sector in*, with *care* as the node. In corpus linguistics, the words either side of the node are denoted by N+1 if the word is immediately to the right, N+2 if it is two words to the right and so on. Conversely, words to the left begin with N–1. This system is a useful way to identify the position of collocates relative to the node.

The collocates of a word are words which are most frequently co-selected in the vicinity of that word. If two words collocate significantly, their presence in the text is the result of a single choice, not two. Stubbs (2002) provides a number of examples of collocations:

- cause collocates with problem(s), damage, death(s), disease, concern, cancer, pain, trouble

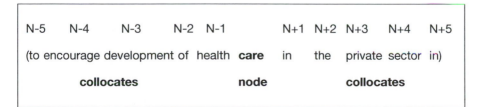

N-5	N-4	N-3	N-2	N-1		N+1	N+2	N+3	N+4	N+5
(to	encourage	development	of	health	**care**	in	the	private	sector	in)
	collocates				**node**			**collocates**		

Figure 4.4 Identifying collocates

- provide collocates with information, service(s), support, help, money, protection, food, care
- applause collocates with loud, thunderous, rapturous, spontaneous, polite, warm, enthusiastic

(Stubbs, 2002: 64–5)

An interesting finding by Sinclair (1991) is what he terms 'upward collocation' and 'downward collocation'. Upward collocates are collocates that are more frequent in the corpus than the node, and downward collocates are less frequent than the node. There are also node word neutral collocates, which have a frequency similar to the node. Sinclair finds that upward and downward collocates provide different information about the node. Sinclair (2003) illustrates this finding with the example of *back*: *back* collocates with *at, down, from, into, on* and *then*, all of which are more frequent words than *back* (upward collocation), and collocates with *arrive, bring* and *climbed*, all of which are less frequent than back (downward collocation). As Sinclair (1991) explains:

> There appears to be a systematic difference between upward and downward collocation. Upward collocation, of course, is the weaker pattern in statistical terms, and the words tend to be elements of grammatical frames, or superordinates. Downward collocation by contrast gives us a semantic analysis of a word.
>
> (p. 116)

In Sinclair's study of *back* (1991), upward collocates tend to be elements of grammatical frames, and the upward collocates of *back* are mainly prepositions, adverbs, conjunctions and pronouns, e.g., *It was really like being back at school.*, *When our parent come back from Paris.*, and *He turned back to the bookshelf.* The downward collocates of *back* are mainly nouns and verbs, revealing the semantics of *back*, e.g., *I flew back home, the girl stared back, go back to bed* and *the back streets of Glasgow.* For neutral collocates, they have to be assigned to the upward or downward categories on a case by case basis.

Another example of upward and downward collocation is given by Sinclair *et al.* (2004):

> If a word like *very* collocates with *confused*, it adds very little to the meaning of *confused* because it is so much more common. But if *utterly* collocates with *confused*, and *confused* is more frequent than *utterly*, then *utterly* influences the meaning or prosody of *confused*. If *very* collocates with almost any adjective that only tells us that *very* comes with very few semantic restrictions.
>
> (p. xxiii)

Task 4.5

Table 4.8 lists the top collocates of 'cold' which has 4,898 instances in the 56-million-word corpus on COBUILD's Concordance and Collocations Sampler website. Use the table to identify upward, downward and neutral collocates and see if your findings confirm Sinclair's (1991) observations. You will need to check the concordances to back up your findings, and so you will need to search for combinations of words. This function is described above and is also described on the website.

Table 4.8 Top 20 collocates of 'cold'

Collocate [based on t-score]	Corpus frequency	Joint frequency	Significance
war	16,618	613	24.190254
water	13,608	292	16.413404
and	1,129,483	1,603	16.139652
the	2,313,407	2,727	14.692721
hot	4,431	195	13.695440
weather	3,173	148	11.944580
it	494,702	679	9.975101
winter	4,190	103	9.799155
air	10,570	111	9.685771
in	765,730	936	9.391803
was	340,423	496	9.322434
wet	1,646	85	9.068305
cold	4,898	88	8.938525
a	973,489	1,096	8.196030
ice	2,923	72	8.193466
too	29,066	107	7.963741
end	22,091	96	7.887995
or	156,128	254	7.638689
wind	2,598	59	7.394623
blooded	140	51	7.124822

Source: COBUILD's Concordance and Collocations Sampler website, 23 March 2010.

Most concordancing software is able to list the collocates for search words and also give varying amounts of additional information on the collocates. In Table 4.9 we can see the top collocates for *tax* in the HKFSC using WordSmith 5.0 and the extensive amount of additional information which is provided.

In Table 4.9, the collocates of *tax* are listed in rank order based on frequency. We can also see whether the collocates are fairly evenly spread to the left and to the right of *tax* (all the function words, *the*,

Table 4.9 Most frequent collocates of tax and their positions relative to the node

N	Word	With	Total	Total left	Total right	L5	L4	L3	L2	L1	Centre	R1	R2	R3	R	R5
1	TAX	tax	8,303	594	593	178	233	131	42	10	7,116	10	42	131	232	178
2	THE	tax	3,497	1,950	1,547	313	365	309	559	404	0	24	340	466	335	382
3	OF	tax	2,338	1,244	1,094	253	173	222	409	187	0	83	434	107	245	225
4	AND	tax	1,704	784	920	124	156	172	257	75	0	195	415	60	113	137
5	DEFERRED	tax	1,667	1,497	170	50	29	11	114	1,293	0	20	22	44	49	35
6	TO	tax	1,441	739	702	112	207	183	159	78	0	49	166	163	194	130
7	INCOME	tax	1,348	1,141	207	58	52	20	10	1,001	0	19	35	48	53	52
8	IN	tax	1,208	536	672	135	105	105	128	63	0	97	228	120	101	126
9	PROFIT	tax	1,025	685	340	35	24	185	430	11	0	173	36	24	58	49
10	FOR	tax	959	445	514	60	86	62	143	94	0	84	170	81	104	75
11	ASSETS	tax	877	183	694	44	53	68	14	4	0	576	10	50	26	32
12	LIABILITIES	tax	686	91	595	10	16	39	25	1	0	359	15	130	36	55

of, *and*, *to*, *in* and *for*, plus one lexical word, *tax*), or whether the collocates occur mainly to the left (e.g., *deferred*, *income* and *profit*), or to the right (e.g., *assets* and *liabilities*). The table also details where the collocates occur relative to the node. Thus, we see, that, when *tax* self-collocates it is most likely to be at either N–4 or N–4. The collocate *the* is most often found at N–2 as is *profit*. The collocates *deferred* and *income* are usually at N–1, and *assets* and *liabilities* are typically at N+1. All of this information helps to build up a very detailed collocational profile for *tax*.

Task 4.6

Study the sample concordance lines in Figures 4.5–4.7 and identify as many collocates as you can and note down their positions relative to the node. In this task, two or more instances of a word will suffice for it to be classified as a collocate. Discuss how you have handled different word forms with the same stem.

```
1 owledge economy with high value added economic activities
2 mic powerhouse where high value added economic activities
3 d processes that will add value to and boost the productiv
4 veness and achieving high value added depends very much on
5 glad to see concrete high value-added technology-based act
6 ency and productivity add value and enhance the competitiv
7  to move upmarket and add value we have established a five
```

Figure 4.5 Sample concordances lines for *value*

```
1 lean government totally committed to (.) low taxation and
2 nless of course you are committed to a deadline of July B:
3  Delta but Hong Kong is committed to be Asia's world city
4 ies and you know we are committed to China we think we hav
5 the Mainland (.) we are committed to continuing the develo
6 ework with a government committed to ensuring a level play
7 cts and services we are committed to make innovation techn
8  good governance we are committed to smoothing the passage
9  city the government is committed to spending up to six hu
10speed the Government is committed to supporting the Hong K
```

Figure 4.6 Sample concordances lines for *committed*

```
1   partnership er with the private sector in terms of hospit
2   is er to encourage more private hospital development and
3  their obligation to help private sectors and we we look at
4  e know it needs a lot of private resources to put in diffe
5  inking with the with the private sector not against even o
6  the government to assist private sectors er even in during
7  f investment er from the private sector as well as the gov
8  ple and buying beds from private sector hospitals not just
9  res so the hospitals are private hospital in mainland Chin
10 e the development of er  private sector when I was in UK e
11   promote development of private hospitals because this wi
12 ng waiting time promote private provision of hospital ser
```

Figure 4.7 Sample concordances lines for *private*

Colligation

Collocation is the lexical company a word or phrase is associated with, while colligation is the grammatical company that a word or phrase is associated with. In other words, colligation is the co-selection of certain word classes or structural patterns in the span to the left and right of the node word. Colligation is similar to collocation as they both concern the co-selection of linguistic features in a text. However, analysing concordance lines for colligates requires the analyst to operate at a level of abstraction in order to determine the word class of the colligate or its structural pattern or grammatical category. Figure 4.8 illustrates the span within which the identification of colligates takes place, which is the same as that for collocates.

Colligation includes grammatical categories such as negative, possessive and modal. For example, *cases* often co-occurs with the

N-5	N-4	N-3	N-2	N-1		N+1	N+2	N+3	N+4	N+5
(to	encourage	development	of	health	**care**	in	the	private	sector	in)
		word classes			**node**		**word classes**			
		<u>or</u> **structural patterns/**					<u>or</u> **structural patterns/**			
		grammatical category					**grammatical category**			

Figure 4.8 Identifying colligates

1 e left for Strasbourg, Mrs Thatcher refused to **budge** in her hostility to the EC Social Charter and the
2 it down, so they're obviously not prepared to **budge**. <u who=PS1D2> No. Well <u who=PS1CX> So <u who=PS
3 u who=PS1CX> Because they, probably they won't **budge**. You see, Neil's already put his side about, we w
4 areas of fat that dieting may reduce but won't **budge** completely, like saddlebag thighs or a pot-
5   solutions, but, since Baghdad refuses to **budge**, it is eventually forced to take a stand. The
6 her knees twisted painfully; her feet didn't **budge**. The grasping hands of the mud held her
7 better than Errol. Roberts, however, did not **budge**. 'On the third time of making my appeal",
8 this year", but the Frenchman refused to **budge**. Foch, he concluded, 'is suffering from a
9   were exhausted by their vain attempts to **budge** even one of the great monoliths, Merlin
10 rages. Once his mind was made up he would not **budge**.2 He was thought of as a [118] modern man".
11   to meet American Michael Moorer – and won't **budge** despite Moorer's willingness to step aside
12 little prayer for Miss dede." [p] Emma didn't **budge**. 'You sure?" [p] Yes, dear. Now leave me
13 kicked at the stone. 'Samson hisself couldn't **budge** them cinders." He stomped on the jacks at his
14   or something worse. The bundle would not **budge**. Father set the emergency brake, and then
15 my mind is made up. Not another step will I **budge** on this errand. What if a wretched old woman
16 Department spokesman said Iraq has refused to **budge** on the question of when Secretary of State
17 and neither side seems particularly ready to **budge** at this point. [p] Cochran: California has
18 whittled and whittled away because she won't **budge**. I mean she says she won't pay for this roof.
19 any interest but their own. Their refusal to **budge** over the World Cup is a reflection of their
20 irport. It was only when the group refused to **budge** that staff chartered a coach to Manchester.

Figure 4.9 Sample concordance lines for *budge*

grammatical category of quantifier, such as *in some cases, in both cases* and *in most cases* (Stubbs, 2002: 65). A good example of the co-selection of the 'negative' grammatical category is provided by Sinclair (2003: 83–90) in his very thorough analysis of *budge*. Figure 4.9 illustrates this example with a selection of concordance lines from the online COBUILD Concordance and Collocations Sampler website.

This kind of analysis provides us with a fuller description of the language which can then feed into language learning materials and activities. A fuller understanding of the meaning of *budge* and its co-selections should also improve dictionary entries.

Task 4.7

Study the concordance lines in Figure 4.9 and identify the 'negative' grammatical category. Where is it found relative to the node and what forms does it take? Given this strong colligational pattern, evaluate the definition of 'budge' in a few dictionaries and suggest improvements where you think it might be necessary.

Task 4.8

Study the sample concordance lines in Figures 4.10–4.12, from the Hong Kong Corpus of Spoken English, and identify patterns of colligation based on word class.

```
1 ects er require intensive care admission and only about fo
2  development of er health care er in the private sector er
3  er to improve er primary care er to provide more services
4 ome care outside hospital care like the ambulatory service
5 e in terms of out patient care er in fact we don't have to
6 orm of er care er nursing care but not really a kind of er
7 panding programme in home care cut down the waiting time a
8 ders to set up outpatient care on a contracting basis now
9 oice in obtaining quality care at affordable level now in
```

Figure 4.10 Sample concordances for *care*

```
1 in partnership er with the private sector in terms of hosp
2 re is er to encourage more private hospital development an
3 s their obligation to help private sectors and we we look
4  we know it needs a lot of private resources to put in dif
5  linking with the with the private sector not against even
6 eople and buying beds from private sector hospitals not ju
7 dures so the hospitals are private hospital in mainland Ch
8 hich start with government private sector professionals ac
9  to promote development of private hospitals because this
10 cing waiting time promote private provision of hospital s
```

Figure 4.11 Sample concordance lines for *private*

```
1  er are treated er in a hospital in mainland China er and tha
2  can be done not by the hospital side but by the private sect
3  y can make use of this hospital services which cover both in
4  Chinese) now this is a hospital that erm er if you go to er
5  phasis is to shift the hospital base services to community s
6  ardens er you see this hospital er which just open about a y
7  on and especially in a hospital setting where it might be th
8  egetarian diet in that hospital er so it's a good to er disc
9  ested interest in this hospital er but I have been er invite
10  the hospital now that hospital er open about a year ago the
11  actual running of the hospital and discuss with them the pr
```

Figure 4.12 Sample concordance lines for *hospital*

Searching annotated corpora

Annotation is an umbrella term for tagging and parsing, and other kinds of information that can be added to a corpus, all of which aim to enhance the corpus contents. There are a number of reasons for annotating a corpus based on the kinds of language research being undertaken, such as natural language processing (NLP), speech synthesis and recognition, natural language generation and understanding, text summarisation and machine translation. For example, annotation can enable the user to distinguish words which have the same spelling, but different meanings. If a word in a corpus is spelled *box*, annotating the word in context will clarify for the user whether it is a noun or a verb. There are various methods for doing annotating, ranging from manual annotation, computer-assisted annotation where the researcher edits the computer-generated output, and fully automated annotation using a computer program. The levels of annotation are many and some of the main ones are listed below:

- Syllable, word segmentation and sentence segmentation.
- Part-of-speech (POS) tagging.
- Syntactic parsing.
- Semantic annotation.
- Pragmatic annotation.
- Phonetic and prosodic annotation.
- Parallel corpora: sentence alignment.
- Learner corpora: error annotation.
- Multi-modal corpora: multi-level annotation.

The most common kind of annotation in corpora is POS tagging which adds a code to each word in a corpus, indicating its part of speech status which can then be read by the software searching the corpus. This process is done using an automatic tagger which tags the words based on rules governing word-classes, coupled with complex algorithms based on the probability that in a particular context a word is, for example, a noun and not a verb. Taggers work very quickly and have levels of accuracy of over 90 per cent, and as high as 96–97 per cent in the case of CLAWS (see http://ucrel.lancs.ac.uk/claws/), but there are always tagging errors. Spoken corpora are especially problematic in this respect because of, for example, the higher use of ellipsis, speaker overlap, repetitions, the use of fillers (e.g., *er*, *um*), and discourse markers (e.g., *well*, *so* and *now*).

An example of POS tagging is given on the website of COBUILD's Concordance and Collocations Sampler. The tagging means that the user can search for combinations of words and tags and the list below is an illustration of the additional information these tags provide:

NOUN   a macro tag: any noun tag
VERB   a macro tag: any verb tag
NN   common noun

Task 4.9

Discuss why a tagger might be useful if you are interested in studying words such as 'burn' or 'claim'.

NNS	noun plural
JJ	adjective
DT	definite and indefinite article
IN	preposition
RB	adverb
VB	base-form verb
VBN	past participle verb
VBG	-ing form verb
VBD	past tense verb
CC	coordinating conjunction (e.g., *and*, *but*)
CS	subordinating conjunction (e.g., *while*, *because*)
PPS	personal pronoun subject case (e.g., *she*, *I*)
PPO	personal pronoun object case (e.g., *her*, *me*)
PPP	possessive pronoun (e.g., *hers*, *mine*)
DTG	a determiner-pronoun (e.g., *many*, *all*)

(adapted from www.collins.co.uk/Corpus/
CorpusSearch.aspx, 24 March 2010)

Figures 4.13 and 4.14 illustrate the results of searches which combine a word, *storm*, with POS tags for adjective to the left and noun to the right, respectively.

The website hosted by Fletcher, 'Phrases in English', was mentioned earlier in relation to n-grams. It also offers users the ability to search for 'PoS-grams' (http://pie.usna.edu/, 24 March 2010), which are based entirely on POS tags irrespective of the specific words represented by the tags. The most frequent PoS-grams depend on whether the frequency is type-based or token-based. Fletcher finds that the most frequent type-based three-word PoS-gram is 'ART ADJ NOUN, e.g. *the other hand*'. When token-based, the most frequent three-word PoS-gram is 'PREP ART NOUN as in *at the end*' (http://pie.usna.edu/, 24 March 2010).

```
1   of silence, then an angry storm from his father. `Borrowed?
2   ert flooded from a recent storm; unable to dig in, the team
3   ane Klaus. That tropical storm was upgraded today. It has
4   newscaster: [p] A severe storm lashed the North Carolina co
5   survives every political storm. [p] Simon: Well, help us co
6   r this is a really strong storm." Those kinds of things are
7   arently, it is a very bad storm. The storm has kept the eva
8   got inside, a torrential storm broke.  A 10-year-old neighb
9   made before another heavy storm hit the Shetland Islands, wh
10  ent through a tremendous storm got over there and this guy
```

Figure 4.13 Sample concordance lines for adjective tag + *storm*

```
1   ers on a preliminary Desert Storm target list, with plans to
2   ain. We're moving through a storm system," the pilot called
3   eported ashigh as 16 feet.   Storm warnings extend north the
4   00 US soldiers sent to help storm victims there two weeks ag
5   million home is insured for storm damage.   This is NPR News.
6   th and Midwest. The unusual storm system swept from Texas th
7    That seems likely. Another storm front is headed toward Cal
8   epresent the calm after the storm, beauty, good fortune, pea
9   TES. [ c] telephone [ /c] [ p] STORM DOORS WITH SCREENS, ALUMIN
10   llow tucked in here on the storm tracks which nothing at al
```

Figure 4.14 Sample concordance lines for *storm* + noun tag

Since POS tagging is the most commonly used form of annotation, studies based on these tags are more commonplace. For example, a study comparing NS versus NNS language use by Granger and Rayson (1998) is a good example of a POS tag-based analysis in which they found that NNS used more determiners, pronouns and adverbs but fewer conjunctions, prepositions and nouns than NS, probably due to the NS using more complex and abstract noun phrases. In another study, Aarts and Granger (1998) find that compared to native English writers, Dutch, Finnish and French writers of English use fewer of the following 'tag sequences' (Hunston, 2002: 82):

preposition-article-noun (e.g., *in the morning*)
article-noun-preposition (e.g., *a debate on*)
noun-preposition-noun (e.g., *part of speech*)
noun-preposition-article (e.g., *concern for the*)

(Aarts and Granger, 1998: 82)

This kind of information can be very useful for language teachers and learners.

In Biber *et al.*'s (1999) study of the grammar of different registers, they were able to take advantage of the POS tags to compare the comparative frequencies of different word classes. Their findings are summarised in Table 4.10.

Parsing

The annotation of a corpus in terms of its constituents, such as phrases and clauses, is termed 'parsing' (i.e., syntactic annotation). Corpora such as the Polytechnic of Wales corpus of children's spoken language (10,000 words), the 44-million-word Child Language Data Exchange System (CHILDES), and the 1-million-word London Oslo Bergen

Table 4.10 The comparative frequency of word classes in three corpora (Biber *et al.*, 1999)

	Conversation	Newspapers	Academic
More common	pronouns verbs adverbs auxiliaries particles	nouns determiners prepositions	nouns determiners prepositions
Less common	nouns determiners prepositions	pronouns verbs adverbs auxiliaries particles	pronouns verbs adverbs auxiliaries particles

(LOB) Corpus are examples of parsed corpora. Automatic parsing is not 100 per cent accurate, and so additional manual editing may be required. Leech and Eyes (1997) at Lancaster University parsed a small corpus manually and then used the resulting output to train the automatic parser. An example of the annotation is provided below:

- *The victim's friends told police that Krueger drove into the quarry* – sentence

- *The victim's friends* – noun phrase

- *The victim's* – genitive

- *told police that Krueger drove into the quarry* – verb phrase

- *police* – noun phrase

- *that Krueger drove into the quarry* – nominal clause

- *Krueger* – noun phrase

- *drove into the quarry* – verb phrase

- *into the quarry* – prepositional phrase

- *the quarry* – noun phrase dependent on the preposition

(Leech and Eyes, 1997: 51)

Semantic annotation aims to indicate the semantic relationships between items in a corpus (e.g., agents or patients of particular actions), or the semantic features of words in a text, which involves the annotation of word senses in one form or another. This level of annotation once had to be done manually, but can be done using corpus annotation tool such as the UCREL Semantic Analysis System

(USAS) (http://ucrel.lancs.ac.uk/usas/). Wilson and Thomas (1997) provide an example of this kind of annotation based on the sentence *Joanna stubbed out her cigarette with unnecessary fierceness*, which is reproduced below:

- *Joanna* – a 'Personal Name'
- *stubbed out* – the class 'Object-Oriented Physical Activity' and the class 'Temperature'
- *cigarette* – the class 'Luxury item'
- *unnecessary* – the class 'Causality/Chance'
- *fierceness* – the class 'Anger'
- *her* and *with* – 'Low Content Words', not assigned to a semantic category

(Wilson and Thomas, 1997: 61)

Software exists that can cover or combine a range of annotation functions. For example, Wmatrix (Rayson, 2009) combines both part of speech and semantic tagging, and key word frequency analysis to identify conceptual domains, such as semantic categories of 'location and direction' (e.g., *centre, east, west, top, overseas*), 'time: period' (e.g., *year, day, period, generation*), and 'government' (e.g., *council, civil, state, president, authority*).

Annotating a corpus for speech acts is a form of annotation that is typically done manually, although the Speech Act Annotated Corpus for Dialogue Systems (Leech and Weisser, 2003) was done, in part, automatically (Baker *et al.*, 2006: 147). Other speech act annotation programs include the Edinburgh Map Task annotation scheme of Human Communication Research Centre Map Task Corpus (Carletta *et al.*, 1997), the Dialogue Act Modeling for Automatic Tagging and Recognition of Conversational Speech (Stolcke *et al.*, 2000), the Dialog Act Markup in Several Layers (Allen and Core, 1997) and Verbal Response Modes Annotated Utterances Corpus (Stiles, 1992).

A speech act-based corpus linguistic program, SpeechActConc (Greaves and Warren, 2010a), requires the user to manually input the speech act annotation, which identifies each speech act as SA001 through to SA999. Below the annotation is illustrated with speech act examples based on Stenström's (1994) speech act typology:

```
<SA001 accept>
<SA002 acknowledge>
<SA003 agree>
<SA004 alert>
<SA005 answer>
```

<SA006 apology>
<SA007 call-off>
<SA008 check>
<SA009 closer>
<SA010 confirm>

(adapted from Stenström, 1994: 39–46)

Once annotated, SpeechActConc can perform automated and user-nominated searches for speech act co-occurrences in a corpus in a similar fashion to the concgrams searches described elsewhere.

Prosodic annotation is relatively rare in spoken corpora. It is very time-consuming to implement since it has to be handled manually. This is because naturally occurring spoken data comes with a lot of background noise and, if it involves two or more people, speaker overlap which makes it difficult, if not impossible, for computer programs to handle. The 1-million-word HKCSE (Prosodic) (Cheng *et al.*, 2008) is an example of a corpus that includes this kind of annotation based on Brazil's (1997) description of discourse intonation. This description (see Table 4.11) has four systems – tone, prominence, key and termination – within which a speaker has thirteen choices.

Each of the independent systems is a source of 'local meaning' (Brazil, 1997: xi) by which Brazil seeks to underline that these are moment-by-moment judgements made by speakers based on their assessment of the current state of understanding operating between the participants. The HKCSE (Prosodic) is annotated using the symbols outlined in Table 4.11 and an example of the resulting prosodic transcription is given in the extract below:

Extract from the HKCSE (Prosodic)
1 b: { / good < AFternoon > } (.) { \ < ^ HOW > are you }
2 B: { / < VEry > well } { / < THANK > you }
3   ((pause))
4 b: { = < JUST > } { V < CHECking > out } * { / <_ RIGHT > }
5 B: ** { \ < YES >}
6 b: { = < ER > } { / [HAVE] you got the mini bar < KEY > sir }
7 B: { / < NO > } { \ i didn't < HAVE > one }

Table 4.11 Discourse intonation systems and choices (Brazil, 1997)

System	Prominence	Tone { }	Key []	Termina-tion < >
Choice	prominent syllable – UPPER CASE	rise-fall - ∧	high - ^	high - ^
	non-prominent syllable – lower case	fall - \	mid - blank	mid - blank
		rise - /	low - _	low - _
		fall-rise - V		
		level - =		

Software, iConc, has been specially written (Cheng *et al.*, 2008), to search for a specific feature of discourse intonation, or combinations of features, or combinations of discourse intonation features and words or phrases. Below, Figures 4.15 and 4.16 are sample concordance lines for searches for rise tone plus *well* and fall tone plus *well*, respectively.

The most recent development in the annotation of corpora stems from the building of multi-modal corpora. Knight *et al.* (2009) describe the formidable challenges faced by those compiling and annotating the Nottingham Multi-Modal Corpus, which is a multi-modal corpus of spoken interaction. The aim is for the user to be able to search the corpus via an interface that gives access to 'lexical, prosodic and gestural features' (p. 2), which requires researchers to transcribe and annotate even gestures such as head nods and hand movements. A multi-modal corpus compiled in China (Gu, 2006) includes orthographic transcription, prosody, speech acts, eye gaze, body

```
1    JOB > ] } ((laugh)) B: { / [ < WELL > ] } { \ i don't [ < KN
2    VE > it } ((laugh)) B: { / [ < WELL > ] } { / i [ FIgured ]
3    < YEARS > ] ago } b2: { / [ < WELL > ] } { = [ < THERE'S >
4    CApital > ] movement } { / [ < WELL > ] } { = [ esTAblished
5    ng < HANdle > it } b3: { / [ < WELL > ] } { \ [ WE ] must ge
6    a: { = [ < ER > ] er } { / [ < WELL > ] } { = [ < THIS > ] i
7    \ i [ < _ GUESS > ] } { / [ < WELL > ] } { = [ < YOU'RE > ]
8    ter < proBAtion > } a: { / [ < WELL > ] } { \ [ < ACtually >
9    ^ eCOnomy > here } b2: { / [ < WELL > ] } { = [ < THAT > ] m
10   < ^ TOIlet > tissue } { / [ < WELL > ] } { \ there're [ VAr
```

Figure 4.15 Sample concordance lines for rise tone + *well*

```
1    { = [ < ER > ] } { \ [ < _ WELL > ] } (.) { ? [ < TALK > ]
2    < REALly > ] } B: { \ [ < _ WELL > ] } { = we [ < PUT > ] in
3    < SOME > ] are } { \ [ < _ WELL > ] } { = [ < THEY > ] } {
4    < _ SEE > ] } (.) { \ [ < ^ WELL > ] } { = [ PRObably ] THAT
5    ng [ < KONG > ] } { \ [ < ^ WELL > ] erm } { = with [ < THE
6    < SISter's > ] } { \ [ < _ WELL > ] } { \ [ ^ TWO ] < SISte
7    ] < CAUSE > } (.) { \ [ < ^ WELL > ] } { ? [ < I > ] } { \ i
8    st < TIME > the } { \ [ < _ WELL > ] } * { = there was [ < E
9    im } ((laugh)) b: { \ [ < ^ WELL > ] } { = he look [ < LIKE
10   < ^ HERE > } b: { \ [ < _ WELL > ] } { \ it's a [ < PART >
```

Figure 4.16 Sample concordance lines for fall tone + *well*

language, gestures, elaborate descriptions of participant roles and their relative positioning all combined in a multi-layered system of aligned annotation (p. 161).

Annotated versus plain text corpora

There is some discussion among corpus linguists about the benefits of using annotated rather than plain text corpora (sometimes termed raw corpora). Those in favour of annotation argue that the additional information makes a corpus more useful and increases both the processing speed and the accuracy of the search results. Those opposed counter that, once annotated, a corpus is less readily updated, expanded or discarded. They also claim that using pre-determined categories to annotate a corpus then limits the kinds of questions that are likely to be asked in the subsequent corpus analysis and that most categories (e.g., nominal clauses, anaphoric reference, direct and indirect speech) have been developed in pre-corpus days. These categories are also based on categories of written grammar which do not always fit the realities of spoken discourse. This latter point raises the issue of corpus-based versus corpus-driven corpus linguistics (see Chapter 6 for more on these approaches). For example, phenomena such as semantic prosody and the extent of phraseology tend to have been identified from plain text corpora because they are word-based rather than category-based phenomena. The ideal arrangement is for any annotated corpus to be also available in its pre-annotated form to allow users to have the choice.

Statistics

There are a number of basic statistics measures available in corpus linguistic software. Word frequency lists give the user both frequency counts and percentages for each distinct word (type) and the type/token ratio (TTR) is another simple statistic (both of these are described earlier in this chapter). The process of normalising results in one set of data, in order to allow direct comparisons with findings from a data set of a different size, is another use of basic statistics (see Chapter 6 for an example of this). Some software, such as WordSmith 5.0, provides a visual dispersion plot for a search item, which shows where it is to be found in a text or corpus, so that if a search item is frequent but concentrated in one part of a text or corpus this can be investigated further. Determining key words is another statistical measure (described earlier in this chapter) that is built into WordSmith 5.0, and other software such as ConcGram 1.0. Calculating the lexical density of a text or corpus (i.e., the percentage of lexical words as opposed to grammatical words) is also possible once the user has compiled and inputted a list of grammatical words. One such program, Coverage 1.3, is available at www.danielbinz.org/node/3, and is the work of a student supervised by Professor Michael Stubbs, who authored such a program himself some time ago (see Butler, 1985: 213–26 for details). The log likelihood ratio (also known as G-square), and the chi-squared measure, are often used to compare the findings from two sets of data. For example, if a specialised corpus has more instances of a particular word compared with a general corpus, these measures can be used to see whether or not the higher frequency is significant (see Oakes, 1998, and Gries, 2010 for more details). In addition to these measures, there is a wide range of statistical tests that can be applied in corpus linguistics that this book does not address; for example, 'confirmatory factor analysis', used in Biber's multi-dimensional analyses (mentioned earlier in this chapter), is detailed in Biber (1995: 94–5). There are a number of useful reference books devoted to statistics in corpus linguistics, and these include Barnbrook (1996), Oakes (1998), and Gries (2010). Readers are advised to consult these when considering the use of statistical measures, and McEnery et al. (2006: 52–8) provide a useful summary about making statistical claims. Here, we will focus on statistical measures of collocation.

In corpus linguistics, the two most commonly used statistical measures in collocation analysis are the t-score and mutual information (MI) value. Both are used to try to determine whether two words co-occur by chance or whether they are co-selected by the speaker or writer and so their association is significant. This is because it is generally felt that relying purely on raw frequencies is too unreliable a guide as to the strength of association between collocates. There are other statistical measures such as the z-score and log likelihood; the latter is also used in some software to determine key words. These tests set out to compare the observed and expected frequencies of the collocates; in other words, whether it is a chance happening or it is co-selection that has taken place.

Most concordancing software programs provide either the t-score or MI value, or both, and the user is able to list the collocates according to the strength of the collocation based on these results (significance for the t-score is ≥ 2 and for the MI value ≥ 3). As with any statistical measures, the user needs to be aware that these two tests of collo-cational significance differ in certain respects. Stubbs (1995) gives a clear overview of the problems associated with the t-score and MI. A limitation of the MI value is that collocates that are rare occurrences are more prominent in the MI list, whereas the t-score emphasises the number of joint frequencies (pp. 9–12). The result is that a collocate list based on the t-score is more likely to include function words than one based on MI. Also, the MI-based list is more likely to include lexical collocates which occur relatively infrequently with the search word.

Tables 4.12 and 4.13 illustrate the difference between the *t*-score and MI results. The tables are based on the top 20 collocates of *storm* using COBUILD's Concordance and Collocations Sampler which allows the user to pick either the *t*-score or MI when generating a collocate list.

It can be seen that only four collocates of *storm* – *desert*, *tropical*, *hurricane* and *clouds* – are shared across the two tables, highlighting their different mathematical approaches. Their composition is different in terms of word class with no function words in the MI list while in the *t*-score list they amount to about half of the collocates. Also, the way in which MI highlights relatively rare joint frequencies, as opposed to the *t*-score list, is apparent with fourteen of the top twenty in the MI collocating with *storm* less than ten times, and eight of these only three times. These differences need to be borne in mind when deciding which measure to use, if any.

There is, however, an even bigger issue regarding the use of statistical measures to determine collocational significance outlined by Sinclair (see Sinclair, 2007a and Cheng *et al.*, 2009 for more details). Sinclair makes the important point that the production of language is never a series of chance occurrences, unlike, for example, rolling a

Table 4.12 Top twenty collocates of *storm* based on *t*-score

Collocate	Corpus frequency	Joint frequency	Significance
a	973,489	562	13.223771
the	2,313,407	981	12.465741
desert	1,635	115	10.684884
by	181,034	120	6.735712
operation	4,345	47	6.693864
over	57,386	64	6.168828
hit	6,841	34	5.531454
during	17,418	34	5.068396
caused	3,521	27	5.023172
protest	1,713	26	5.013260
up	104,073	65	4.766961
in	765,730	273	4.692093
clouds	714	22	4.651556
[h]	106,714	64	4.594785
after	57,391	45	4.524214
tropical	717	20	4.431208
hurricane	444	19	4.332896
of	1,100,578	362	4.259727
when	102,483	56	3.987319
rain	2,327	17	3.979032

Table 4.13 Top 20 collocates of *storm* based on mutual information

Collocate	Corpus frequency	Joint frequency	Significance
teacup	26	7	10.043560
derbys	20	5	9.936634
troopers	30	4	9.029653
weathering	28	3	8.714120
weathered	132	13	8.592546
trooper	62	5	8.304203
desert	1,635	115	8.106867
surges	44	3	8.061978
hurricane	444	19	7.389892
sewer	72	3	7.351414
torrential	73	3	7.331513
lull	84	3	7.129000
flap	184	6	6.997742
saturn	227	7	6.917140
clouds	714	22	6.915985
lightning	368	11	6.872199
tropical	717	20	6.772418
halloween	108	3	6.766393
braced	112	3	6.713921
upgraded	113	3	6.701095

dice six times, and so the whole notion of 'happenstance' versus 'statistically significant' is not applicable to collocation. In other words, since we know that we string together words in an utterance or sentence systematically based on patterns of co-selections, it simply does not make sense to use statistical measures that are based on the assumption that we could be stringing together these words purely by chance.

Concgramming

A phraseology-oriented software program, ConcGram 1.0 (Greaves, 2009) has extended our ability to retrieve phraseology, especially phraseological variation, from a corpus. ConcGram 1.0 does this by fully automatically finding all of the co-occurrences of between two and five words in a corpus regardless of constituency variation (e.g., *risk management*, *risk assets management*, *risk controlled approach to portfolio management*) or positional variation (e.g., *risk management*, *management of operational risk*). These co-occurrences are termed 'concgrams' (Cheng *et al.*, 2006) and they are examined in more detail in Chapter 5 (some of the functions available in ConcGram have been added to WordSmith 5.0).

Concgram frequency lists can be fully automatically generated with no prior input of search items from the user. The program also allows

the user to then select a concgram and display its concordance. As
with the single-word frequency lists, concgramming a corpus finds
unique concgrams and their frequencies. For example, concgramming
the 7.3-million-word HKFSC uncovered 268,982 unique two-word
concgrams with 37,288,456 two-word concgrams in total. This is a
very long list and it takes some time to generate the full list, depending
on the power of your computer. The top twenty concgrams in the
HKFSC are shown in Table 4.14.

Just as we have seen earlier, the most frequent words in any corpus
are function words. We find these words co-occurring at the top of
concgram frequency lists. It is not until we get to numbers 18
(*Company/the*) and 20 (*Group/the*) in the list that we begin to find
lexically richer concgrams. Lower down the very long list of concgrams
we find more and more such concgrams. In Table 4.15, there is sample
of concgrams from the middle of the same two-word concgrams list,
all of which have forty-two instances in the HKFSC. Again, this
confirms the continuum which one invariably finds in such frequency
lists from the grammatically rich co-occurrences at the top to the
increasingly lexically rich as one moves down the list.

Once the two-word concgrams have been found, it is possible to
continue to automatically find all of the three-word concgrams, then
the four-word concgrams, and so on. If you find a concgram in the
list to be of interest, you can select the concgram and use the 'specific

Table 4.14 Top twenty two-word concgrams in HKFSC

	Two-word concgram	Frequency
1	of/the	436,870
2	the/to	204,920
3	and/the	204,876
4	in/the	198,052
5	and/of	125,874
6	in/of	106,861
7	of/to	97,632
8	a/the	87,004
9	for/the	85,999
10	a/of	81,978
11	and/to	73,303
12	and/in	71,593
13	on/the	67,951
14	or/the	66,755
15	by/the	62,985
16	in/to	62,659
17	as/the	60,686
18	Company/the	58,152
19	be/the	51,875
20	Group/the	48,036

Table 4.15 Twenty random two-word concgrams from the
middle of the frequency list in HKFSC

	Two-word concgram	Frequency
1	ensure/risk	42
2	functions/perform	42
3	guaranteed/interest	42
4	involve/uncertainties	42
5	listed/liability	42
6	losses/revaluation	42
7	movements/risk	42
8	notes/owned	42
9	outflow/resources	42
10	policies/risks	42
11	provide/shares	42
12	qualifying/recommence	42
13	retirement/year	42
14	rights/variation	42
15	risk/shares	42
16	rules/relating	42
17	statement/summary	42
18	supervisory/under	42
19	term/unexpired	42
20	trading/treasury	42

concgrams search' function to find what words co-occur with that
particular concgram. For example, if you are interested in the two-
word concgram *environmental/waste*, and you want to see all of the
three-word concgrams which include these words, this function will
find them. Table 4.16 shows the results of the search in the HKFSC
with a cut-off frequency set at 5.

The user can also choose to nominate up to five words or phrases
using the 'user-nominated' concgram search function. The concordance
lines in Figure 4.17 illustrate the way in which a concgram display
differs from the traditional KWIC display by highlighting all of the
words in the concgram. This has the effect of focusing the user's
attention on all of the co-occurring words, rather than focusing
primarily on the centred node, *management*.

The concgram concordance display begins with those instances of
risk to the right of the centred word. As *risk* moves further away from
management, it is displayed lower down in the concordance. Once
instances to the right have been exhausted, those to the left are
displayed. This method of arranging the concordance makes it easier
for the user to analyse the various 'concgram configurations' (Cheng
et al., 2009: 5).

Table 4.16 Specific three-word concgram search – *environmental/waste*

	Two-word concgram	Co-occurring word	Frequency
1	environmental/waste	the	35
2	environmental/waste	and	34
3	environmental/waste	on	17
4	environmental/waste	of	16
5	environmental/waste	protection	15
6	environmental/waste	in	13
7	environmental/waste	to	9
8	environmental/waste	with	8
9	environmental/waste	an	7
10	environmental/waste	course	7
11	environmental/waste	festival	7
12	environmental/waste	issues	7
13	environmental/waste	management	7
14	environmental/waste	legislation	6
15	environmental/waste	training	6
16	environmental/waste	compliance	5
17	environmental/waste	is	5
18	environmental/waste	reduction	5

```
1   s form the basis for our management of this risk. With clo
2   isciplined and proactive management of such risk. The fram
3   d the need for effective management of credit risk. Despit
4   e high level centralised management of credit risk for HSB
5   . HSBC aims, through its management of market risk in non-
6   latory requirements. Our management of operational risk be
7   aluation, acceptance and management of some degree of risk
8   m of US$10 billion under management. Foreign exchange risk
9   issioner post, but isn't management of uncertainty and ris
10  ent K H Lee R the Senior Management Statutory Committee Ri
11  r attention by us to the management of foreign currency ri
12  ional risks and the risk management and control thereof. U
13  plementing enhanced risk management systems and practices
14  y the former risk assets management department. The assets
15  ree-tier risk and safety management system, reviews  of tr
16   insurer risk and policy management strategies, constraint
17  iew the risk control and management of our Company and app
18  sive risk monitoring and management of credit and non-cred
```

Figure 4.17 Sample concordance lines for the concgram *management/risk*

Task 4.10

Visit the following website, http://rcpce.engl.polyu.edu.hk/, which has OnlineConcGram, a simplified version of ConcGram 1.0 (Greaves, 2009).

Select the Hong Kong Engineering Corpus (HKEC) and then select 'advanced searches'. Enter two search words, 'risk' and 'management' and select a span of 2. Note down the number of instances. Repeat the search with a span of 5, noting down the number of instances. Discuss possible reasons for the different frequencies.

Select the Hong Kong Financial Services Corpus (HKFSC) and repeat the searches. Compare your results with those from the HKEC.

Repeat the search in the Annual Report sub-corpus of the HKFSC and note down the results.

Repeat the procedure using the Media Release sub-corpus in the HKFSC.

Discuss possible reasons for the different frequencies, bearing in mind the relative sizes of the corpora.

Concluding remarks

In order to get the most out of corpus linguistics, it is important to keep up to date with developments in software development and to be confident that you can fully exploit the many functions they provide. It is also important that the user is able to analyse the results generated by the software and can offer a plausible explanation for them. In this chapter, basic searches such as the generation of word frequency lists, keyword lists, and concordances have been explained and illustrated. Also, the increasing interest in phraseology has been discussed and the importance of including phraseological variation emphasised. A brief overview of statistical measures both highlighted their usefulness, and discussed their limitations with regard to determining the significance of co-selections.

Note

1   The full corpus of budget speeches (1997–2010) is publicly available at http://rcpce.engl.polyu.edu.hk/.

5 Extended units of meaning

This chapter will:

- focus on lexical phraseology, and underline the need to move beyond current understandings of the 'word';

- look at the forms and functions of Biber *et al.*'s (1999) 'lexical bundles', termed 'n-grams' in this book;

- examine Sinclair's (1996, 1998) notion of the lexical item and its five categories of co-selection (i.e., collocation, colligation, semantic preference, semantic prosody and the core) as a framework to describe extended units of meaning;

- explain how meaning creation can best be addressed by looking beyond the 'word' as a unit of meaning; and

- explore problems of vocabulary learning and teaching and the part played by vocabulary in how texts are organised and taught.

Introduction

One of the most influential figures in corpus linguistics is John Sinclair. He conducted the first computer-based study of collocation (Sinclair *et al.*, 1970; Sinclair, 2004), and was behind the well-known COBUILD project and related publications such as dictionaries, grammars, and learning and teaching materials. His influence is based, in part, on two interrelated notions that are central to his corpus linguistic work. These are that language is all about creating meaning and that language has a tendency to be phraseological (Sinclair, 1987). The first notion might be thought to be self-evident, but sometimes it can be lost sight of in studies of language use. The second notion is based on the overwhelming evidence of corpus linguistics and has far-reaching implications for those interested in meaning creation. When Sinclair and other corpus linguists use the term 'phraseology', they use it in an inclusive sense to refer to recurrent patterns of associated words. Importantly, the tendency for words to be associated is a result of speakers and writers co-selecting words in order to create meaning (e.g., *impending + storm*, see discussion in Task 5.5 on p. 105). The kinds of co-selections speakers and writers make and their meaning-making potential are explored in this chapter.

N-grams

Probably the most studied manifestation of the phraseological tendency in language is the n-gram. Language quite often comes in the form of repeated phrases made up of two or more adjacent words, such as *you know, of the, I think, a lot of* and *I don't know*, and these are known as 'n-grams', where 'n' represents the two or more words in the phrase. In this book, we use the term 'n-grams', but these phrases are variously known as 'bundles', 'clusters', 'chunks' and 'formulaic language', among others. Concordancing software is able to identify n-grams and produce lists of them in the same way that it finds single words and generates word frequency lists. The most frequent kind of n-gram is made up of two words and as the size of the n-gram increases the number to find shrinks quite dramatically. For example, in a study of n-grams that occur at least twenty times in a 5-million-word corpus (Carter and McCarthy, 2006: 831), there are 45,015 two-word n-grams as opposed to a mere 31 six-word n-grams. N-grams can tell us interesting things about language use and they have been mainly studied in terms of their structure, language functions, and register- or genre-specificity.

N-gram structures

Two widely used grammar books are based on corpus evidence and they include descriptions of the structural patterns which n-grams have. Biber *et al.* (1999: 996–7) identify the most frequent four-word n-grams, termed 'lexical bundles' in their main study and defined as 'three or more adjacent words' (p. 990), in their corpora and describe a number of frequent structural patterns; for example, personal pronoun plus lexical verb phrase (plus complement clause), *I don't*

Task 5.1

Using WordSmith 5.0 (Scott, 2008), identify a frequently occurring lexical word in a corpus and search for its two-word, three-word and four-word clusters. Note down the frequencies and discuss possible reasons for your findings.

know what; pronoun/noun phrase (plus auxiliary) plus copula *be* (+), *it was in the*; noun phrase with post modifier fragment, *the nature of the*; preposition plus noun phrase fragment, *as a result of*; and (verb/adjective plus) to-clause fragment, *are likely to be* (p. 996). They also identify the grammatical category of the final word in their four-word n-grams – verb, pronoun, other function words, noun and so on (p. 997). Similarly, Carter and McCarthy (2006: 832–3) focus on the structure of the most frequent n-grams in their corpora and, importantly, they do not confine their study to four-word n-grams. This means that their description includes the structures of the most frequent n-grams in any corpus; namely, two-word n-grams. The most frequent structure they find is preposition plus article, *My father's birthday is on the fifth.*, with some frequent three-word instances as well, *We were never allowed out of the school.* Subject plus verb is another common structure in both two-word, *I was* and *do you*, and three-word n-grams, *I don't know* and *do you want*. Longer n-grams of between three to five words are found to often have the structure of subject plus verb with complement items, as in *I mean I, I don't know if* and *do you know what I.* Again, in terms of n-grams of three or more words, they find many instances of noun phrases plus *of*, such as *a bit of, at the end of* and *in the direction of the.*

N-gram functions

In addition to their structures, these grammars are also interested in describing the major functions of n-grams. Five major n-gram functions are identified by Carter and McCarthy (2006: 834–7). The first, and most frequent, of these functions is to express basic relations in texts and this is usually done with n-grams which are 'prepositional expressions' (p. 834). The most common relations are those of time, *I'll see you in the morning* and *In the middle of the night a noise woke Henry*, and place, *There was nobody on the beaches* and *He was waiting at the bottom of the stairs.* Other basic relations such as possession, agency, purpose, goal and direction are also expressed, and these too are often done with preposition-based n-grams, such as *of a/the, to the, with a/the, by the* and *for the* (p. 834).

> **Task 5.2**
>
> Generate a list of the most frequent two- and three-word n-grams in a corpus. Try to identify the most frequent structures in your list and compare them with those discussed above.

Another function of many n-grams is to impart interpersonal meanings which build and sustain the personal and social relations between the participants (Carter and McCarthy, 2006: 835). These n-grams are used to monitor the extent of the shared knowledge between the participants, hedge assertions and opinions, and express varying degrees of tentativeness. Many n-grams used for these interpersonal functions include three verbs, *know*, *mean* and *think*, such as *you know*, *do you know what (I)*, *I know what you mean*, *I mean* and *I think* (p. 835).

Task 5.3

What basic relation is expressed by each of the following (underlined) n-grams extracted from the BNC?

1 *A good meaty texture <u>with a</u> balanced, not too salty flavour.*

2 *A police spokesman said that officers, attacked <u>by the</u> animal, had to fire several rounds to kill it.*

3 *Mr Rafferty worked <u>for the</u> Belfast Telegraph for 25 years.*

4 *The boy turned and pointed <u>to the</u> woman's headband.*

5 *We were <u>at the side of the</u> lake having a bite to eat when it all happened.*

6 *<u>In the</u> evening, I meet friends at the Devonshire for a drink.*

Task 5.4

What is the interpersonal function of each of the following (underlined) n-grams extracted from the BNC?

1 *As she left he patted her on the bum which is, <u>you know,</u> a bit friendly.*

2 *But they're apt to make me feel a bit, I suppose that's what they're for, a bit docile like, <u>you know what I mean</u>?*

3 *<u>I don't know</u> whether we'll keep the individuals on the next one, cos people did talk about group work.*

4 *<u>You know,</u> you can organise them.*

5 *<u>I think</u> an hour of this is about enough isn't it?*

6 *He was in the police <u>you know,</u> and he was a male nurse.*

Another interesting function of n-grams is to be vague, which is when speakers and writers refer vaguely to things rather than being precise or explicit. There are various reasons for being vague. It could be that it is simply not possible to be precise or explicit, or it would be inappropriate in a particular context to be overly precise or explicit. Most typically, vague language is used because the speaker or writer assumes that there is no need to be precise or explicit and what appears to be vague in fact will be understood thanks to shared experiences or points of view, or cultural schemata (Carter and McCarthy, 2006: 835). Examples of n-grams used in this way are *kind of*, *this and that*, and *(or) something like that*.

The need to link clauses and sentences is another function performed by n-grams (Carter and McCarthy, 2006: 836). Many of these n-grams include commonly used conjunctions, such as *and* and *but*, as in *and it was*, *but it was* and *and then*. Others which are frequent include *as well as*, and *at the time*. Complete Task 5.6.

The last function of n-grams described by Carter and McCarthy (2006: 836–7) is related to turn-taking in spoken dialogues. They identify n-grams associated with speakers constraining hearers to take the next turn in the discourse. These n-grams typically expect a response from the hearer and include interrogative fragments, *do you want to* and *what do you*, and tags such as *do you*, *shall I* and *isn't it*. Another group of n-grams are found at the start of speakers turns and serve to introduce what the speaker wants to say, for example, *another thing is*, *just a quick question*, *well I think* and *one thing*. Complete Task 5.7.

Task 5.5

Study the following sentences and utterances from the BNC and try to identify 'vague n-grams'.

1 *It's a different sort of team, but it's a team.*

2 *The column where people advertise second hand bikes, second hand sewing machines, second hand cars and all the rest of it.*

3 *I'd get bags of clothing and stuff for them.*

4 *I used to weigh spuds and fill the shelves and all that sort of thing.*

5 *Recommended course of action and stuff like that.*

6 *Well it involved a lot of things, a bit of everything.*

Task 5.6

Study the following extracts from the BNC and try to identify 'linking n-grams':

1 *Upon closer examination, however, it was revealed that there were at least three ways in which such a conclusion would be misleading. In the first place, half of the non-union green-field site companies did not have a formal system whereby management informed or consulted with their employees.*

2 *I believe in a competitive world, but at the same time I think we have got to be laying sound foundations for future growth ...*

3 *It is understood that no one has been injured as a result of the nurse's alleged actions.*

4 *The problem is that our managerial hierarchies are so badly designed as to defeat the best efforts even of psychologically insightful individuals. Solutions that concentrate on groups, on the other hand, fail to take into account the real nature of employment systems.*

5 *If he is going to have to abandon a dream for the sake of your joint happiness, it's something you need to talk about. In the same way, you need to know if he wants to be Prime Minister.*

6 *One common occurrence, as a consequence of this obsession with secrecy, is that we now have a system of government by leaks.*

Task 5.7

Visit the following website – http://rcpce.engl.polyu.edu.hk/HKCSE/ – and search this spoken corpus for turn-taking boundaries by searching for a colon, ':'. Colons are used to identify speakers at the start of each turn – a:, B: etc. Look either side of the turn boundaries and note down some of the n-grams associated with turn allocation and turn introductions.

N-grams are also categorised by discourse function by Biber *et al.* (1999). They propose four main functions and these are referential, text-organising, stance and interactional. Referential n-grams include time, place and text markers, such as *at the beginning of*, *the end of the* and *at the same time*, whereas n-grams acting as text organisers express contrast, *on the other hand*, inference, *as a result of*, or focus, *it is important to*. Stance n-grams convey speaker and writer attitudes, such as *I don't know why* and *are more likely to*, and interactional n-grams denote, for example, politeness, or are used in reported speech, as in *thank you very much* and *and I said to him*. While the categories for functions differ between the two grammars, it can be seen that they cover similar ground, and the difference can partly be explained by Biber *et al.*'s (1999) focus on four-word n-grams.

N-gram specificity

Findings from studies of n-grams have shown that n-grams, or the relative frequencies with which they occur, can differ depending on the kind of corpus being investigated. For example, in CANCODE, which is a spoken corpus, the most common n-grams differ from those in a written corpus (Carter and McCarthy, 2006: 829–31). In the spoken corpus, the most frequent two-word n-grams are *you know*, *I mean, I think, in the* and *it was*. While in the written the top five are *of the, in the, to the, on the* and *it was*. It can be seen that only one n-gram, *in the*, is in the top five for both. The most common five-word n-grams in the spoken corpus are *you know what I mean, at the end of the, do you know what I, the end of the day* and *do you want me to*. In the written corpus they are *at the end of the, by the end of the, for the first time in, at the top of the* and *at the back of the*. Again, only one n-gram, *at the end of the*, is in both. N-grams, therefore, are a means to describe similarities and differences in language use and these relate back to some of the functions of n-grams that might be more prevalent in spoken or written language. For example, the n-grams associated with the interpersonal function are far more common in a spoken corpus while those associated with the linking function occur more frequently in written corpora.

Academic language use has been the subject of a lot of studies and these studies have shown how the study of n-grams can reveal register- and genre-specific patterns of language use. Thanks to such studies, it is now known that academic language contains distinctive high

Task 5.8

Look back at the functions of n-grams and use some of the examples as search items in a written corpus and a spoken corpus. Allowing for the size of the corpora, what are the relative frequencies of the n-grams and why is there such a variety?

If you don't have corpora available, go to http://rcpce.engl.polyu.edu.hk/HKCSE/ for a spoken corpus, and go to http://rcpce.engl.polyu.edu.hk/HKEC/ for a mainly written corpus.

frequency n-grams due to the conventions of academic spoken and written discourses, as well as enabling us to better appreciate differences between the various academic disciplines. Examples of n-grams typical of academic language include: *for example, the importance of, the nature of, there are a number of, in other words* and *in the case of* (Carter and McCarthy, 2006: 837).

Other studies have compared the use of n-grams across different genres. Hyland (2008), for example, looked at four-word n-grams and compares their structures and functions across three academic genres; namely, research articles, Ph.D theses and Master's dissertations. He found the greatest similarity in the use of n-grams in the research articles and Ph.D theses with five of the top ten shared (*on the other hand, in the case of, on the basis of, at the same time* and *in terms of the*). Next were the writers of Ph.D theses and Master's dissertations with four overlapping (*on the other hand, at the same time, in the case of* and *as well as the*). Writers of research articles and Master's dissertations had only three n-grams in common (*on the other hand, at the same time* and *the results of the*) (p. 51). Hyland has three functions for the n-grams (p. 49), research-oriented (e.g., *at the beginning of, the use of the, the magnitude of the, the structure of the* and *in the Hong Kong*), text-oriented (e.g., *on the other hand, as a result of the, in the present study* and *in the case of*), and participant-oriented (e.g., *are likely to be, may be due to, it is possible that, it should be noted that* and *as can be seen*). He also compared the frequencies with which the three sets of writers used these functions. Master's students' dissertations make most use of research-oriented n-grams and a relatively lower use of participant-oriented n-grams compared with writers of research articles and Ph.D. theses. Conversely, the presumably more expert writers used more text-oriented n-grams than research-oriented n-grams and also relatively more participant-oriented ones. Hyland's study demonstrates how n-grams can reveal similarities and differences both between genres and between different sets of writers.

Others have shown that n-grams provide insights into the phraseology used in different contexts. A good example of such a study is one by Scott and Tribble (2006: 132), in which they examined the top forty three- and four-word n-grams in the whole of the 100-million-word BNC, and three sub-corpora of the BNC: conversations, academic writing and literary studies periodical articles. The top ten n-grams for the whole of the BNC and the sub-corpora (Scott and Tribble, 2006: 139–40) show that the top four three-word n-grams are the same for whole of the BNC and the conversations (*a lot of, be able to, I don't know* and *it was a*), but the top four in academic writing and literary studies periodical articles are different. In these formal written sub-corpora, they found considerable overlap in the top ten (e.g., *as well as, in terms of, it is a, it is not* and *one of the*).

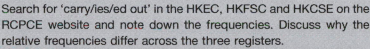

Task 5.9

Search for 'carry/ies/ed out' in the HKEC, HKFSC and HKCSE on the RCPCE website and note down the frequencies. Discuss why the relative frequencies differ across the three registers.

Search for 'assets + liabilities' at http://rcpce.engl.polyu.edu.hk/HKFSC/advanced.htm and note down the relative frequencies in the annual reports sub-corpus and the media releases sub-corpus. Again, discuss the relative frequencies in these two genres.

Scott and Tribble (2006) also found that certain structures occur with differing frequencies across the four corpora and they investigated one structure in particular, i.e. noun phrase with *of*-phrase fragment (e.g., *one of the*). Through their study, they discovered a set of terms which seems to be important in academic language and which are to be found at the end of this n-gram, *one of the* (p. 141); examples of these n-grams are *one of the most*, *one of the main*, *one of the major*, and *one of the first*. With the exception of *one of the most*, all of these n-grams are more frequently found in academic discourse and, therefore, can be said to be register-specific.

Idioms

While studies of n-grams make up the majority of the studies of phraseology, another form of phraseology which is studied is the idiom, although the dividing line between n-grams and idioms is not easy to draw. The use of idioms in a language is interesting because they are a special kind of phraseology which can often provide insights into the culture, and the use of idioms across cultures may reveal differences in cultural values.

O'Keeffe *et al.* (2007: 82–3) suggested two useful ways to find idioms in a corpus, given that idioms can be difficult to find automatically using corpus linguistic software. They pointed out that certain words are 'idiom-prone' (p. 83) because they are 'basic cognitive metaphors' and give the examples of parts of the body, money, light and colour. They illustrated one method by first searching for *face* in CANCODE and then studying the 520 concordance lines which revealed fifteen different idioms; for example, *let's face it*, *on the face of it*, *face to face* and *keep a straight face* (p. 83). The second method is to first sample texts from the corpus in order to study them qualitatively to identify idioms. The idioms found are then searched for in the corpus as a whole. This method has led to the identification of many idioms in CANCODE and the five most frequently occurring are *fair enough*, *at the end of the day*, *there you go*, *make sense* and *turn round and say* (p. 85). Also, idioms, like n-grams, can be described in terms of their functions and register- and genre-specificity (McCarthy, 1998).

A study (Li and MacGregor, 2009) that looked into the register-specificity of metaphors compared colour terms in business English between Hong Kong (Hong Kong finance corpus, HK-F) and the UK (BNC-F), with each corpus comprising approximately 7 million words. The study examined eight colour words: *black*, *white*, *green*, *red*, *yellow*, *blue*, *brown* and *grey*, and found that they are used literally and metaphorically in both corpora but quantitative and qualitative differences were apparent (see Table 5.1; Li and MacGregor, 2009: 16). Colour words appear more frequently overall in the BNC-F than in the HKC-F, with the exception of *yellow*, but more often as metaphors in the HKC-F, with the exception of *red*. The ratios of literal to metaphoric use of colour terms showed large variation between colours and corpora.

Li and MacGregor's (2009) study identified these general categories by first generating a word list, and then examining it for words which look as if they might be used metaphorically in the corpus. These words, and related words, were then used as the search items. This method adds one more to the two described above and is another useful way to extract metaphors from a corpus. Now complete Tasks 5.10 and 5.11.

Lexical items

One of the most interesting and important findings from corpus linguistics has been to provide evidence for meaning creation being phrase-based rather than word-based. This evidence is largely thanks to the ideas of Sinclair. What does phrase-based meaning mean?

Table 5.1 Comparison of the frequencies of colour words per million words

Colour term	BNC-F			HK-F		
	Total #	Metaphoric #	Use %	Total #	Metaphoric #	Use %
Black	124	27	22	6	4	63
White	106	26	25	39	2	4
Red	58	16	28	29	20	68
Green	52	29	56	23	10	42
Yellow	12	<1	<1	38	<1	0
Blue	36	17	48	14	4	26
Brown	14	<1	<1	1	<1	20
Grey	26	11	45	2.1	1.9	88

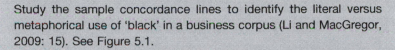

Task 5.10

Study the sample concordance lines to identify the literal versus metaphorical use of 'black' in a business corpus (Li and MacGregor, 2009: 15). See Figure 5.1.

```
1   t. Auditors deal with the black and white of reconciling c
2   sparent, and came from a "black box", based offshore in the
3   oduced through the use of "black boxes" and the removal of
4   estore our finances to the black. For that year I am forecas
5   lped keep the bank in the black. If we see no big changes i
6   y colour as long as it is black. In short, the local indust
7   68 agents, the HKFI put a black mark on their records, ind
8   t to 5 per cent above the black market  exchange rate for t
9   s and has clamped down on black market activities. Despite
10     (1249) Black marks for black market CLARA LI Hundreds of
11  al exchange rate and the black market is also a factor. Wi
12  official exchange and the black market rate at 7 to 8 per
13  le being  referred to as "black people". Well, I do not pe
14  d that China still raised black questions marks in the min
15  oon Signal or higher or a black rain storm warning or othe
16  both the Binomial and the Black-Scholes option pricing mod
17  t year, but stayed in the black thanks to one-off gains fr
18     23 October 1997 – The Black Thursday? The financial turm
```

Figure 5.1

Task 5.11

Search for 'red', 'green', 'blue', 'attack', 'defend', and 'surrender' in a financial services corpus – http://rcpce.engl.polyu.edu.hk/HKFSC/. List some of the metaphor-related n-grams you find and see if you can classify some of their functions in financial services contexts.

This concept is best illustrated with an example. If we consult a dictionary, such as the 2006 COBUILD dictionary, to find out what the word *impending* means, we find the following entry:

imǀpendǀing
An **impending** event is one that is going to happen very soon. (FORMAL)

On the morning of the expedition, I woke up with a feeling of impending disaster.
ADJ: ADJ n

(Cobuild, 2006)

From the above entry, the meaning of *impending* might be summarised as 'will happen soon'.

If we now study the concordance lines in Figure 5.2, which are based on a search for *impending* using the online concordance sampler of the Bank of English, the above dictionary definition can be seen to be lacking because it does not focus on the words associated with *impending*.

A search of a corpus enables us to see multiple instances of *impending* and this then shows up interesting patterns of usage. In Figure 5.1, we can see that *impending* does indeed convey the meaning 'will happen soon', but this concordance also shows us that what is going to happen soon is most likely going to be either unwelcome or unpleasant (e.g., *disaster, air raids, doom, nightmares, death, scandals*). There are occasional exceptions to this (and this is to be expected), and, in line 10, we find one such exception where the *impending*

```
 1 a month's notice of impending charges and were invited to d
 2 is, Thatcherism and impending world-wide environmental disa
 3 ive aid to avert an impending economic disaster and thus se
 4 cise location of an impending quake. With the proviso that
 5 ed disturbed by the impending presence of a third. Two was
 6 m it, and a sign of impending illness when someone fails to
 7 for any sign of an impending ambush. Then, as the Land Rov
 8 in the warnings of impending moral catastrophe. It would b
 9 's concern about an impending election. [p] In 1996 for the
10 l be boosted by an impending agreement with John Swift, th
11 t the taskforce to impending air raids, but they would hav
12 es try to fend off impending nightmares. At the heart of i
13 ok with a sense of impending doom, but the conclusion is s
14 ible factor was an impending court case - now resolved - a
15 t appears to be an impending scandal. He argued in the Bri
16 rder. Rumors of an impending Putsch began to spread throug
17 readers) about an impending assault in Congress against t
18 prepared for Mom's impending death. The 9-year-old was exc
19 n they were facing impending loss and a need for role chan
20 bation, and to the impending scandals. Basically, they've
```

Figure 5.2 Sample concordance lines for *impending*

agreement would seem to be welcome rather than unwelcome. Interestingly, the example provided in the COBUILD dictionary – ... *a feeling of impending disaster* – conforms to the typical pattern of usage but this pattern of use, and its impact on meaning, is not mentioned in the entry. Also, one example in a dictionary entry[1] is unable to implicitly foreground the meaning of *impending*, which is better summarised as follows: '*impending* + noun phrase = something (i.e., the co-selected noun phrase) unwelcome or unpleasant will happen soon'. The meaning of 'impending' given by Cambridge Dictionaries online contains the semantic prosody (Sinclair, 1996, 2004) 'something unpleasant or unwanted':

> **impending**
> adjective [before noun]
> describes an event, usually something unpleasant or unwanted, **that**
> **is going to happen soon:**
> *impending disaster/doom*
> *Lineker announced his impending retirement from international*
> *football before the 1992 European Championships.*
> (Cambridge Dictionaries online,
> accessed 26 August 2008)

The point being illustrated here is that meaning is created through combinations of associated words and not by individual words. In the case of *impending*, only by examining the words it associates with is it possible to begin to move beyond a partial description of meaning to a fuller description, and it is not the meaning of individual isolated words, but the meaning of co-selected words which has to be described. Hence, the notion of lexical item (Sinclair, 2004), which is an extended unit of meaning, which conveys the idea that meaning is created through the co-selection of words.

Task 5.12

Look up the word 'duplication' in a dictionary and note down the definition. Then search for 'duplication' using the online BNC concordancer. Study the results of your search and discuss whether the dictionary entry could be improved upon to more fully represent the meaning taking into account the patterns of co-selections you have found.

Five categories of co-selection

The fact that speakers and writers co-select the words which make up extended units of meanings termed 'lexical items' (Sinclair, 1996, 1998, 2004) then leads us to the following questions:

> What kinds of co-selections are made by speakers and writers?
> How do we find them in a corpus?

Lexical items can be comprised of up to five categories of co-selection (Sinclair, 2004: 141–2). These are the core and semantic prosody, which are both obligatory, plus semantic preference, collocation and colligation, which are optional. The core is the word, or words, always present in every instance of a lexical item and the semantic prosody is the overall functional meaning of a lexical item. The term 'semantic prosody' is used by Sinclair to emphasise that meaning is created across co-selected words in the lexical item and does not reside in only the core, just as the prosody of spoken language is based around larger units, tone units, rather than individual words. Collocation and colligation are related to the co-selection of words and grammatical choices with the core, respectively. The semantic preference of a lexical item refers to the tendency for lexical items to be restricted to identifiable semantic fields.

All of the co-selections are also described by Sinclair in terms of the process by which each category is selected. It is the selection of semantic prosody by the speaker that then leads to the selection of the core and the other co-selections of a lexical item. This process is summarised below:

From the point of view of the speaker/writer, the process of co-selection is:

1 First the speaker/writer selects a **semantic prosody** of *x* [applied to a **semantic preference** *y*].

2 The **semantic preference** in turn controls the **collocational** and **colligational patterns**.

3 The final component of the **lexical item** is the **invariable core**.

(adapted from Sinclair, 2004: 34)

In a detailed study of a lexical item (Cheng *et al.*, 2009) based on 259 instances, the co-selections of the lexical item with PLAY[2] + *role* as its core are identified. A sample of thirty instances of this lexical item is in Figure 5.3 below.

The core of this lexical item consists of *PLAY* and *role* because these are the words which are invariably co-selected in all of the concordance

```
1    spur game what else played a role in that is the two people
2    But I'm not here to play that role. We must please be clear
3    ard (IDB) hope will play a key role in financial regenerati
4    ated that it should play a full role in a UN conference to
5    this reason it will play a vital role in our later construc
6    potential and could play a major role as the bridge between
7    l authorities still play a crucial role in the shaping of t
8    the banks. 4. Banks play a central role as consultants, adv
9    urage the pupils to play an active role in learning. 17.71
10   family may come to play a pivotal role in all major expend
11   cal considerations play a decisive role in location choice
12   should be ready to play a positive role in a Nato that was
13   nisation and hence play an important role as "gatekeeper"
14   rest. Expectations play an important role in this theory o
15   fessional advisers play an essential role in the managemen
16   ch, some additives play a very useful role in slowing down
17   private sector can play a more prominent role in local and
18   iduals just listed play a very important role in giving yo
19   nalities that PPBs play a much more significant role in pu
20    briefly the roles played by the Comptroller and Auditor G
21   increasing role to play in environmental quality during th
22    important role to play in developing our understanding of
23   undamental role it plays in good business practice.    Ever
24   e critical role is played by the ruwang. It is the latter
25   a positive role to play in an organisation, and that role
26   ignificant role to play in helping corporations to achieve
27   t role for them to play is that of a co-ordinator. An exam
28    role they have to play in securing a healthier and safer
```

Figure 5.3 Sample concordance lines for the lexical item with *PLAY* and *role* as its
core

lines. Some of the most frequent collocates (and here we report the findings from the original study) are *important* (23 instances), *significant* (15), *major* (8), *leading/lead* (8), *central* (8), *key* (7), *crucial* (6), and *vital* (5). The main colligational patterns are the co-selection of a modifier, determiner and preposition. In terms of semantic preference, this lexical item is found in the context of business or economic activities, and organisational or societal relationships. The semantic prosody of the lexical item is revealed by the consistent choice of modifier found to the left of *role* and is summarised as 'to participate and/or contribute in a weighty/meaningful manner' (Cheng *et al.*, 2009: 248–9).

Task 5.13

Study the concordances below and try to identify the co-selection in the lexical item.
What is the core? (See Figure 5.4)
What are the collocates? (See Figure 5.5)
What are the colligates? (See Figure 5.6)
What is the semantic preference? (See Figure 5.7)
What is the semantic prosody? (See Figure 5.8)

```
1 uis-Dreyfus will have to work hard to recover the company's
2  is happy to jump-to and work hard on a new factory opening
3 eally is an incentive to work hard and perform well, says T
4 ouraged to take risks to work very hard on our behalf to en
5 red members generally do work very, very hard. But I can th
6 ful preparation and hard work. It comes from taking a genui
7 heir reputation for hard work and honesty, Goans have alway
8 ife. Determination, hard work, commitment and family unity
9 ntiality, dynamism, hard work, the ability to sell a produc
10 fluence comes from hard work in a well paid job, and permi
```

Figure 5.4 Concordance lines for *work*

```
1 owledge economy with high value added economic activities s
2 mic powerhouse where high value added economic activities i
3 d processes that will add value to and boost the productivi
4 veness and achieving high value added depends very much on
5 glad to see concrete high value-added technology-based acti
6 ency and productivity add value and enhance the competitive
7  to move upmarket and add value we have established a five
```

Figure 5.5 Concordance lines for *value*

```
1  re has been increasing concern expressed in recent years o
2 pectorate has expressed concern over driver's behaviour at
3 t already has expressed concern about the effect of any air
4 axe NALGO has expressed concern at the effect of job losses
5 rew Tickle, Greenpeace. Concern has been voiced over the pl
6 o all viewpoints. "Some concern has been voiced at our deci
7 he public.11.2 BIG BANG Concern had been voiced for some ti
8 (1987) point out, most concern has been voiced about incre
9 be so affected and much concern has recently been voiced in
10  of England has voiced concern at increasing debt defaults
```

Figure 5.6 Concordance lines for *concern*

1   of injecting quality into the products and **services** provided. It means that every decision or action

2 attractive [unclear] employer. We in the public **services** provide a higher standard of efficiency and

3   not the way forward, what is needed is quality **services** provided by a quality workforce. The G M B must

4 ve done much over the last decade to improve the **services** we provide for the people we serve and   the

5   is using, and who are the beneficiaries of the **services** being provided. Closer analysis reveals a shaki

6 to live in communities that provide high quality **services**. However, this test has attracted criticism -

7   employees perform in providing the goods and **services** their customers and clients want depends on the

8   business sector by providing more effective **services**. Strategic Planning "Strategic planning"

9   available to provide efficient and effective **services** to the consumer. Congress, the, the blatant

10   who are providing effective and efficient **services** to appreciative (and preferably paying) customers

Figure 5.7 Concordance lines for *services*

1 mming the size of the civil service, eliminating **red** tape and over-regulation, and sourcing services are

2 to enhance fair competition. Apart from cutting **red** tape and promoting fair competition, the Government

3 a has been trying hard to trim down bureaucratic **red** tape in recent years, with one-stop service counters

4 minbi business in Hong Kong; removing regulatory **red** tape in general and reviewing our competition policy

5 k force that will look at how we can further cut **red** tape, outsource services and develop public-private

6 put forward policy recommendations on how to cut **red** tape, streamline procedures, de-regulate and generall

7 nt for our companies to thrive and grow. Cutting **red** tape. Streamlining procedures. Reducing compliance co

Figure 5.8 Concordance lines for *red*

Task 5.14

Study the following three extracts and one scenario. Identify a marked use of language in each one and, using an online corpus such as the online concordance sampler of the Bank of English, provide evidence for your choice. Is the use of language marked because of semantic preference or semantic prosody?

Extract 1

This extract is from a formal invitation to a very senior government official in Hong Kong to attend an exclusive reception and to give a formal speech to the distinguished guests.

Dear XXXXXXX
Invitation to be Guest-of-Honour of a Special Reception for XXXXXX

In this connection, I have great pleasure in writing to cordially invite you to be the Guest-of-Honour of this important event and to deliver an address to a capacity crowd, comprising distinguished guests, industry leaders in Hong Kong and the mainland as well as media representatives.
. . . . . .

Extract 2

This extract is from a Ph.D thesis written by a research student who is studying the discourse particles 'so' and 'well'.

4.1 Previous studies of *well*
Of all the discourse particles, *well* has probably attracted much more attention than any other in linguistic research. As a highly versatile word which occurs frequently in the spoken language, there appears to be an incessant interest in this linguistic item. This section reviews the treatment of *well* in the literature, examining how the particle is analysed from different approaches. It describes some major studies of *well* in the field and in particular gives special attention to areas which have not been thoroughly examined.

Extract 3

This extract is from an editorial in The Hong Kong Standard *dated 19.12.03.*

It is clear that Hong Kong's economy is on the path to recovery and we can look forward to considerably better prospects next year.
   This good news is compounded by recent surveys of business conditions. A survey conducted by Grant Thornton showed that

business confidence had soared in Hong Kong compared with last year and businesses were optimistic with respect to the economy and positive on turnover, profits and business expansion.

Scenario

At a recent university graduation dinner, students had prepared badges with a one-word description of each teacher. One female teacher was given the 'trendy' badge and another female teacher was given the 'elegant' badge.

Assuming the students wished to compliment their teachers, were these words good choices?

Accounting for phraseological variation

In this chapter, we have looked at n-grams and we have looked at the co-selections that together comprise lexical items. We can now try to link up the two and the link is, in fact, the rationale for looking beyond n-grams to better account for the phraseological tendency in language. Sinclair (2001) is concerned that focusing on the n-grams in corpus linguistics has led to other forms of phraseology being ignored. He points out that by only looking at words which are adjacent, n-gram studies do not take into account phraseological variability with regard to the relative position of the words (e.g., *concern expressed* and *expressed concern*) and also whether other words intervene between the core words (e.g., *work hard, work very hard, work very very hard*) (p. 353). To be fair to those who have studied n-grams, it should be noted some researchers have bemoaned the lack of corpus linguistic software able to fully automatically retrieve such variations. Sinclair also criticises attempts to relate n-grams to grammatical structures because 'a grammar must remain aware of lexis, and that the patterns of lexis cannot be reconciled with those of a traditional grammar' (p. 353).

Sinclair's own model for identifying and describing lexical items obviously encompasses the variation that exists in phraseological patterning, but how can we find these co-selections in a corpus unless we are already aware of their existence? As described in Chapter 4, Cheng *et al.* (2006) have developed software able to fully automatically retrieve the co-selections which comprise lexical items from a corpus along with other forms of phraseology. The software is ConcGram (Greaves, 2009) and it finds concgrams (Cheng *et al.*, 2006, 2009) which are co-occurring words. Crucially, this is done fully automatically because it is important to be able to identify concgrams without relying on single word frequency lists, lists of n-grams, or some form of user-nominated search. The reasons for this are that single word frequencies are not a very reliable guide to frequent phraseologies in a corpus because the co-selections of words are the source of meaning creation. Also, n-grams miss all of the instances of phraseologies which exhibit any kind of variation, and, most phraseologies are not fixed, this means that n-grams can only show part of the picture.

After the concgrams have been found by the program, there is still important work to be done by the user who must distinguish between 'co-occurring' words (i.e., concgrams) and 'associated' words (i.e., phraseologies) in the concgram concordances. This is because the software identifies all of the co-occurrences of two or more words in a wide span and not all of these instances are necessarily meaningfully associated. Determining the parameters of 'associatedness' can be an interesting and enlightening activity (see Task 5.15 opposite). In order to illustrate this point, a sample of the concgram *different/people* is provided in Figure 5.9.

In the concordance, most of the instances of *different/people* are meaningfully associated with the same canonical meaning, but the one in line 10 is best described as a co-occurrence rather than as associated.

```
 1 like, finding out what different people believe, finding out
 2 t a few a times though different people, look and see how fa
 3 round to payments that different people have opt out of the
 4 and there there were a different sort of people. Near our ho
 5  information about the different types of people living in a
 6  the press. Of course, different kinds of people read differ
 7 ent itself, predispose different groups of people towards ce
 8 itions, and that these different groups of people come to li
 9 rm I presume you' re no different from other people? Planning
10 , irrespective of the different activities in which people
11 portions of people of different ages of each sex in each et
12 at schemas  people at different locations hold. There may b
13 ngs between people of different races has necessitated the
14 on between  people in different countries, just as much as
15 e number of people in different socioeconomic classes(see 1
17  variety of people of different personalities are capable o
18 hip between people of different races: an affinity is sugge
19 mple of how people of different cultures and a different la
20variety of people with different characteristics and the con
```

Figure 5.9 Sample of the two-word concgram *different/people*

Task 5.15

Study the concordances below and decide whether the words in bold are meaningfully associated or only co-occurrences.

economic/provide (See Figure 5.10)
additional/provide (See Figure 5.11)
development/promote (See Figure 5.12)
economic/new (See Figure 5.13)
business/Hong Kong (See Figure 5.14)

Another consideration when searching for words in a corpus is whether or not to include all the word forms containing the same stem in your corpus search. For example, the word forms *nag*, *nags*, *nagged* and *nagging* are all from the stem *nag*, which, in corpus linguistics, is termed 'lemma'. Corpus linguistic software can allow you to view all 'lemmatised forms' in one concordance (see Figure 5.3, where *play*, *plays* and *played* are included in the concordance). However, you should be aware that there is evidence (see Stubbs, 2002: 26–9) that this inclusive approach is not always for the best because different word forms can exhibit quite different patterns of co-selection. Stubbs (2002: 28) illustrates this with the word forms *seeks* and *seeking* which have no shared collocates, and the same is the case for the forms *seeks* and *sought*, while others share collocates, for example *seek* and *seeking* and *seek* and *sought*. Figures 5.15 and 5.16 on p. 125 illustrate this point further by separating *nag* and *nagging* in order to make it easier to study their respective co-selections.

In Figure 5.15, we find that 14 (70 per cent) of the instances of *nag* are used in the context of a person communicating with another person (lines 1, 2, 4, 6–14, 16, 18). In 3 instances (15 per cent), it is the colloquial and derogatory denotation for a horse (lines, 3, 15, 17). There is one instance where it is someone's name (line 5). There is no instance of it being co-selected with some kind of negative physical condition. The findings are very different when the instances of *nagging* are examined. The most common co-selection is with a mental state (10 instances) in lines 1, 3–6, 8, 10, 13, 14 and 18. Physical condition, which was not found co-selected with *nag*, has 3 instances (lines 7, 12, 20) and those instances of *nagging* co-selected with a person communicating are in lines 2, 9, 11, 15–17 and 19.

This comparison illustrates why it is best to be cautious before conflating word forms in a concordance. This is because each word

1 infrastructure projects cannot support all **economic** activities and **provide** all employment
2 the future directions for Hong Kong's **economic** development and **provide** a suitable platform for
3 ce expenditure for the disadvantaged during **economic** downturns and should instead **provide** them with
4 ght measures that promote a more sustainable **economic** development, tap new opportunities, and **provide**
5 tap new opportunities, and **provide** new **economic** drivers to benefit Hong Kong in the long run.
6 t. I shall **provide** an update on the overall **economic** condition in the middle of this year. I
7 **provide** a suitable platform for sustainable **economic** growth where necessary. There are times when the
8 **vide** a full, clear and honest account of our **economic** prospects. Through clear appreciation of the

Figure 5.10

1 f life through the Internet. We will **provide** **additional** recurrent funding of about $37 million to
2 arning and self-development. I will **provide** **additional** recurrent funding of about $19 million to
3 Point and Kwun Tong. We will also **provide** **additional** funding to facilitate the work of the
4 victims of domestic violence, I will **provide** **additional** recurrent funding of about $25 million to
5 rsons with disabilities, I will also **provide** **additional** funding of about $7.7 million to increase the
6 4000 graduates. Fourth, I will **provide** an **additional** $1.1 billion non-recurrent funding to **provide**
7 and we will also progressively **provide** 800 **additional** places for postgraduate research programmes in
8 wo years. Second, I will **provide** $13 million **additional** funding for the Labour Department to adopt a
9 about $55 million to **provide** a total of 650 **additional** subsidised residential care places through the
10 recent years, I will **provide** funding for 10 **additional** medical social workers. This will allow more

Figure 5.11

1 onomy. My key strategies for **promoting** the **development** of our economy include: Promoting development

2 elopment of our economy include: **Promoting development** of the regional economy and continuing econom

3 owledge-based economy. We will **promote** the **development** of new technologies to enhance the

4   and mechanisms, so as to **promote** the **development** of bond products. Agreements for the avoidance

5 and creativity into education, **promote** the **development** of the local film industry through the Film

6 sectors of the community.   **Promoting** the **development** of the bond market is important to reinforcing

7 Arts, culture and sports can **promote** social **development** and enhance people's quality of life. The

8 timulate consumption and **promote** economic **development**. It is expected that such activities will create

9 usiness opportunities and **promote** economic **development** more proactively. For example, we will **promote**

10 bond programme is to **promote** the further **development** of our bond market and to provide more choices

11 ntrate on **promoting** medium and long-term **development**, strengthen our economic foundations, bolster

12 that **promote** a more sustainable economic **development**, tap new opportunities, and provide new econom

13 s. To **promote** the further and sustainable **development** of our bond market, we intend to implement a

Figure 5.12

1 ght measures that promote a more sustainable **economic** development, tap **new** opportunities, and provide

2 posed by the financial turmoil. The drastic **economic** changes have fostered **new** roles for the

3 far-sighted in encouraging high value-added **economic** activities that open up **new** sectors for

4 logistics and tourism hub; Reaching into **new economic** territory such as new technology-based economy,

5 rrent strengths and advantages to create **new economic** drivers. All of this requires us to play our

6   that open up **new** sectors for sustainable **economic** growth. I will elaborate on our way forward in

7   tap **new** opportunities, and provide new **economic** drivers to benefit Hong Kong in the long run.

8 tap **new** opportunities during this worldwide **economic** slump. The financial turmoil has impacted on the

Figure 5.13

1 reover, we are encouraging the industrial and **business** sectors and Taiwan businessmen in **Hong Kong** to

2 competitiveness of **Hong Kong.** We will tap **business** opportunities and promote economic development

3 in wine fairs in **Hong Kong** and to set up **business** here. To upgrade the software and the hardware

4 in Hong Kong to set up a **Hong Kong**-Taiwan **Business** Co-operation Committee to provide opportunities

5 **Hong Kong**'s position as an international **business** and financial centre. To this end, I signed the

6 f **Hong Kong.** At the end of last year, I led a **business** delegation, travelling by land from Nanning in

Figure 5.14

```
1 get going. Aunt Molly is a nag about regular meals. If I'm
2  seen by themselves, don't nag them to tell you what happen
3 , don't begrudge it him or nag him for the mess he makes. H
4 ould say, to comfort her. `Nag, nag, nag, night and day. Pa
5 , where to start? They nag nag nag nag, but then nagging is
6 s. The question which will nag at readers of `God: A Biogra
7 . [p] Frustration began to nag at the visitors. Quite unnec
8  business. Her mother is a nag, her daughter is a diabetic,
9 im, don't vote for him". A nag she may be, but this is a ro
10 orget insurance. Your old nag may appear to be the most do
11  in my bathchair, while I nag him. But all the same, I thi
12   pretty? Did your mother nag and scold you when you got m
13  vors of him, he couldn't nag me like other adults. I lear
14  alarm. Cotton mouth, the nag of some unspecified dread, f
15    Yeah man. Shit, what a nag you are Jus" wait `til we ma
16 to change. Sally began to nag me more and more about `The
17 in Gregor's back began to nag at him afresh when his mothe
18 g time since Iona and his nag have budged. They came out o
19 you've just [ZGY] sort of nag them. [F01] Yeah. [F02] Well
20 ould be the one who would nag at us to get our homework do
```

Figure 5.15 Sample instances of *nag* using online Bank of English concordancer

```
1 d, but there is always a nagging doubt in my mind when cast
2 you want to stop a woman nagging you to wash your hair or t
3 ss about sentiment and a nagging hollowness in the main cha
4 t help much, leaving the nagging suspicion that if this is
5 nother, there's always a nagging fear that something import
6 ng with their mixture of nagging, feedback-drenched melodie
7  if he'd touched an old, nagging wound. No. At first, I did
8 his mind and with it the nagging feeling he'd had of someth
9 e I will. Harriet's been nagging to get away for the winter
10 d, as we have seen, the nagging awareness that tropical cl
11  easier for her without nagging or criticizing. If you hav
12 y important in lumbago, nagging low back pain, sway-back (
13 tidy. The hormones were nagging away: do [50] your bit for
14 me on myself for weeks. Nagging guilt may ultimately lead
15 er. But never resort to nagging which cannot build charact
16 ase in point. Combining nagging, fiercely rhythmic repetit
17 and size, is called the Nagging Wife's Tongue. [p] Auden,
18   [p] There is also the nagging precedent, first mentioned
19      In the workplace, nagging is likewise gender-free. B
20  saying that it was the nagging accuracy of Ambrose and fr
```

Figure 5.16 Sample instances of *nagging* using online Bank of English concordancer

form can have different co-selections, and so be part of different extended units of meanings, with, of course, different meanings.

Types of phraseological variation

Studies of concgrams suggest that they can provide the raw data to find three main kinds of phraseology (Warren, 2009; Greaves and Warren, 2010b); collocational frameworks (Renouf and Sinclair, 1991), lexical items (Sinclair, 1996, 1998, 2004), and organisational frameworks (Warren, 2009; Greaves and Warren 2010b).

We have seen in Chapter 4 that grammatical words are the most frequent in any corpus and co-selections of these words are the most frequent phraseologies. Renouf and Sinclair (1991) call these co-selections 'collocational frameworks' and, to date, they have not received much attention. One study has found that the five most frequent are *the . . . of, a/an . . . of, the . . . of the, the . . . in* and *the . . . to* (Li and Warren, 2008). A sample of one of the most frequent collocational frameworks is in Figure 5.6.

The widespread use of collocational frameworks suggests that they should be studied more. Over twenty years ago, Sinclair and Renouf (1988) proposed that they should be included in a lexical syllabus, but they are still excluded, if they are considered at all. As we have seen, recent grammars (Biber *et al.*, 1999; Carter and McCarthy, 2006) describe n-grams, but collocational frameworks, with their inevitable constituency variation, are not among them. Carter and McCarthy (2006: 503–5) list four-word n-grams from their written texts, for example, *the end of the, the back of the* and *the top of the*. However, the collocational framework in all of these n-grams (i.e., *the . . . of the*) is not mentioned.

The original idea behind searching for concgrams was to be able to identify and describe lexical items (Warren, 2009), the second

```
1 ur Village (top) behind the waterfront in Puerto Sotogrande
2 ccurate, form of words. The difficulty in developing a sing
3  otball hooliganism and the crime rate in general. In count
4  land. This would imply the acceptance in principle of payi
5 ! Newspapers do develop the discussion in much more detail,
6 ideo from Playback. For the first time in their history the
7 workers aiming to raise the share of wages in the national
8  negligence, and indeed the biggest change in civil law thi
9 es must be addressed by the business units in their plans.
```

Figure 5.17 Sample concordance lines for the collocational framework *the . . . in*

Task 5.16

Study the sample concordance lines on p. 128, and identify a second organisation-oriented element that forms an organisational framework with 'because'. See Figure 5.17.

major kind of phraseology to be found in the concgrams raw data, and these have been described and illustrated earlier in this chapter.

The third type of phraseology, organisational framework, can exhibit considerable constituency variation. Hunston (2002: 75) mentions phraseologies that result from clauses being co-selected, and she provides an example: *I wonder . . . because*. She notes that these co-selections, which she terms 'clause collocations', can be hard to find because the intervening clause can be very long (p. 75). Using the notions of organisation-oriented elements and message-oriented elements proposed in linear unit grammar (Sinclair and Mauranen, 2006), Warren (2009) uses the term 'organisational frameworks' for these phraseologies to capture how organisational elements, such as conjunctions, connectives and discourse particles, are sometimes co-selected.

Certain organisational frameworks are listed in grammars as correlative conjunctions, such as *either . . . or* and *both . . . and*. However, there are no doubt other combinations of conjunctions, connectives and discourse markers; for example, *I think . . . because*, *and . . . and*, *or . . . or*, etc., which are less well-known, and probably many more which are not so familiar, and possibly others that we are not aware of. These need to be given greater priority in studies of phraseology because, at the moment, the full extent of their use, the forms that they take and their functions are under-investigated.

Concluding remarks

Our understanding of both the extent of phraseology in language and how it is realized have been significantly impacted by corpus linguistics. This chapter has shown how meaning creation is phrase-based rather than word-based. In other words, meanings are created by co-selections of words and not by the selection of single words. The main pioneer of this notion in corpus linguistics, Sinclair, has been the focus in the chapter, and elsewhere in this book, because it is his idiom principle and categories of co-selection that, to date, best account for phraseology. Again, in this chapter the importance of including phraseological variation in any study of phraseology has been underscored by discussing the implications of concgramming.

1   years. I mean it comes as no surprise to me er **because** of the lack of Health and Safety provision

2   that off. I think it might need burning off **because** if you leave it on it's gonna be a bit oddish!

3   that's fine, so I'll have to get it in soon **because** I won't be able to get him in till about <u

4   Er and I think frankly erm we won the election **because** she was not leader of the party. That was my

5   undreds of years. So he brought his family over **because** negotiations were taking **so** long, and he

6   t the moment. I mean, fixed rates are dangerous **because** once you've fixed, if interest rates then go up,

7   Away. I think Bryony likes erm Smarties **because** she's always sucking the juice out of beans. <u

8   this year. So we have to keep ahead of that, **because** we're planning the benefits for you, twenty or

9   mean they really didn't understand, you know **because** food to them is just food, you know it was just

Figure 5.18

Notes

1 To be fair, the CD which comes with the dictionary allows the user to view corpus examples, but the user would then have to analyse these to arrive at the fuller meaning.
2 Small capitals indicate that all word forms of the lemma *play* are included.

Part III

Approaches to and models of corpus linguistic studies

6 Data-driven and corpus-driven language learning

This chapter will:

- describe the procedure for students to conduct a corpus-driven language project;
- suggest methods for preparing the research report, both oral and written; and
- suggest a set of criteria for assessing the quality of the research report.

Introduction: from theory to practice

Chapter 3 describes the rationale for studying corpus linguistics as a discipline and using corpus linguistics as a method of linguistic inquiry. It also describes different types of corpora and their specific uses, the mechanics of corpus design and construction, and corpus applications. These applications include the tracking of variation and change in the English language, the production of dictionaries and other reference materials, and the study of different aspects of linguistics, including lexis, grammar, lexico-grammar, literal and metaphorical meanings, discourse structure, pragmatics, and discourse intonation, the study of linguistic variation across modes (speaking and writing), registers (e.g., academic, business, social, scientific and legal) and genres (e.g., university textbooks, financial reports, conversation, plays and contracts), and the study of multilingual and parallel texts.

Chapter 4 describes corpus search functions and methods of analysis used in corpus linguistics, namely the generation of word frequency lists and profiles, keyword lists and keyness, n-grams, examining collocation and colligation in concordance lines, searching annotated corpora, concgramming, and text analysis statistics. Chapter 5 is about lexical phraseology, and describes multi-word units in terms of their structures, functions, specificity and idioms.

This chapter describes how students conduct, and teachers assess, a corpus-driven language project. It begins by describing the objectives and intended learning outcomes of such an assignment, and these are followed by step-by-step guides for the student-researchers to design and undertake their language projects. The chapter also suggests methods for preparing the research report, both oral and written, and how to assess the quality of the report.

Data-driven learning

The notion of 'data-driven learning' (DDL) (Johns, 1991a, 1991b, 2002) has been explored in a growing number of classroom-based research studies, showing how data from corpora can be used by students to extend and enhance their language learning (Tribble, 2000; Tribble and Jones, 1990). DDL advocates that language learners can be both active learners and language researchers by accessing corpus data directly so that they can critically analyse examples of authentic language in various ways. Johns (1991a, 1991b) explains the assumption behind DDL as follows:

> What distinguishes the DDL approach is the attempt to cut out the middleman as much as possible and give direct access to the data so that the learner can take part in building his or her own profiles of meanings and uses. The assumption that underlines this approach is that effective language learning is itself a form of linguistic research, and that the concordance printout offers a unique resource for the stimulation of inductive learning strategies – in particular, the strategies of perceiving similarities and differences and of hypothesis formation and testing.
>
> (Johns, 1991a, 1991b: 30)

In Johns' view, 'research is too serious to be left to the researchers' (Johns, 1991a, 1991b: 2), and DDL represents 'research-then-theory' (Johns, 1991a, 1991b: 30), which is the essence of the corpus-driven approach to language research (Tognini-Bonelli, 2001). This view is radical, and both students and teachers need to take on new roles for DDL to succeed.

Conducting corpus-driven language projects

The main benefit of combining DDL with a corpus-driven approach in language studies is the development of corpus linguistic techniques and procedures that directly link up theories about language and the facts revealed by natural language (Tognini-Bonelli, 2001). In other words, corpus linguistic techniques and procedures can be applied to different types of language corpora in order to acquire knowledge and gain insights about a wide range of linguistic features. In addition, conducting language projects can help the student-researcher to develop generic attributes such as analytical reasoning, critical thinking, and problem-solving, which are highly valued in any university programme. Analytical reasoning involves thinking in a logical manner, supporting ideas with well-reasoned arguments and evidence. Critical thinking involves evaluating information and evidence critically and being able to recognise flaws or inconsistencies in an argument. Problem-solving involves understanding the problem, exploring plausible answers, and selecting the most appropriate solution to the problem. In a university context, students working on corpus-driven language projects in groups can develop their intellectual curiosity and learn to work independently or as part of a team.

To begin planning the corpus-driven linguistic research, the first question is usually: what kinds of linguistic study are possible for the project? It is useful to begin by thinking about an aspect of English language use that you find of interest or problematic. Swales (2004), for example, suggests several starting points for analysing the academic speech in the MICASE corpus:

> One of the more obvious ones is starting with a word – or more exactly a lemma (a word in all its forms). Other starting points would be some grammatical structure (if-clause; utterances with missing subjects) or some discoursal function (making suggestions; introducing a speaker).
>
> (http://micase.elicorpora.info/using-micase-tips-tutorials/ doing-micase-based-investigations-i-s, accessed 22 April 2010)

There are many online resources that describe a variety of language problems in the areas of lexis, grammar, discourse and a combination of one of these areas, kept in 'kibbitzers'. Kibbitzers were originated by Tim Johns. The MICASE Kibbitzers website contains a number of kibbitzers. A few examples are given as follows:

1 Criteria/data: Uncountable or Countable?

Do MICASE speakers prefer to say 'the data is' or 'the data are'?

2 Among or Between?

The traditional rule recommends 'between' for two things and 'among' for more than two. Do MICASE speakers follow this rule?

3 Hyperbole in Academic and Research Speech

In ordinary speech, hyperbole (or exaggeration) is common. Do we still find these exaggerations in academic speech?

> (http://micase.elicorpora.info/micase-kibbitzers, accessed 16 April 2010)

All of the above kibbitzers are good research topics for DDL projects.

1. Step-by-step guides for the corpus-driven language project

In the classroom context, the corpus-driven language project usually involves a small-scale research study, which can be an individual or a group project. The procedure of preparing for a corpus-driven language project is described below in eight steps:

1 Choose a linguistic feature that you find either interesting or problematic.

2 Conduct a literature review on the selected linguistic feature by reading, for example, books, journal papers or book chapters that report on some corpus linguistic research studies. Then write a summary of the reading and evaluates how useful it is for your own project. This helps you to understand the scholarly literature relevant to the linguistic feature you are interested in studying, to formulate your research question(s), to design the method of your study, and to lay the foundation for understanding your findings and appreciating their value.

3 Write a research question, or research questions.

4 Decide on the method that you will use to answer the research question(s).

5 Either compile your own corpus of 20,000–40,000 words, or use a ready-made corpus. In addition, you might want to use a reference corpus (e.g., the British National Corpus or the Corpus of Contemporary American English) to study the keyness of your self-compiled corpus (i.e., study corpus), depending on the purpose and research question(s) of your own project.

6 Follow the procedure of a corpus-driven study (see Task 6.9).

7 The project can be done in a group or individually. You might like to share the compilation of the corpus but conduct your own individual study.

8 Report, in the form of an oral presentation and a written report, on the study that you have conducted. The length of the oral presentation varies, with an average of five minutes for each speaker, depending on the scale and scope of the project and whether the project is individual or group work. The individual report can be 1,500 to 2,000 words, excluding end-of-text references and appendices.

2. Assessing the corpus-driven language project report

The following assessment criteria for oral presentation (Figure 6.1) and written research report (Figure 6.2) may be used to assess the quality of the corpus-driven language project:

1. Clear research question(s) of the corpus-driven language study, supported with reasons (10%)
2. A clear description of the corpus or corpora and method of analysis (20%)
3. A clear description of the main findings of the study to date (50%)
4. Logical conclusions linking the research question(s) of the study and the findings to date (10%)
5. Effective verbal delivery (10%)

Figure 6.1 Suggested oral presentation assessment criteria

1. **Introduction (20%)**
   - A clear and logical rationale for the choice of linguistic feature, supported by what the literature says about it
   - A critical review of the literature
   - A clear description of the research question(s) of the corpus-driven language study
   - An effective link between the literature review and the research question(s)
2. **Method of study (10%)**
   - A clear description of the corpus (and other corpora, if applicable) studied: procedure in building (finding) it, corpus size, type of data, etc. (i.e. data collection methods)
   - A clear description of the procedure taken to conduct the study and the method to analyse the corpus or corpora (i.e. data analysis methods)
3. **Discussion of findings (50%)**
   - An effective description, interpretation and explanation of the findings with reference to the research question(s) of your study
   - An effective description, interpretation and explanation of the findings to the literature review (10%)
4. **Conclusion (10%)**
   Logical conclusions drawn from the findings with reference to both the research question(s) and the literature review
5. **Related to the written report (10%)**
   - Appropriate and complete in-text and end-of-text referencing
   - Appropriate and accurate language
   - Effective expression of ideas and arguments

Figure 6.2 Suggested report structure and assessment criteria

Figure 6.2 describes the structure and assessment criteria of the project report, as well as the relative distribution of marks across the different sections.

3. Activities that guide the corpus-driven language project

The following describes nine activities that are useful for the student-researcher to prepare for the corpus-driven language study project. All of the activities have been used in a subject called 'Corpus-driven Language Learning' to English major and non-English major undergraduate students in a university in Hong Kong. Most of these activities can be introduced and finished in forty-five minutes by most students, and so they can be quite readily adapted for different learning and teaching contexts (e.g., in a computer laboratory under the supervision of a teacher) or for blended learning with students doing the activities outside class, or independently by students.

Task 6.1

This activity introduces some basic corpus analysis methods: comparing the frequencies of selected words in a corpus and studying co-occurring words in a concordance. Any two, or more, corpora, online or ready-made, can be used, for example:

1 Go to BYU-BNC: British National Corpus at http://corpus.byu.edu/. Select the whole corpus. Enter a word, click on 'SEARCH', and record the frequency (e.g., the frequency of 'funny' is 4,315). Repeat searching for word frequencies by entering other words.

2 Enter *British*. The frequency of *British* in the British National Corpus is 35,428. Now click on 'BRITISH' to see the concordance lines. Study the first thirty lines and find out the three most common nouns that occur in the 'slot' immediately to the right (i.e., N+1) of *British*. Then note down the three most frequent nouns that occur within five words to the right (i.e., N+1–N+5) of *British*.

Task 6.2

Many online corpora provide very useful real-world data to examine different linguistic features, and so it is important to learn more about the online corpora in terms of why they are constructed, the nature of corpus data contained in them, and the design features and functions. A set of free online corpora created and maintained by Prof. Mark Davies of Brigham Young University can be accessed at http://corpus.byu.edu/. Spend ten to fifteen minutes navigating the website to understand its content and structure. Then select the COCA (Corpus of Contemporary American English) → More information → Where do I start? → Brief tour for non-linguists.

Now read the information on the website, and see if you can do the following:

1 Describe the five types (genres) of contemporary American English (1990–2008) in the COCA.

2 On the COCA page, click on the links that are specified in column 1 below and find out the frequency over time (column 2) and the frequency in different English genres (column 3).

3 For each search item, after completing the table, click on 'Chart' to look at the graphic information of the findings.

See Grid A, p. 140

4 Write down what you think the commonest collocates of the word *smile* are.

5 Still using COCA, enter *smile* to read the collocates of the word. Compare what you have written down in 4 above to discover any similarities and differences.

6 Search for *democrats* and *republicans* in COCA, and compare their collocates. Based on the COCA texts (from newspapers, magazines, TV talk shows, etc.), which of the two political parties, 'democrats' or 'republicans', is *electable*, *open-minded* and *fun*, and which is *extremist*, *mean-spirited* and *greedy*?

See Grid B, p. 140

7 Compare the adjectives used to describe the words *women* and *men* in COCA. Who are *grumpy*, *impotent*, *masked*, *burly* and *armed*, and who are *glamorous*, *petite* and *voluptuous*?

See Grid C, p. 140

1. Search item: What to click on	2. Most frequent over the past 15–20 years	3. Most frequent in genre of American English
Word: *funky*		
Part of speech: suffix *–dom*		
Phrase: global warming		
Grammatical constructions: *get + V-ed*		

Grid A

Word	Collocates
	electable, open-minded, fun
	extremist, mean-spirited, greedy

Grid B

Word	Collocates
	grumpy, impotent, masked, burly, and *armed*
	glamorous, petite, and *voluptuous*

Grid C

Task 6.3

A word has a colligate when a particular word class co-occurs in the vicinity of the word (Stubbs, 2001) and colligation can only be observed after assigning 'a word class to each word under examination' (Sinclair, 2004: 142).

1. On page 142 is a sample of twelve concordance lines for *development* from the Hong Kong Budget Speeches Corpus 1997–2010 (176,515 words) at http://rcpce.engl.polyu.edu.hk/Budgets/default. htm. Study N–1–N–5 and N+1–N+5 positions. Record the words in each of these positions below, and then describe any patterns and associated meanings that are observed.

See Figure 6.1 and Grid D (pp. 142–3)

2. From the co-occurring words recorded in the table above, do you observe any colligational patterns of the word *development* in the Hong Kong Budget Speeches Corpus 1997–2010? Write down the colligational patterns of *development* in the table below.

See Grid E

Task 6.4

Go to the online *Cambridge Advanced Learner's Dictionary* and study the different entries for the word *attack* used as a verb and a noun (http://dictionary.cambridge.org/search/british/?q=attack&x=49&y=6).

1. Which uses are literal and which are metaphorical?

2. Now study the concordance lines for *attack* from a specialised corpus of financial news reports in 2009. Make a note of all the metaphorical uses of the word.

See Figure 6.2

1　ahead. While formulating our economic **development** and fiscal policies, we should be alert to all such

2　of pushing ahead with infrastructure **development** and am prepared, if necessary, to increase the estimate

3　lion to establish a Youth Sustainable **Development** and Engagement Fund. Our determination to introduce

4　rge-scale projects, including Kai Tak **Development** and the Central-Wan Chai Bypass. 61. Madam Presiden

5　lion. Proposals covering the scope of **development** as well as financing arrangements will be announced

6　nning progress of these projects. The **Development** Bureau and the Transport and Housing Bureau will play

7　ly essential for Hong Kong's economic **development** but also an effective means of tackling the wealth gap

8　land for long-term commercial or hotel **development**; (c) Launching a two-year pilot scheme whe

9　e Mainland. 28. I have asked the Trade **Development** Council to enhance its support for SMEs. Specifically,

10　dertaken by the Civil Engineering and **Development** Department will cover the whole of Hong Kong Island a

11　 Forum, with the support of the Film **Development** Fund, will be held in April to help the industry to a

12　et up steering committees to promote **development** in each of these four important economic sectors. I

Figure 6.1

Words co-occurring with *development* in N-5-N-1 and N+1-N+5 positions.

Line no.	N-5	N-4	N-3	N-2	N-1	Development	N+1	N+2	N+3	N+4	N+5
1											
2											
3											
4											
5											
6											
7											
8											
9											
10											
11											
12											

Grid D

L1-L5 (with frequency)	R1-R5 (with frequency)

Grid E

```
 1 for all. Sir, The "heart attack" affecting markets (front p
 2 ased that fees are under attack. And given the potential of
 3 ted to the risk of heart attack and heart-related death in
 4 ing protecting data from attack and unauthorised access," i
 5 t buy-out or a terrorist attack. But when the big wave stru
 6 d Mugabe's price-cutting attack "completely fractured the s
 7 xpenses or for terrorist attack.  Consumer protection About
 8 y campaigns that seek to attack employers through their cust
 9 anisation has come under attack from poorer countries which
10 cy has since come under attack from the European Commission
```

Figure 6.2

Task 6.5

O'Keeffe *et al.* (2007: 83) describe a few everyday words that are 'idiom-prone' because 'they are the foundations of basic cognitive metaphors':

- parts of the body, e.g., *eye, shoulder, hand, nose* and *head*

- money, e.g., *money talks, put your money where your money is, the smart money*

- light and colour, e.g., *be in the dark, shed light on, give the green light, have green fingers,* etc.

O'Keeffe *et al.* (2007) searched the 5-million-word Cambridge and Nottingham Corpus of Discourse in English (CANCODE) made up of spoken English for the word-form *face*. Out of 520 occurrences, they identified fifteen idiomatic expressions (p. 83). The idioms listed in the table below are those which occur three times or more. Find out the meanings of these idiomatic expressions from online references or dictionaries, e.g., *Cambridge Advanced Learner's Dictionary, Collins English Cobuild & Thesaurus, Longman English Dictionary Online,* and so on.

Idioms with 'face'	Frequency	Meaning
let's face it	20	
on the face of it	10	
face to face	6	
keep a straight face	4	

Idioms with 'face'	Frequency	Meaning
face up to	4	
till you're blue in the face	3	
fall flat on one's face	3	
shut your face	3	

Search for *face* in two corpora of different registers:

1 Hong Kong Corpus of Spoken English (HKCSE) (1 million words)
http://langbank.engl.polyu.edu.hk/HKCSE/

2 Hong Kong Financial Services Corpus (HKFSC) (7.3 million words)
http://langbank.engl.polyu.edu.hk/hkfsc/

Note that corpora of different sizes cannot be compared directly, and the frequencies of occurrence need to be normalised. Study the words surrounding *face* (left and right) to make sense of the use of the idioms in the corpora.

Hong Kong Corpus of Spoken English (1 million words)

Idioms with the word-form face	Frequency	Meanings

Hong Kong Financial Services Corpus (7.3 million words)

Idioms with the word-form face	Frequency	Meanings

Describe any similarities and differences in the findings that you think are due to register variation.

Task 6.6

As Biber (2006: 56) notes, the noun *thing* is extremely frequent in all academic spoken registers (classroom teaching, class management talk, office hours, and study group), occurring about 3,000 times per million words, but only 300 per million words in written registers. Biber (2006: 56) also describes three major uses of *thing*:

1 Refer to a physical object, but rarely used this way in spoken university registers.

2 Refer to actions, activities, or events.

3 Refer to ideas or informational points to consider.

These major uses can be regarded as three semantic preferences (see Chapters 5 and 8 for more on semantic preference).

Search MICASE for the word *thing*, following the Speaker Attributes and Transcript Attributes described below. See Table 6.1.

Choose any ten concordance lines for *thing*, and classify each instance into any of the three major uses: a physical object; actions, activities, or events; and ideas or information points to consider (Biber, 2006: 56).

Table 6.1 Search for *thing* in MICASE: speaker and transcript attributes

Speaker attributes	Transcript attributes
Gender: Male	Speech Event Type: All
Age: All	Academic Division: Humanities and Arts
Academic Position/Role: All	Academic Discipline: All
Native speaker status: Native speaker, American	Participant Level: Senior Faculty
First language: All	Interactivity Rating: All

Task 6.7

Sinclair (1991: 141–51) examines the phrase *true feelings* in the Bank of English as a lexical item. Below are his findings about the meaning and function of *true feelings*:

- An invariable CORE which consists of the two words <u>true feelings</u>.

- A colligation 'possessive' which is realized by a possessive adjective modifying the core in most instances, but in some is replaced by the definite article <u>the</u> followed by an <u>of</u>-phrase on the other side of the core.

- A word or phrase meaning the expression of one's true feelings, usually a verb to the left of the possessive. This is a semantic preference.

- A word or phrase meaning reluctance or difficulty, usually placed to the left of the semantic preference; this is the semantic prosody. In several cases the meaning of the verb puts together 'expression' and 'reluctance', e.g., in the verb <u>conceal</u>.

(Sinclair, 1991: 148–9)

Now search for *true feelings* in the British National Corpus at http://corpus.byu.edu/. The phrase occurs fifty-three times. Study all the fifty-three concordance lines for *true feelings* and do the following tasks:

1. List all the words immediately to the left (L1) and record their frequency. What is the commonest word class?

2. Look at the words in L2 and record their frequency. What is the commonest word class?

3. List all the verbs to do with expressing things. Write the verbs that have the meaning of 'reveal' and those of 'conceal' (Sinclair, 1991: 146) in the table below:

'reveal'	'conceal'

4. Study the lines with the verbs in the 'reveal' class and look for those that are associated with the meaning of 'reluctance'. Write all of the verbs in the 'reveal' class and the words in the same line that expresses 'reluctance' in the table below:

Line number	Verb	Reluctance

Task 6.8

Go to MICASE at http://micase.elicorpora.info/ and find MICASE Kibbitzers, which show the discussion of different language problems to do with lexis, syntax and discourse. Now click on the second MICASE Kibbitzer, 'Among or Between'. Read the paper published online (Reinhard and Swales, 2003) (a PDF of the paper is also available) and answer the questions below:

1 What is the linguistic feature that the authors are interested in investigating, and why?

2 What do grammar books, writing manuals and college student handbooks say about the linguistic feature?

3 Do the authors have any research questions for their corpus-based study of *among* and *between*?

4 What are the patterns observed in the MICASE corpus data?

5 How do the authors compare the patterns in the data with those described in reference materials?

6 What conclusions do the authors draw from their corpus-based study of *among* and *between*?

Task 6.9

Task 6.9 provides six steps for carrying out a corpus-driven language project.

Step 1: Identify a linguistic feature that you are interested in or find problematic. According to Sinclair (1991), 'lemma' is not equal to 'word-forms' or 'inflected forms' and each inflected form of a lemma is clearly associated with a specific pattern of usage. He suggests that 'each distinct form is potentially a unique lexical unit' (Sinclair, 1991: 8).

You are interested in knowing more about this linguistic phenomenon and in finding out how different inflected forms of a lemma behave in terms of their collocational profiles. With the help of a dictionary, identify the inflected forms of the word. Below, write down the lemma and its inflected forms:

Lemma: _____

Inflected forms: _____

Step 2: Read about the lemma and its inflected forms in some online grammar books and dictionaries. Write down what you find about their meanings and uses and any descriptions and examples of collocations of the lemma and its inflected forms.

Step 3: Record corpus findings
You will work with the *Time Magazine* Corpus of American English at http://corpus.byu.edu/time/. Study the collocational profile of the chosen lemma, and that of each of its inflected forms in the *Time Magazine* Corpus of American English. Write down the language facts that you have observed.

Step 4 Formulate a hypothesis to account for the language facts. (This has been done, see below.)
Hypothesis: Each inflected form of a lemma has its own unique collocational profile.

Step 5: Discussion of corpus findings
Further analyse what you have noted in Step 3 and make a general statement about what you find in order to answer your hypothesis.

Step 6: From your observations and generalisations, produce a theoretical statement about the linguistic feature. (This has been done, see below.)

Theoretical statement: Each inflected form of a lemma has its own unique collocational profile.

Concluding remarks

As Tim Johns (1991a: 2) points out, 'the language-learner is also, essentially, a research worker whose learning needs to be driven by access to linguistic data'. Following the guidelines, students will do their corpus-driven language projects 'without knowing in advance what patterns they would discover' (Cheng *et al.*, 2003: 183). The projects effectively 'cut out the middleman as far as possible' and give students 'direct access to the data, the underlying assumption being that effective language learning is a form of linguistic research, and that the concordance printout offers a unique way of stimulating inductive learning strategies – in particular the strategies of perceiving similarities and differences of hypothesis formation and testing' (Johns, 1991a: 30).

7 Corpus linguistics and our understandings of language and text

This chapter will:

- describe some significant research findings of corpus linguistic studies across a range of linguistic phenomena, features and fields;

- cover, for example, phraseology, extended units of meaning, local grammars, spoken and written language organization, pragmatics, specialised corpora, register variations, genre analysis, and learner corpora; and

- return to issues raised in Chapter 1 by making use of corpus findings.

Introduction to phraseology

In corpus linguistics, it is now firmly established that, to fully understand a word, we need to examine 'the company that it keeps' (Firth, 1957: 11) rather than examining it in isolation. Firth gives his famous example of *dark night* where 'one of the meanings of *night* is its collocability with *dark*, and of *dark*, of course, collocation with *night*' (p. 196). Corpus linguistics provides lots of evidence for the ways in which words have distinct and describable patterns regarding the company they keep, and the company they do not keep. For example, we can say both *Happy + Christmas* and *Happy + Birthday*, but, while we can also say *Merry + Christmas*, we cannot say *Merry + Birthday* (Renouf and Banerjee, 2007) because the collocability of *Christmas* and *Birthday* (and, of course, of *Merry*) differ in this respect. The search for those words that do collocate is a central concern in corpus linguistics and has led to many significant findings.

In Chapters 4 and 5, we looked at the most commonly studied kind of phraseology in corpus linguistics – the n-gram – recurrent adjacent words (*lots of, you see, I mean, I don't know*, etc.). These have been found to be linked to certain functions and to vary across registers and genres. However, as Sinclair repeatedly points out (see Sinclair, 2008), the main task of corpus linguists studying phraseology is to account for all the co-selections in a lexical item. Sinclair (2008: 409) notes that scholars have focused on invariable multi-word items because their 'repetitions were easily noticed', but more attention needs to be given to phraseological variation.

One attempt to classify different kinds of phraseological variation is provided by Philip (2008), who describes the notion of 'phraseological skeletons' (pp. 97–100). These skeletons would include collocational frameworks (e.g., *the ... of*) and organisational frameworks (e.g., *because ... so*) (Warren, 2009) described in Chapters 4 and 5. These skeletons basically provide a core component of a phraseological unit and come in a variety of forms (p. 97). They represent one way of categorising the kinds of phraseological variation often to be found in patterns of language use. In Figures 7.1–7.4 below, the collection of phraseological skeletons described by Philip is illustrated using sample concordance lines from COCA (www.americancorpus.org/).

One of these phraseological skeletons is the lexico-grammatical frame (Moon, 1998) that consists of a fixed component and a variable component (see Figure 7.1).

Philip gives the example of the preposition *beyond* as the fixed part of such a frame, which is then followed by variable nouns such as *surprise, tears, question* and *belief.*

Another phraseological skeleton is the semi-prepackaged phrase (Francis, 1993). This is a skeleton where variants can replace one of the elements (Figure 7.2).

```
1 ation run riot. They are beyond surprise. ROS: And how much
2 nfected eyes of children beyond tears. Dysentery, malaria a
3 had gone for help, it is beyond question we would have been
4 you think about the days beyond work. I know what he feels,
5  death had shattered him beyond repair. Suicide was also cl
6 less than an hour, bored beyond belief. Still he wasn't sur
```

Figure 7.1 Sample COCA concordance lines for *beyond*

```
1 o reason at all you haven't the faintest idea how to spell
2 ere beautiful. They had not the least idea that their love.
3 his head as a hat I haven't got the slightest idea what the
4 hotocopy of a map I haven't the remotest idea cos I don't k
5 ! My little foot! I haven't the foggiest idea, but it's blo
6  the act, do I?" "I have not the remotest idea what you mea
```

Figure 7.2 Sample COCA concordance lines for *HAVE + not + the + idea*

In the above example, the stable ingredients are the lemma *have* plus *not/n't* plus *idea* plus a variable element which precedes *idea*, but always adds meaning in a similar fashion, such as *faintest*, *slightest*, *remotest* and *least*.

Idiom schemas (Moon, 1998) are another kind of phraseological skeleton and are defined by their semantic prosody rather than word form co-occurrence, although the example in Figure 7.3 does have an invariant core (*short of a*).

In the example of an idiom schema in Figure 7.3, the formula is basically to state that somebody or something is stupid or incompetent by stating that they lack (i.e., *short of*) the desired quantity of some specified whole (e.g., *a picnic*, see line 1) by a small amount (e.g., *one sandwich*, see line 1). As we can see, what occurs either side of *short of a* is restricted only by the speaker's imagination, the idiom's schema guarantees that each new creation is understood.

The last phraseological skeleton is the idiom theme plus variations (Philip, 2008: 100), and the example in Figure 7.4 is based on the idiom *like a red rag to a bull*.

Above, we can see that the form *like a red rag to a bull* is never found and, instead, we find many small variations, all of which conform to the same semantic prosody.

Extended units of meaning

There is one form of phraseology that we look at separately here. As we have seen in Chapter 5, the search for 'units of meaning' is

```
1 sgow, is one sandwich short of a picnic. So clueless and in
2 right", "a few bricks short of a full load"). In short, gou
3 ly a few co-ordinates short of a bearing, and starts to bac
4  a couple of currants short of a teacake. Not only did the
5  in y' know one marble short of a whatever yeah or okay er D
```

Figure 7.3 Sample COCA concordance lines for *short of a*

```
1 oh well I mean that was red rag to the bull I don't think h
2 ple community arts is a red rag to a bull because there is
3 hase it." It was like a red rag to a big, black bull. Or, g
4 since April, is another red rag to dollar bulls looking for
5 A missile, once again a red rag to the Israeli bull. Sensin
6  to one person can be a red rag to another. We can all be e
```

Figure 7.4 Sample COCA concordance lines for *red rag to*

prioritised by a number of influential corpus linguists. The idea that meaning is represented in individual words has been abandoned and the evidence shows that meaning resides in extended units. Not all phraseologies represent specific units of meaning. Phraseologies such as *and I, to be, to the, with a, the ... of the, a ... of, either ... or, I mean ... because, one of the, there is a, what do you* and *to be a* are not extended units of meaning in themselves, although they may well be among the co-selections comprising extended units of meaning. The composition of an extended unit of meaning, termed 'lexical item' (Sinclair, 1996, 1998), and described in detail in Chapters 5 and 8, has to include an identifiable semantic prosody (i.e., functional pragmatic meaning). Here, we only review two examples of the realisations of lexical items, as this notion is covered elsewhere in this book (see Chapters 4, 5, 8). The examples are chosen to illustrate the advice from Sinclair (2008) that corpus linguists need to account for more than the invariable (i.e., fixed) core word(s) in lexical items because there are 'other components of a meaningful phrase lurking around, less obvious because more variable, but playing a number of important roles in the creation of meaning' (Sinclair, 2008: 409).

The word *veritable* is examined by Sinclair (2003: 91–6), and in Figure 7.5, below, we illustrate his analysis using a sample of concordance lines from COCA (www.americancorpus.org/).

We can see that *veritable* is always followed by a noun and is an attributive adjective. Sinclair also notes that *veritable* is almost always preceded by the indefinite article. The exception is line 10, where the speaker is quoting a previous speaker and so uses the definite article. From this pattern, he concludes that the noun group, of which *veritable* is a part, is almost always new information. Also, *veritable* greatly emphasises the nouns which already tend to convey large-scale things using metaphor (e.g., *emporium, army* and *torrent*). Sinclair (2003: 101) also notes there is often an *of* phrase after the noun group (lines

```
 1 r potatoes? Now it is a veritable battleground of competing
 2 on my bet. It will be a veritable investment. " # " By sedu
 3 stilence of insomnia, a veritable miasmic funk endemic to t
 4 r. " # Dimm let loose a veritable torrent the one time he s
 5 or would never visit, a veritable army of lesser demons had
 6  covering his eyes as a veritable font of tears gushed down
 7  so on, and so forth, a veritable torrent of angry question
 8 a meticulous archive, a veritable emporium of mementos. Eac
 9 g, it bubbled over in a veritable pandemonium: # ... There
10 us and addictive - the veritable crack of the nut world? "
```

Figure 7.5 Sample COCA concordance lines for *veritable*

1, 5–8, 10), which is linked to the metaphorical noun group in that the *of* phrase clarifies meaning, which may be obscured by the newness of the metaphorical noun group. Finally, the semantic prosody of the lexical item is 'strongly dramatic, exaggerated' (p. 103).

The word *provide*[1] is discussed briefly by Stubbs (2002: 24, 65) in terms of its most frequent collocates (*information, service*(s), *support, help, money, protection, food* and *care*) and its semantic prosody resulting from these collocates: 'desirable or necessary' (p. 65). On p. 156 we study a sample of concordance lines for *provide* taken from the HKEC (http://rcpce.engl.polyu.edu.hk/HKEC/) to see if a more detailed look at its co-selections can usefully add to Stubbs' (2002) initial findings. From the sample concordance lines, we can find a number of components that Sinclair (2008: 409) says will be 'lurking around', each playing an important role in the meaning created in the extended unit of meaning (lexical item) with *provide* as its core.

From the sample concordance lines on p. 156, we find that colligational patterns to the left are strong; *provide* is typically part of a *to*-infinitive (twenty-five instances) and preceded by a modal verb in eight of the remaining instances (e.g., *can, shall* and *will*). These patterns indicate future time reference or obligation in terms of what is provided. To the right, the determiners, where the goods or services provided is not plural or uncountable, are mainly indefinite (exceptions are found in lines 35–7) and so what is provided is typically new information. The provider is normally a company, the government or an organisation of some kind and so the semantic preference is for this lexical item to be used in an institutionalised context (i.e., institution to institution, or institution to person, rather than person to person). The use of modifiers in front of the good(s) or services provided helps us to identify the semantic prosody of this lexical item: *best, efficient reasonable, reliable, additional, adequate, effective, excellent, further, more, qualifies, regular, safe, support* and *simple*. All of these components help us to refine the semantic prosody, which Stubbs (2002: 65) notes as being 'desirable or necessary', so that it is more specific (i.e., promise/commitment to enhance perceived needs).

Local grammars

The term 'local grammar' was first used by Gross (1993: 26, 29) to describe similar features shared across time expressions (e.g., *on May 2nd, on Tuesday May the 2nd, on Tuesday the 2nd of May*). Gross' point is that there is a limit to the ways one can express time, and, since the components of these expressions do not fit easily into general descriptions of English grammar, why not describe the ways in which time expressions share similar features? This description is, in effect, the local grammar of time expressions, and this local grammar could

```
 1 n, this reservoir could provide a daily supply of 2,000,000
 2 side the plant house to provide a neater appearance.  Photo
 3  and variable costs and provide a reasonable return to inve
 4 , this code  intends to provide a reasonable standard and s
 5 zone and low zone.  To provide a reliable and efficient em
 6 and conservation and to provide additional incentives to po
 7  The end supports can  provide adequate lateral and torsio
 8 he flaps up and down to provide an even distribution of air
 9   The objectives are to provide an opportunity to enhance t
10  for the applicant to  provide and maintain the best pract
11  for the applicant  to provide and maintain the best pract
12  the Administration to provide, before the relevant Public
13 ck-wiring cables shall provide connections between:-(a) Th
14  (see Section 7.2). To provide consultants with the opport
15 nd approved design. To provide design flexibility, the Bui
16  Lok  Ma Chau. It will provide domestic passenger service
17 age tunnel schemes can provide earlier flood relief in the
18 void dust emission and provide effective wheel washing fac
19 void dust emission and provide effective wheel washing fac
20 ve a partner that will provide excellent customer relation
21 riff burden; and  - To provide financial incentives to the
22 quest the applicant to provide further information. The Ve
23 nt was also seeking to provide incentives for a whole rang
24 , Be Happy" intends to provide insights into the  essence
25 iary won a contract to provide IT infrastructure, networki
26 ompany is committed to provide long-term career developmen
27 from the control band. Provide maximum loads on equipment
28 enants to sign on.  To provide more applied research to su
29 erformed by them; and  provide qualified specialists in th
30 d. Step 5 The AP shall provide records of material quality
31 uction team replied to provide regular irrigation for all
32 stand-by services also provide road support to the Police
33 o project planning, to provide safe plant, safe system of
34 d in the late 1980s to provide simple design rules to eval
35 pace, and the other to provide the added illumination for
36 nternational standards provide the means by which principl
37 unction can be used to provide the squeezed video signal a
38 residents' housing and provide them either with cash compe
39 exchange scholar shall provide to the Organizers and his s
```

Figure 7.6 Sample HKEC concordance lines for *provide*

then be the basis for writing a computer program for automatically retrieving time expressions from a corpus. For Gross (1993), local grammars have a two-fold purpose. They are seen as a better way to describe language use and, because they are better descriptions of particular uses of language, local grammars can be used to automatically retrieve all such instances of language use from a corpus because each local grammar is specific to a particular use of language.

While the study of local grammars is still a relatively new phenomenon, the main argument in favour of them is that they describe 'the resources for only one set of meanings in a language, rather than for the language as a whole' (Hunston, 2002: 90). Hunston (2002: 90–1) describes how it is possible to build up a detailed description of the resources used by speakers and writers for specific sets of meanings by using examples of the ways in which it is possible to talk about sameness and difference. First, she identifies the words that indicate these meanings (e.g., 'equate', 'match', 'contrast', 'differentiate') and the patterns in which they are used (e.g., verb + plural noun group as in 'equate two things', verb + *between* + plural noun group as in 'differentiate between two things'). Next, she identifies elements in the local grammar such as 'comparer', 'comparison', 'item 1' and 'item 2', and these elements are then mapped on to the pattern (p. 90). In another study, Hunston and Sinclair (2000: 93–7) describe the local grammar of evaluation made up of the following elements: evaluative category, evaluated entity and affected entity. For example, 'he (evaluator) is (hinge) adamant (evaluating response) that he does not want to enter politics (thing evaluated)' and 'they (evaluation carrier) were (hinge) lucky (evaluative category) that we scored when we did (thing evaluated)' (p. 89).

Such an approach has been used successfully by others. In an earlier study, Allen (2005) describes the local grammar of cause and effect, and Barnbrook (2002) describes the local grammar of dictionary definition sentences. In addition to describing the local grammar of dictionary definitions, Barnbrook and Sinclair (2001) show how a computer program based on the features of the local grammar can be used to search for definitions in corpora comprising non-dictionary texts because the structures used in dictionary definitions are not unique to dictionaries, but are frequently used for definitions generally – in other words, all definitions share the same local grammar.

Hunston and Sinclair (2000) argue that by adopting such an approach, corpora can be analysed using local grammars and such analyses would be more simple, precise and useful than using a general grammar:

It would be simple in that each local grammar would use a limited number of terms, although the number of local grammars would be fairly extensive. It would be precise in that each local grammar could be stated in its own terms, without the need to fit in with more general statements. It would be useful because the terminology used would be reasonably transparent and would immediately relate the grammar and lexis of each part of the text to its discourse function.

(p. 101)

From the point of view of language learners and teachers, Hunston (2002: 157) argues that local grammars can be superior to general grammars because it is more useful to know 'that a clause is an 'Evaluated Entity' than that it is an object etc.'.

It is apparent from the local grammar studies conducted so far that the underlying assumption is that specific language uses have describable phraseologies and hence a local grammar. Indeed, Hunston (2002: 157) states that 'local grammars remain one of the ways that an emphasis on phraseology will contribute to different descriptions of English in the future'. Sinclair's work on the phraseological tendency in language leads him to take the argument in favour of local grammars even further. Sinclair (2007b) argues that lexical items (i.e., the products of the five categories of co-selection described elsewhere) which exhibit variation – in other words, phrases that are not fixed – are best described using a local grammar. Sinclair's rationale for this is that, when one studies the phraseological variation in a lexical item, it is possible to identify the most common form and its meaning. This can then be used as a benchmark against which it is possible to describe variations of the phrase which still share this meaning. Sinclair (2007b: 8) claims that phraseological variations that share a local grammar are likely to share the same meaning, and those that do not are likely to have a different meaning. Studies investigating local grammars are still few and far between, but as they increase they are likely to give us a better understanding of how phraseology is organised to create meaning.

Discourse organisation

Researchers interested in how spoken and written discourses are organised use corpora to find recurrent features which contribute to this aspect of language use. There is an imbalance between written and spoken corpora. The difficulty in obtaining and transcribing spoken language means that written corpora are destined to always be more numerous than spoken corpora. This is unfortunate given that we use language to speak a lot more than we do to write, and it means that corpus studies of discourse tend to be based on written discourse.

Some corpus linguists have compiled specialised corpora based on a particular genre, for example, fund-raising letters, and then identified the moves in each of the texts (Biber *et al.*, 2007). Once the texts have been broken up into their respective moves, all the instances of each move are combined to form *move* sub-corpora. This kind of study not only allows the study of the move structure of a genre, it also permits the analysis of language patterns associated with particular moves.

Biber *et al.* (2007: 62–72) identify a total of seven possible moves across the texts in a corpus of philanthropic fund-raising letters: get attention, introduce cause/establish credentials, solicit response, offer incentives, reference insert, express gratitude, and conclude with pleasantries. Using a corpus allows the researchers to identify the most common sequencing of moves in the genre and which moves are obligatory and which are optional. It is also possible to see how patterns of language use vary across the seven moves, including the extent to which different moves occupy different positions along Biber's (1988) dimensions.

Another application of corpus linguistics is the investigation of how information can be structured in discourse (Conrad, 2010: 232–3). Conrad (2010) gives the example of *that*-clauses when they are in subject position, especially at the start of a sentence. This is illustrated in Figure 7.7 with examples of the phrase *that there are* taken from the BNC.

Conrad (2010: 232–4) notes the phrase *that there are*, in the kinds of contexts illustrated in Figure 7.7, repeats information previously mentioned in the discourse. Such connections across a discourse are cohesive in nature because they provide a link to prior discourse and, it is argued, these cohesive devices play an important role in contributing to the overall coherence of the discourse.

Another important contributor to the cohesion of a discourse and its overall coherence for readers and hearers is the ways in which speakers and writers explicitly position a discourse relative to prior and future discourses. No discourse exists in isolation. Each discourse is part of a chain of discourses which intertwine and, in order for each discourse to make sense, speakers and writers have to make it clear

```
1 at has gone on here. That there are three, three issues tha
2 very confused about. That there are two basic different typ
3  everyone's devious. That there are people alive as straigh
4 s-roots development. That there are now 40-odd rugby develo
5 re is no third kind. That there are no hybrid statements wh
6 time has come about. That there are, for instance, kangaroo
```

Figure 7.7 Sample BNC concordance lines for *that there are*

how each new discourse in the chain fits in relation to previous discourses, and also predicted discourses. This process by which a discourse makes reference to prior and future discourses is termed 'referential intertextuality' (Devitt, 1991). Failure to appropriately signal this kind of intertextuality might result in miscommunication if the hearer/reader is unable to relate the current discourse to prior discourses. A corpus of email discourse chains (i.e., interconnected series of emails) has revealed phrases used by the writers for this discourse function (Warren, 2010). For example, the most common phrases used contain the words *please* followed by an imperative, as illustrated in Figure 7.8.

These phrases usually refer to future discourses (e.g., *please advise*, *please check* and *please see*), but there are examples when the phrases refer the reader to prior discourses (line 4, *please find*).

Another word that is frequently used in phrases to refer to prior discourses is *as* (Warren, 2011), as shown in Figure 7.9.

These phrases explicitly position the current discourse relative to prior discourses and, according to Warren (2011), it is not uncommon for more than 50 per cent of a business email to consist of references to either prior or future discourses. It would be interesting to see whether there are so many intertextual references in informal emails.

Discourse markers (e.g., *anyway*, *now*, *okay*, *right*, *so* and *well*) are a distinctive feature of spoken discourse and have an overarching organisational function, plus they can signal the speaker's feelings towards the interaction and the formality of the context of interaction

```
1 e our misunderstanding, please advise us where are the prob
2 essfully. Please check. Please send all log files to us whe
3  regards, XXXX Hi XXXX, Please confirm all the requirement
4 ks JXXXX TXXXX Hi JXXXX, Please find attached the maintenanc
5 ely.  In the mean time, please kindly concentrate on prepar
6 X to modify the coding. Please see whether our logic below
```

Figure 7.8 Examples of *please* signalling intertextuality

```
1 / FCEV /@XXX where XXX=' 0' As advised by AXXXX & AXXXX, for
2  Regards, CXXXX LXXXX  Hi, As agreed, we will be delinking
3 we have prepared two lists as attached for the purpose of e
4 s the update to XXX domain as confirmed by HXXXX and LXXXX.
5 . Regards, EXXXX Hi VXXXX, As discussed this morning, pleas
6 Decision needs to use rule as specified under column 'XXX CA
```

Figure 7.9 Examples of *as* signalling intertextuality

(Carter and McCarthy, 2006: 212). In a corpus-driven study, Lam (2009) looks at the discourse marker *well* in the prosodic version of the HKCSE (Cheng *et al.*, 2008), and below are two examples of how *well* functions to organise the discourse:

(1)
... but yet at the same time not violate our group harmony (.) yea it can be done (.) it can be done okay well let's talk a little bit about conflict why is conflict management so important ...

(2)
... so I start er to er write a proposal and I talk to my er supervisor er well he's a lecturer ...

(Lam, 2009: 270)

In Example 1, the speaker uses *well* to introduce a new topic and, in Example 2, *well* is used to signal the addition of information. In her study, Lam (2009: 266) compares the use of *well* in the HKCSE and a database of English language textbooks used in secondary schools in Hong Kong. She finds that the frequencies, the positions of *well* in the utterances, and the functions performed by *well* are very different. For example, *well* is under-represented in the sample oral presentations in the textbooks compared with real word presentations, and over-represented in the sample discussions offered as models for students in the textbooks (pp. 266–7). Similarly, the position of *well* in utterances in the HKCSE, while tending to be utterance initial (57.9 per cent), is also in medial (38.1 per cent) and final (0.7 per cent) positions, and can occur on its own (3.3 per cent). In the textbooks it is only ever in initial or final positions and is overwhelmingly found at the start of utterances (89.8 per cent) (p. 268). In terms of the six functions of *well*, the textbooks only include two of them (framing, 24.3 per cent, and responsive, 69.2 per cent) in any significant numbers, with the other functions (linking, emotive, processing and turn managing) having just seven instances in total. In the naturally occurring spoken language of the HKCSE all of the functions are to be found, although framing (32.9 per cent), responsive (37.5 per cent), and processing (17.7 per cent) are more frequent. Lam (2009) concludes that there are two major problems with the textbooks. First, they do not explicitly teach the important role of discourse markers such as *well*. Second, the instances of *well* in the textbooks do not reflect how often it is used, where it is used, and for what purposes it is used in the real world, and this needs to remedied in language learning.

Pragmatics

Pragmatics is the study of how meaning is created (and interpreted) in context. It is a field of linguistics which is not interested in what is literally said or written, but how it derives meaning in context. For example, if somebody says *I'm tired*, what does this mean in the context in which it is said? The meaning potential of this utterance is huge, although in context, it is unlikely to be ambiguous. The concern of pragmatics, then, is primarily the function of the language not the formal features of its words and sentences. One area of interest to pragmatists is the identification of what they term 'speech acts' based on the notion that a particular speech act function (e.g., apologizing, thanking, requesting) can come in a variety of forms. Studies using corpora have helped to identify types of speech acts and the forms that they might take. Below we look at two such studies.

A study of request markers by Aijmer (1996) looks for combinations of words associated with speakers making requests in the London Lund Corpus. Table 7.1 presents some of her findings, excluding those request markers with fewer than five instances.

In another study of speech acts using the CANCODE corpus, Adolphs (2008) studied how speakers make suggestions. As in Aijmer's (1986) study, Adolphs (2008) went in search of pragmatic patterns associated with this speech act. Not surprisingly, she started by searching for the lemma *suggest* and found phrases used by speakers to make suggestions. Two of these, *I suggest* and *suggestion*, are

Table 7.1 Most frequent request markers in the LLC

Request marker	Frequency
could you	25
can you	20
let me	20
would you	13
may I	11
can I	10
will you	10
you can	8
could I	6
could you . . . please	6
I would be grateful if you could	6
I wonder if you could	6
if you could	6
you had better (you'd better, better)	6
could I . . . please	5
may I just	5
you must	5

Source: Adapted from Aijmer (1996: 150, 157, 161)

illustrated using examples from the HKCSE (http://rcpce.engl. polyu.edu.hk/HKCSE/) in Figures 7.10 and 7.11, which confirm the findings from CANCODE. Adolphs (2008) finds that the more widespread way to make suggestions in spoken discourse is for speakers to use what look like introductions to questions to introduce suggestions: *why don't you, why not, how about, why don't we* and *why don't I*. Again, these findings are confirmed in the HKCSE and are shown in Figures 7.12–7.16.

The phrase *I suggest* always introduces a suggestion by the speaker in the HKCSE (Figure 7.10), but *suggestion* may be linked to other functions (e.g., *do you have any suggestion to improve this situation* and *well er if the suggestion is we should introduce mainland con concepts . . .*) (Figure 7.11). However, any potential ambiguity surrounding the use of *suggestion* seems to be taken care of by two frequent collocates to the left: *my* and *I*. These collocates make the source of the suggestion clear to the hearer.

```
1 onward but it is only I suggest a recommendation * to the Fi
2 of little things that I suggest changing apart from here P__
3 ay  B2:  okay so what I suggest is * for the next two or thre
4 inutes as well er can I suggest that we have a ten minute bre
5 to another department I suggest you talk to the Personnel  b:
6  video  b:  mhm   A:  I suggest that you pick up the featured
7 tight schedule and er I suggest them to use the airport hotel
8 (.) well that's what I suggest we should u: uhuh * yes  x:
9 discussion (.) if not I suggest yes  b2: yes erm (.) er are t
10agree with it so what I suggest you find something as your un
```

Figure 7.10 HKCSE concordance lines for *I suggest*

```
1 ember (.) that's er one suggestion (.) and again the famili
2 a6: mm  a4: and er so a suggestion about the machine because
3 f seeing yourself so my suggestion as a new comer * with er
4 nd I and I have another suggestion from patients that is apa
5 cultural thinking so my suggestion is maybe you would like t
6 ay be I I I just make a suggestion is two months food and be
7  er cohesive devices my suggestion is um if you well as it i
8 ike to point out er one suggestion is we can use memo more e
9 working (.) right so my suggestion is you should actually mo
10 t way so er so what my suggestion would be  a: mhm b:er for
11 round them and what my suggestion would be um if you'll be
```

Figure 7.11 HKCSE concordance lines for *suggestion*

```
 1 ooks   a: er okay (.) why don't you ask them to do some part
 2 w you are don't know why don't you come up * remember what
 3  need to but  b: but why don't you cover it up you know lik
 4 or your food but why why don't you do likewise for your bev
 5  yes  A: * ((laugh)) why don't you do something about it po
 6  * ((laugh))  A2: ** why don't you do the introduction firs
 7 b: yes  B:  okay um why don't you er okay basically why do
 8 : okay superb um (.) why don't you er tell me a little bit
 9 B: oh * Chin  b2: ** why don't you feel hungry  B: I'm not
10  Tshirt Tshirt  B: why don't you get one of the you know
11  ((Cantonese))  B:  why don't you go and ask  (break)  a1:
12 )) b: but after RIU why don't you go er RCU or  B: they wo
13 lease ((inaudible)) why don't you guy call me ((pause)) qu
14 ld has got a figure why don't you (inaudible) Donald  b4:
15 ssioner * why don't why don't you insist to banks that the
16 l town planning (.) why don't you join the er (.) Planning
17 A: ** okay  A: okay why don't you just write that it's my
18 mself ((laugh))a1:  why don't you keep it  B: what am I go
19 I going to do  a1:  why don't you keep it D__  a2:  why wh
20 y don't you let erm why don't you let A__ start his lesson
21 to pick up N__  A2: why don't you let erm why don't you le
22 we have the ability why don't you outsource as you say sep
23 ord it   b: oh okay why don't you put this down we will ju
24 A: * and  B: ** and why don't you say a sentence like I li
25  okay yeah (.) okay why don't you say A__ is handsome  b1:
26 the past one  A: so why don't you say that b: mm  A: why d
27  it says reasons to why don't you say the reasons I'm appl
28  one bottle of wine why don't you set targets in terms of
29 bit on that area um why don't you share some of your hobbi
30  ((laugh))  B:  so why don't you sing a song to us  a2: n
31 rofile okay so then why don't you so you could say you wor
32 ound noise here  B: why don't you stop and play it and see
33 hen water  B: yeah  why don't you talk about your your fam
34 u er okay basically why don't you tell me a little somethi
35 m))  ((a girl says: why don't you wear socks ((people talk
36  did you write this why don't you write that last paragrap
37  work for that then why don't you (.) you what you can do
```

Figure 7.12 HKCSE concordance lines for *why don't you*

```
1 t bored so we said well why don't we change that and do thi
2 ion to class (.) but er why don't we er try the exercise an
3 (.) okay anyway (.) now why don't we just jump to the next
4 fferent a: yeah   B: * why don't we talk about  a: ** and
```

Figure 7.13 HKCSE concordance lines for *why don't we*

```
(.) * and then I said oh er why don't I just you know   a1:
```

Figure 7.14 HKCSE concordance lines for *why don't I*

```
1  of glasses I also said why not do other things like someth
2 ate two buildings (.) * why not just one building a4: ** er
3                      ** why not just say something B: er I
4  b: ((laugh)) then then why not just tape why not use casse
5 that particular residue why not other residue to begin with
6 virus itself already so why not others so I'm not surprised
7 augh))  a: I asked them why not they try the mm * you know
8 twenty eight and twenty why not twenty four and twenty four
9 ions of mixed grill why why not twenty portion of fish (pau
10 then why not just tape why not use cassette (pause) A: whe
```

Figure 7.15 HKCSE concordance lines for *why not*

```
1 yeah (.) okay  b2: but how about if we just (.) er sell one
2 couple nights okay how how about let's buy a beer B: yeah (
3   B: and two o'clock * how about morning a: ** (inaudible)
4  you know sort of like how about putting on courses instead
5 )  b: ** ((laugh))  B: how about something honest like I'm
6 ght degrees  A1: well how about that season from September
7  yeah  that I like  b: how about the the steamed barbecue p
8 not sure in Hong a: ** how about you go to the Kong tourist
```

Figure 7.16 HKCSE concordance lines for *how about*

The phrases *why don't you/we/I* combined are the most frequently used in the HKCSE to introduce suggestions Figures 7.12–7.14), and, interestingly, although they are, in theory, also a means to introduce a question, they are never used in this way in the HKCSE. The phrase *why not* (Figure 7.15) and *how about* (Figure 7.16), however, do sometimes introduce questions as seen in the following examples:

Example 1
B: well it's not applicable in your case
A: why not

Example 2
A: so how about the Prada bag is he going to buy that for you
(HKCSE)

The above examples show that the local context determines whether these phrases are interpreted as questions or suggestions. In the case of Example 1, we see that instances of *why not* alone are typically questions, and Example 2 is a good example of the way in which *how about the Prada bag* serves to introduce the later question, *is he going to buy that for you*, and so, in context, there is no ambiguity.

Specialised corpora

In corpus linguistics, a corpus is often described as being either 'general' or 'specialised'. General corpora are usually much bigger than specialised corpora. For example, the Bank of English is over 600 million words; COCA is more than 400 million words; and the BNC is 100 million words, and all are general corpora. Specialised corpora, on the other hand, can usually be measured in the thousands or low millions of words, although there are some that are very large. However, size is not the main factor distinguishing the two types of corpora. What distinguishes general corpora from specialised corpora is the purpose for which they are compiled. General corpora aim to examine patterns of language use for a language as a whole, and specialised corpora are compiled to describe language use in a specific variety, register or genre. The selection of the contents of a specialised corpus often requires the corpus linguist to seek advice from experts in the field to ensure its representativeness and balance.

Specialised corpora cover a wide range of registers, genres, language forms and language varieties, and they have grown in recent years. As corpus linguistics has grown, so too has the demand for more specific studies and applications that specialised corpora are often best designed to meet. Having a specific focus can also mean that they can be used to inform the learning and teaching of language for specific purposes, especially when the patterns of language use are benchmarked with a general corpus to highlight similarities and differences.

Register

There are corpora that are built to be representative of a register. The description of English grammar by Biber *et al.* (1999) is a very good example of a register-based study of grammar. As has been mentioned before, it makes use of four corpora representing four different registers collected from US and UK sources (Biber *et al.*, 1999: 29–35): conversation, academic writing, newspapers and fiction. Using these corpora enables Biber *et al.* (1999) to highlight the ways in which patterns of language use vary across different registers. For example, they look at the frequencies of different kinds of lexical words (nouns, verbs, adjectives and adverbs) across the four registers (pp. 65–6) and find that the different word classes are not evenly spread. Nouns are most frequent in newspapers and academic writing and are much less common in conversations. Conversely, verbs are more common in conversations and fiction than in the other registers. These frequencies then have consequences for the occurrence of adjectives and adverbs, which are co-selected with nouns and verbs respectively. Adjectives are most common in academic writing and then fiction, with conversation having the fewest, which is in line with the frequencies of nouns found in the four registers. Conversely, adverbs are more common in conversation and fiction, both of which have more verbs. The proportions of nouns and verbs in each register also vary. Biber *et al.* (1999: 65–6) note that, in conversation, there are roughly as many nouns as there are verbs, whereas, in newspapers and academic writing, there are about three or four nouns for every lexical verb. This difference is partly explained by the much higher use of demonstrative and personal pronouns in conversation, with seven times more personal pronouns in conversation compared with academic writing (p. 333).

This point can be further illustrated by referring back to Tables 4.3 and 4.4 in Chapter 4, which list the most frequent words in the 9.3-million-word HKEC (a corpus of engineering English, mostly written) and the 0.9-million-word HKCSE (a spoken corpus). There are no personal pronouns among the top twenty most frequent words in the HKEC, but there are five in the HKCSE (*you*, *I*, *it*, *we* and *they*). If we compare the use of *I* in the two corpora, we find it ranked 6th in the HKCSE, accounting for 1.99 per cent of all of the words, while *I* is ranked 89th in the HKEC and makes up only 0.11 per cent of the corpus. In other words, *I* occurs about seventeen times more often in spoken English than in written engineering English.

Other examples of register variation findings from Biber *et al.*'s (1999) corpus-based grammar are the use of modal and semi-modal verbs. They find that the use of *have to* to indicate personal obligation is five times more frequent in conversation than in academic writing (p. 494), while *may* is used twenty times more often in academic writing to express possibility than in conversation (p. 491). The use of passives also shows conversation and academic writing to be the most different among the four registers. Passives are more than four times more common in academic writing than in conversation, which is, in part, because in academic writing there is a strong convention to not express the agent (e.g., *it was found that* . . . rather than I *found that* . . .) because of an emphasis on generalisations rather than who performs the action (p. 938). Throughout their very informative grammar, Biber *et al.* (1999) detail many more similarities and differences they find across the four registers.

In a different study that looks at n-grams (Scott and Tribble, 2006), academic writing and conversation are, again, the corpora used. They are interested in examining similarities and differences between novice academic writers and expert writers in their use of three-word n-grams. The novice writers are Polish postgraduate students of English literature and the corpus is made up of their MA dissertations. The expert writers are extracted from the literature sub-corpus of the BNC. Scott and Tribble (2006) uncover similarities in the use of n-grams such as *the end of, the nature of, the fact that* and *in order* to. They also find quite a lot of differences. The novice writers, for example, use *a kind of* and *a number of*, which are not used frequently by the expert writers, while the experts make frequent use of *a sense of, in terms of, the use of, the work of.* Where they found differences in n-gram use, Scott and Tribble (2006: 149–52) searched for them in other BNC sub-corpora representing other registers. The results of these searches are interesting. They found that the n-grams used by the novices, but not the experts, were more likely to be used with similar frequencies in the conversation corpus. Conversely, those n-grams used by the experts and not the novices were more likely to be used with similar frequencies across all of the academic registers in the BNC. In other words, the different uses of n-grams by the expert writers conform to academic norms whereas those of the novices conform to conversation norms. Scott and Tribble (2006: 152) conclude that such findings should lead to the teaching of alternative n-grams to the novices, which they could then choose to make use of to bring their writing more in line with that of expert academic writers. For example, instead of *a kind of* and *a number of*, the novices could use *a variety of, a form of*, and *a type of*, all of which are to be found more frequently in the written academic register corpus of the experts (p. 152).

Genre analysis

Specialised corpora based on a particular genre (i.e., text type) have become very common and can vary with regard to both the number of texts collected and the specificity of the text type collected.

Online gaming has become very popular, with millions of players around the world meeting online to play with, or against, each other. Ooi (2008) has compiled a 1-million-word gaming blog corpus to look at language use specific to the gaming web-blog genre where gamers discuss games, strategy and so on. His study focuses on the semantic prosodies of several key words in this gaming genre – words that are either unique to it or that occur more frequently than in general English use. Ooi (2008: 317–21) examined the words *vertically*, *frag* and *shmup* (short for *shootemup*, which is short for *shoot them up*). The word *vertically* is found to have the following collocates: *scroll(ing)*, *flip*, *advance*, *shmup*, *stages* and *game*. By far the most frequent of these collocates is *scroll(ing)*. The semantic prosody of *vertically* and its co-selections in gaming language is 'forward movement' (p. 318). The word *frag* means to violently kill, according to dictionaries (p. 319), but in gaming, with collocates such as *easy to*, *attempt to*, *can*, *enable* and *well-placed*, Ooi concludes that the lexical item made up of *frag* and its co-selections has the semantic prosody of 'positive violence'. The word *shmup* has collocates such as *horizontal(ly) scrolling*, *vertical(ly) scrolling*, *side scrolling*, *cool*, *favourite*, *encompassing*, *fine*, *great* and *debut* (p. 317). Ooi arrives at the semantic prosody of 'encompassment' for the lexical item comprised of *shmup* and its co-selections (p. 317).

Another genre-based study is conducted by Friginal (2009), who is interested in the language patterns in a corpus of phone calls to outsourced call centres in the Philippines. The outsourcing of call centres has grown in recent years, and he collected his corpus to better understand language use in the industry to then enable him to be more effective in his work in the quality assurance department of a call centre company. One thing he is interested in is key word analysis, and he compares the differences in key words used by the call centre agents to those used by the callers (p. 141). He finds that the agents use more second person pronouns (*your*, *you*), while the callers use more first and third person pronouns. Callers use more past tense verbs (*was*, *said*, *went*, *did*), contractions (*I'm*, *I've*, *didn't*, *doesn't*), progressives (*saying*, *trying*, *looking*), question words (*what*, *where*) and informal words (*guys*, *stuff*, *yeah*, *yup*). The call centre agents, on the other hand, use more formal, respectful words (*please*, *sir*, *ma'am*, *apologise*, *Ms*, *Mr*) and words that relate to their roles in the provision of a service (*calling*, *check*, *verify*, *assist*, *kindly*, *inconvenience*) (p. 141). Based on his findings, Friginal (2009: 296) intends to develop a 'reliable rating and assessment instrument' to ensure the qualifications and ability of current and prospective call centre agents.

An example of a corpus based on a very specific text type is Quaglio's (2009) 604,767 word *Friends* corpus comprised of nine seasons (206 episodes) of the well-known television programme. He compares his *Friends* corpus with the 4-million-word American conversation sub-corpus of the Longman Grammar Corpus to uncover what similarities and differences there are between scripted conversations and naturally occurring conversations. Quaglio uncovers interesting similarities and differences between the two. He finds *Friends* has the same core linguistic features as conversations using Biber *et al.*'s (1998) involved versus informational dimension (Quaglio, 2009: 57–69). Both have a high incidence of first- and second-person pronouns, contractions, present tense verbs, demonstrative pronouns, hedges, private verbs, general emphatics, stranded prepositions and discourse particles.

The use of vague language is commonly found in naturally occurring conversations. It comes in a variety of forms such as hedges (e.g., *kind of (like), sort of (like)*), vague coordination tags (e.g., *or something (like that), or anything (like that), (and) stuff (like that)*), vague nouns (e.g., *thing(s), stuff*), discourse markers (e.g., *you know, I mean*), stance markers (e.g., *probably, perhaps, maybe*), modals (e.g., *could, might*), copular verbs (e.g., *seem, appear*), and utterance final *so* (Quaglio, 2009: 73). Apart from the use of *perhaps* and *maybe*, which are more frequently used in *Friends*, and the use of copular verbs, and *could* and *I mean*, which are used with similar frequencies in the two corpora, vague language is much more frequent in the conversation corpus than in the *Friends* corpus. Quaglio (2009: 86) argues that the reason for this difference is that, in conversation, the participants rely heavily on shared knowledge to be able to interpret vague language in contexts where specificity and precision are not required, or would not be appropriate. If participants are unsure, they can seek clarification. These conditions are not met in TV dialogues in which the actors communicate for the benefit of a third party (the audience). Therefore, the shared knowledge is less and the audience is unable to clarify vague usage, which is hard to interpret, hence the higher level of specific language use in *Friends*.

Features associated with emphatic or emotional language are much more frequent in the *Friends* corpus than in the conversation corpus. Emphatic or emotional language covers language use, such as intensifiers (e.g., *very, so, really, too, totally*), emphatic markers (e.g., *oh, wow*), stance markers (e.g., *of course*), responses (e.g., *wow, sure, fine*), copular verbs (e.g., *look, feel, sound*), expletives (i.e., mild and strong use of swear words), and lexical bundles (e.g., *I can't believe, thank you so much*). The *Friends* dialogues are more exaggerated in the use of these language features than conversation in the real world, except for the use of strong expletives and the use of *wow* as a response. Quaglio (2009: 105) states a number of possible reasons for this. One reason is that this heavy usage is probably due to the nature of TV entertainment and entertainment discourse in general. *Friends* is also a comedy TV show and it is possible that jokes function better with a higher level of emphatic/emotional content. The absence of strong expletives can be explained by the censorship regulations imposed on TV broadcasters in the US. Quaglio (2009: 121) also argues that the scriptwriters have deliberately tried to make the dialogues informal and the result is an overcorrection. For example, *so* is twenty-three times more frequent in *Friends* than in the conversation corpus (e.g., *that's so great, I'm so over him*) and its overuse has come to be associated with the TV series (Quaglio, 2009: 116). From Quaglio's study we can conclude that if the scriptwriters had access to a reference conversation corpus, this problem might be avoided and the dialogues would be more realistic.

While conversation has a relatively low score on the narrative-non-narrative dimension compared to fiction (Biber *et al.*, 1999), it is still in the middle of this dimension. *Friends* and conversation are similar in terms of the involved versus informational dimension, but they are different in terms of the narrative versus non-narrative dimension. *Friends* is characterised by what Quaglio (2009: 132) terms 'immediacy' – a lack of concern with past events. In *Friends*, the focus is on the present and near future. The turns in *Friends* are also found to be more even in length, and spread more evenly across all of the participants. *Friends* tends to be about the here and now, interspersed with evaluative comments (often using emphatic and emotional language). These features make the TV dialogue more lively in terms of involving all the participants and are probably also a product of the comedy aspect of the programme in which hearers will often humorously evaluate one another (p. 137).

Learner corpora

Specialised learner corpora are corpora made up of texts written or spoken by novice rather than expert writers or speakers of a language. They are usually texts spoken or written by learners of the target language (typically, the target language is English). Indeed, these corpora are aimed specifically at language learning and teaching. For example, Flowerdew (2001: 370–1) studied a 200,000-word corpus of written reports by university students and finds that, while students know key vocabulary, they are less familiar with co-selections made with these vocabulary items resulting in 'collocational mismatches' (p. 371).

One of the best-known learner corpora is the International Corpus of Learner English (ICLE) (Granger *et al.*, 2009). ICLE is a written learner corpus made up of 3 million words of EFL (English as a foreign language) writing by university students from 21 mother tongue backgrounds. Each sub-corpus contains 200,000 words written by third or fourth year university students, who each contribute two 500-word essays – one argumentative and the other a literature examination paper. The guidelines for the corpus stipulate that 'descriptive, narrative or technical subjects are not useful for the corpus' (http://cecl.fltr.ucl.ac.be/Cecl-Projects/Icle/icle.htm, 12 May 2010). A complementary corpus exists, which is a corpus of spoken learner language, the Louvain International Database of Spoken English Interlanguage (LINDSEI). Each mother tongue represented in the corpus contains approximately 100,000 words based on university students giving brief monologues on a topic of the student's choice, a short interview based on general topics such as university life and hobbies, and the narration of a story based on four pictures. In total, each student contributes about fifteen minutes of data, which is approximately 2,000 words.

Mukherjee (2009) examined the verb-noun collocates used by German learners in both of these corpora. He found a number of verb-noun collocates, which he terms 'deviant', in that they do not conform to native speaker norms. Several of these are ascribed to mother tongue interference, such as using the plural form of *difficulty* and *chance* in contexts such as *I had most difficulties* and *I will have excellent chances there*, because in German the plural form is used. Another collocational problem uncovered from the learner corpora (pp. 213–14) is that German learners often produce *make + experience* as collocates when they should say or write *have + experience* (e.g., *I wouldn't want to miss the experiences I've made* versus *I want to talk about an experience I had in a foreign country*). Mukherjee (2009) concludes that efforts should be made to improve German learners' 'collocational competence' (p. 212) by including frequently occurring verb-noun collocations in English language learning materials. He also cautions against always using instances of non-deviant language use from native speaker corpora because he finds it better motivates learners if they are given positive evidence from a learner corpus (p. 214). This avoids the danger of learner corpora being seen only as a means of identifying errors when they can also be the source of positive feedback.

Another study that makes use of these two learner corpora (Granger, 2009: 26–7) highlights some of the learner errors to be found across all of the learners represented in them. Granger (2009: 26) found that there is an overuse of *important* in the corpora compared with comparable corpora of native speaker university students. The latter use other adjectives in addition to *important*, such as *critical, crucial, major, serious, significant* and *vital*. Another common phenomenon is the overuse of *which* with non-personal subjects, and the subsequent underuse of *that*. N-grams are another source of both overuse and underuse (p. 27) by learners with, *for example, on the other hand* and *on the contrary* overused, while others, such as *is an example of* and *as discussed* are underused relative to their use by native speaker university students. Since these problems are all pervasive, Granger (2009: 27) argues that they provide useful content for future English language learning textbooks and reference books.

Concluding remarks

Corpus linguistics has become well-established and this chapter has reviewed a number of corpus linguistics-related studies that illustrate the breadth of the field. These areas include register variation, local grammar, and language learning and teaching. A number of these areas were first discussed in Chapter 3 when considering the applications of corpus linguistics. It is intended that the studies reviewed here go some way to addressing the problems outlined in Chapter 1 and also serve as a source of ideas for the corpus linguistic project outlined in Chapter 6.

Note

1   The choice of *provide* is inspired by Sinclair's analysis of *incur* (Sinclair, 2003: 57–62), which has similar colligational patterns and semantic preference, but very different collocates and semantic prosody.

8 Corpus approaches to language and text

This chapter will:

- cover some of the main concepts and models that underpin corpus linguistic research, namely:

  - trust the text: the importance of corpus evidence in language description;

  - naturally occurring contexts of use;

  - inseparability of form and meaning;

  - corpus-driven and corpus-based approaches;

  - model for the analysis of extended units of meaning and lexical priming; and

- underscore the importance and value of the above to teachers, researchers and learners who wish to become competent and reflective language users and researchers.

Trust the text: corpus evidence in language description

Few people these days would want to argue that we can describe a language based on introspection or by fabricating examples. As Sinclair (1991: 6) states: 'one does not study all of botany by making artificial flowers'. Trudgill (1996) is even harsher in his criticism of those who do not base their descriptions on actual language use: 'in the final analysis if linguistics is not about language as it is actually being spoken and written by human beings, then it is about nothing at all' (p. xi). Even so, why go to all the trouble of compiling a corpus? One of the main advantages of a corpus is that it provides better quality evidence because it allows the user to empirically (i.e., scientifically) establish the regularity of patterns based on their repetition throughout a corpus. Single instances of real world language use do not permit the systematic analysis of language use afforded by multiple instances contained in a corpus.

Importantly, a corpus is not just any collection of texts; a corpus is 'a collection of naturally-occurring language text, chosen to characterize a state or variety of a language' (Sinclair, 1991: 171). In other words, a corpus is designed and compiled based on corpus design principles. Another feature which is fundamental to corpus linguistics is that a corpus is 'machine-readable' (McEnery and Wilson, 2001: 31). This means that it is stored on a computer and can be searched using specially written computer programs. This is important in order to do the quantitative analyses associated with corpus linguistics such as generating word frequency lists, concordances, key word lists, collocate lists and statistical tests. However, it is important to point out that corpus linguists can also conduct more qualitative kinds of analysis where they access the larger context, or the whole texts held in the corpus, in which various forms of language use occur. Of course, many combine both quantitative and qualitative approaches in their studies. It is also useful to remember that the use of a corpus in linguistics and literary studies has a long history that predates computers, and quantitative studies were done manually in the past. Admittedly, such studies took a long time and would simply not be possible today, with corpora totalling hundreds of millions of words.

As we have seen throughout this book, corpus linguistic studies have contributed significantly to a better understanding of language, especially meaning creation. However, when we engage in corpus linguistics, we also need to be aware of the limitations of investigating corpora. These have been detailed by Hunston (2002) and are summarised below,

- Corpora can tell us whether something is frequent, or not, but they are not able to tell us if something is possible in a language.

- Corpora can only show us what they contain.

- Corpora can give us evidence but the user must then interpret this information.

- Corpora contain examples of language outside of divorced from their original 'visual and social context'.

(adapted from Hunston, 2002: 22–3)

Nonetheless, despite the limitations of corpora, the advantages of corpus linguistics outweigh the limitations and, as O'Keeffe and McCarthy (2010: 12) state, corpus linguistics is 'a healthy, vibrant discipline'. The key to its success remains the same basic method: 'large quantities of "raw" text are processed directly in order to present the researcher with objective evidence' (Sinclair, 1991: 1).

Naturally occurring contexts of use

Corpus linguistics aims to adopt an empirical approach by basing its descriptions of language on data collected from naturally occurring contexts of use (Tognini-Bonelli, 2001: 2). This approach is 'inductive' (p. 2) because observations are made first and then statements of theory are put forward. The process known as the corpus-driven approach (p. 87), is summarised in the flow chart (Figure 8.1).

Later in this chapter, the corpus-driven approach (p. 87), is revisited and contrasted with the corpus-based approach (p. 65), but here we are concerned with the importance attached to basing language description on actual attested instances of language use in corpus linguistics. By attested examples, we mean language that has been used in the real world rather than invented or contrived examples. One of the main arguments in favour of using a corpus is that it provides a much more reliable guide to how language is used than relying on intuition (Hunston, 2002: 20).

Hunston (2002: 20–2) provides examples drawn from four aspects of language where intuition is known to be very unreliable: collocation, frequency, semantic prosody and phraseology. She cites Granger (1998), who notes that language textbooks typically do not include commonplace examples of adverbs collocating with adjectives (e.g., *keenly felt, readily available* and *vitally important*) and that are rarely used by learners of English. Hunston (2002: 21) argues that this is because many textbooks still tend to be written based on the writers' intuitions, and so they contain unattested examples; whereas, if all textbooks were written based on corpus evidence, writers would be able to include such collocations. The relative frequencies of words also defy intuition, and so whether, for example, *big* or *large* is more frequent is hard (or impossible) to know intuitively. However, a quick

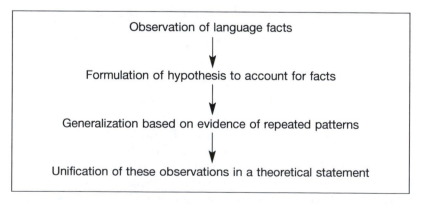

Figure 8.1 An empirical approach to language description

search of the BNC held at Brigham Young University (http://corpus. byu.edu/bnc/) tells us that it is *large* (33,037) that is more frequent than *big* (24,852), although, of course, this might vary depending on the kind of corpus used for the searches (e.g., written versus spoken). Fully identifying the semantic prosodies of lexical items based on intuition is also problematic (Hunston, 2002: 21). Hunston (2002: 21) gives an example from Channel (2000), *par for the course*, which not only means that something often happens, but also negatively evaluates whatever it is that often happens. The sample of concordance lines in Figure 8.2 confirms the semantic prosody described by Channel that uncovering the full semantic prosody of lexical items can only be achieved when it is possible to study multiple instances.

Similarly, the full details of phraseology are unlikely to be arrived at through intuition. We have seen in Chapter 5 how a particular phraseology may consist of up to five kinds of co-selection, and how it often exhibits considerable variation. All of this information can only be retrieved by careful examination of actual use. As Tognini-Bonelli (2001: 89) writes, 'the typical cannot be severed from actual usage, and "repeated events" are the central evidence of what people do, how language functions and what language is about'. This is why it is important that corpora contain texts collected from naturally-occurring contexts of use.

Finally, a word of caution from Sinclair (2005b: 101), who says that no corpus is perfect and none can claim to constitute a truly representative coverage of language use. He reminds corpus linguists that 'the results of corpus research so far are indicative of patterns and trends, of core structures and likely contributions to theory and description, but they are not yet definitive' (p. 101). He says that a key objective in corpus linguistics is to 'improve the procedures and criteria and so that the reliability of the descriptive statements increases' (p. 101). This is not to discredit the advances made by corpus linguistics, but it always has to be borne in mind that, as in all scientific studies, findings need to be replicable to ensure their validity. In other words, it has to be possible for others to be able to confirm or refute the findings of fellow corpus linguists.

```
1 on the Health Service, par for the course. Lord Mayor, the
2 don but I daresay it's par for the course round here. I wou
3  in his voice. "It was par for the course. Two of them succ
4 man not her husband is par for the course, eh?" He saw my e
5 ads is well-rooted and par for the course. Despite the grow
6  sarcastically. "About par for the course." "There's more,"
```

Figure 8.2 Sample BNC concordance lines for *par for the course*

Inseparability of form and meaning

'There is ultimately no distinction between form and meaning', according to Sinclair (1991: 7). What does this mean?

Sinclair (1991) has an answer to this question, but it comes in the shape of another question: 'Is it wise to divide language patterning into grammar and something else (be it lexis or semantics or both) before considering the possibility of a co-ordinated choice?' (p. 3). While it looks like he is asking a question, in fact he is declaring a strong theoretical standpoint. This standpoint is that meaning creation in language is done by the co-selection of what many see as two distinct systems: grammar and lexis.

What evidence is there from corpus linguistics to support this theoretical position?

One finding of corpus linguistics is that semantic prosodies may vary greatly depending on particular co-selections of grammatical choices. For example, Louw (1993: 171) points out that, when *build up* is used transitively with a human subject, it has a typically positive semantic prosody (e.g., *build up organisations*, *build up relationships* and *build up better understanding*). However, when *build up* is used intransitively (i.e., when things or forces build up of their own accord), it has a semantic prosody that is overwhelmingly negative (e.g., *cholesterol build up*, *toxins build up* and *armaments build up*).

Sinclair (1991: 8) warns that the word forms of a lemma should only be conflated 'when their environments show a certain amount and type of similarity'. In other words, it is best to assume that the word forms of a lemma have different co-selections, and hence create different meanings, unless there is evidence to the contrary. Sinclair (2003: 64–72) illustrates this point with the lemma *border* (+ *on*). To illustrate his findings, sample concordance lines for each word form, *border* (+ *on*), *borders* (+ *on*), *bordered* (+ *on*) and *bordering* (+ *on*), taken from COCA (www.americancorpus.org/) are shown in Figure 8.3 to further discuss the phenomenon.

As we move down the different word forms in Figure 8.3, we find a steady movement away from the predominant meaning of geographical, physical borders, found most frequently in the instances of *border on*, towards a very different meaning that is abstract and refers to mental borders (Sinclair, 2003: 70), found most frequently in the instances of *bordering on*. Most of the instances of *border on* have the former meaning (lines 1–4, 6), *borders on* has two (lines 3–4), and *bordered on* has one (line 1). All of the instances of *bordering on* have the abstract meaning; and, in all these cases where the meaning is abstract, the co-selection is typically with extreme mental and character traits and unacceptable behaviour (p. 69), such as *blackmail*, *harassment*, *hilarity*, *fraud*, *lie* and *contempt*.

```
1 from the French-Spanish border on a road that looked like no
2  Only three dishes even border on deserving criticism, and t
3 orces rolled across the border on Oct. 6,1973, Israeli tanks
4 , just outside the park border on River Road in Gatlinburg,
5 , whose size and weight border on that of a full-fledged ult
6 pon tagged the Canadian border on July 25, he simply turned
```

```
1 f anything of substance borders on the impossible. The idea
2  the lane, which almost borders on the neurotic, would seem
3 ry is in Nigeria, which borders on Cameroon in western Afri
4 rieties of rice. # Isan borders on Laos, and regardless of
5 mier self-made hedonist borders on self-inflicted caricatu
6 fort to our enemies and borders on treason, but most of all
```

```
1 ad. The neighborhood is bordered on the east by Rockaway Ba
2 Idris standards, and it bordered on flamboyant. This could
3  no access. " Her laugh bordered on giddy at the thought o
4 n, and the Supernatural bordered on obsession, surpassing
5 , and a confidence that bordered on cockiness. He was the b
6 rnatural intensity that bordered on the obsessive. He never
```

```
1 o be helpful; this was bordering on blackmail. # # " Listen
2 for this shit. This is bordering on harassment. " # " Haras
3 rgy with an enthusiasm bordering on hilarity. (More than o
4  corrected. It must be bordering on fraud to lead people t
5 t is absolutely false, bordering on a lie. Harsanyi knows
6 developed a skepticism bordering on contempt toward the "
```

Figure 8.3 Sample COCA concordance lines for *border, borders, bordered and bordering (+ on)*

Another very interesting and significant observation from Sinclair (1991: 44–8) is that, when the different forms of a lemma are searched for in a corpus, the distribution of the various forms often very uneven, and the collocates, and hence the lexical items and the potential of each form for meaning creation, are likewise very different. This can be illustrated with an example based on an analysis of the frequencies and collocates of *devote, devotes, devoted* and *devoting*. A search of the BNC via the website at Brigham Young University (http://corpus.byu.edu/bnc/) gives us the following frequencies: *devoted* (2,741), *devote* (593), *devoting* (129) and *devotes* (95). These frequencies confirm Sinclair's (1991) observation. The word form *devoted* (77.2 per cent) is by far the most frequent with more than four times more instances than the next most frequent; *devote* (16.6 per cent), which has nearly five times more instances than *devoting* (3.6 per cent); and the least frequent, *devotes* (2.6 per cent), is almost twenty-nine times less frequent than *devoted*.

If we now study the collocates of these words using the COBUILD Concordance and Collocations Sampler (www.collins.co.uk/Corpus/CorpusSearch.aspx), we find, as one might expect, that the number of significant collocates (i.e., those collocates with a *t*-score above 2.0)

Table 8.1 Most frequent collocates of *devote* from the online COBUILD Concordance and Collocations Sampler

Collocate	Frequency of collocate in corpus	Co-occurrence of collocate with devote	t-score
to	1,104,731	328	15.209561
time	74,161	86	8.893266
his	184,325	42	5.127986
will	111,798	27	4.172832
much	41,484	21	4.152019
more	94,468	25	4.101384
attention	4,748	17	4.068335
resources	2,374	16	3.971772
life	30,746	18	3.897964
their	108,479	24	3.845807
we	191,233	27	3.445740
himself	12,254	13	3.443905
able	12,322	12	3.294921
energy	4,287	10	3.097799
herself	4,837	9	2.923314
space	5,133	9	2.918622
myself	5,856	9	2.907159
all	130,977	18	2.774329
her	111,700	16	2.671833
whole	12,104	8	2.624890
papers	2,360	7	2.603326
could	59,556	11	2.462564
must	21,837	8	2.461223
spare	1,231	6	2.425587
pages	2,221	6	2.406364
full	14,868	7	2.378473
itself	7,157	6	2.310522
considerable	1,939	5	2.194825
entire	2,759	5	2.177383
our	52,043	9	2.174912
some	70,139	10	2.107359
themselves	8,861	5	2.047591
hours	9,809	5	2.027427

increases as the frequencies of the words increase. This is because the more frequent the word form, the more productive it is likely to be with regard to meaning creation. In Tables 8.1–8.4, the collocates of each word form are listed.

Tables 8.1–8.4 confirm the inseparability of form and meaning. It can be seen that the numbers of significant of collocates increase with the frequencies of the words as the frequencies of the word form increase. Thus *devotes* and *devoting* both have nine significant collocates, *devote* has thirty-three, and *devoted* has eighty-three. We can also see the meaning creation potential changing and, while all the lists share some collocates (e.g., *time*, *to*, *his*, *life* and *much*), it is only in the collocates of *devoted* that we find, for example, nouns referring to people which tell us something about who is devoted to who – *wife*, *husband*, *followers*, *fan*, *fans*, *family* and *mother*. In other words, each word form adds new collocates, and so makes a distinct contribution to meaning creation. This further confirms the potential problems of conflating all the word forms of a lemma when studying the co-selections of lexical items mentioned in Chapter 5, unless there is evidence that they do share the same meaning.

Similarly, Stubbs (1996: 172–3) looks at the lemma *educate* in a corpus of 130 million words and finds very different frequencies and collocates for different word forms, *education*, *educated*, *educate*, *educating* and *educates*. The most frequent word form is *education* with 27,705 instances and it collocates with *further*, *higher*, *university* and *secondary*; *educated* has 3,450 and collocates with *at* (e.g., *he was educated at . . .*); *educate* has 858 and collocates with *enlighten*, *entertain*, *help*, *inform* and *train*; *educating* has 463; and *educate* only twenty-nine instances.

The lemma *decline* is examined in detail (Sinclair, 1991: 44–51) in a 7.3-million-word general corpus that has 245 instances of the lemma.

Table 8.2 Most frequent collocates of *devotes* in online COBUILD Concordance and Collocations Sampler

Collocate	Frequency of collocate in corpus	Co-occurrence of collocate with devotes	t-score
to	1,104,731	37	4.292333
his	184,325	12	2.939542
he	299,113	12	2.612873
its	53,185	7	2.447580
time	74,161	7	2.369421
space	5,133	5	2.213438
times	16,389	5	2.163813
life	30,746	5	2.100516
much	41,484	5	2.053175

Table 8.3 Most frequent collocates of *devoted* in online COBUILD Concordance and Collocations Sampler

Collocate	Frequency of collocate in corpus	Co-occurrence of collocate with devoted	t-score
to	1,104,731	797	21.571572
is	407,114	150	6.590370
his	184,325	92	6.321178
life	30,746	43	5.759487
her	111,700	64	5.623789
a	973,489	233	4.410709
of	1,100,578	253	4.130391
solely	422	17	4.105687
he	299,113	89	4.038103
entirely	2,260	17	4.029822
who	104,737	44	3.946077
whole	12,104	19	3.886320
page	4,663	16	3.801607
are	198,957	63	3.671353
exhibition	1,691	14	3.664744
attention	4,748	15	3.664348
has	124,665	46	3.654181
section	3,665	14	3.574959
time	74,161	33	3.547510
space	5,133	14	3.508188
entire	2,759	13	3.475324
subject	6,020	14	3.467844
was	340,423	90	3.379952
were	110,611	39	3.230688
wife	8,189	13	3.219023
chapter	2,054	11	3.211228
much	41,484	22	3.185226
pages	2,221	10	3.042749
resources	2,374	10	3.034515
himself	12,254	13	3.027152
years	45,988	22	3.021805
husband	6,083	11	3.004489
exclusively	721	9	2.959099
research	7,649	11	2.924133
an	136,157	42	2.905237
she	127,836	40	2.884662
totally	3,046	9	2.827205
most	43,653	20	2.810940
loyal	759	8	2.782758
father	10,631	11	2.771119
fan	1,273	8	2.751831
following	7,900	10	2.737121
each	22,468	14	2.719725
mother	12,633	11	2.668391
lives	6,231	9	2.646525
energies	244	7	2.630056
magazine	3,314	8	2.629025
and	1,129,483	231	2.551450
herself	4,837	8	2.537387
shop	5,149	8	2.518614

Table 8.3 *continued*

Collocate	Frequency of collocate in corpus	Co-occurrence of collocate with devoted	t-score
been	105,013	32	2.497561
family	21,020	12	2.431426
care	10,080	9	2.428178
sections	924	6	2.385292
absolutely	4,244	7	2.372760
coverage	1,151	6	2.369521
column	1,232	6	2.363893
study	5,458	7	2.294671
mainly	2,234	6	2.294276
fans	2,720	6	2.260510
books	6,095	7	2.253697
their	108,479	31	2.251977
series	6,606	7	2.220827
special	10,351	8	2.205612
electoral	496	5	2.198318
followers	500	5	2.198013
protecting	534	5	2.195426
large	10,599	8	2.190690
energy	4,287	6	2.151638
staff	7,773	7	2.145761
book	11,372	8	2.144179
spare	1,231	5	2.142378
single	7,916	7	2.136563
work	35,426	14	2.130344
charity	1,744	5	2.103334
considerable	1,939	5	2.088492
cause	5,270	6	2.083342
reform	2,270	5	2.063300
beauty	2,328	5	2.058886
meeting	9,561	7	2.030750
museum	2,723	5	2.028823
dwight	2,855	5	2.018776
hours	9,809	7	2.014798
speech	3,087	5	2.001119

Table 8.4 Most frequent collocates of *devoting* in online COBUILD Concordance and Collocations Sampler

Collocate	Frequency of collocate in corpus	Co-occurrence of collocate with devoting	t-score
time	74,161	25	4.817866
to	1,104,731	45	4.685951
his	184,325	14	3.136727
life	30,746	9	2.874150
all	130,977	10	2.653673
much	41,484	8	2.648324
her	111,700	8	2.343481
spare	1,231	5	2.229308
whole	12,104	5	2.169597

The distribution is uneven: *decline* (122), *declined* (76), *declining* (38) and *declines* (9). Sinclair (1991) then studies their usage and, again, finds differences: *decline* (12 per cent verbal; 88 per cent nominal), *declined* (100 per cent verbal), *declining* (33 per cent verbal; 67 per cent adjectival), and *declines* (89 per cent verbal; 11 per cent nominal). The two main senses of the lemma *decline* found in dictionaries, 'refuse' and 'reduce', also tend to be associated with particular usages. The sense of 'reduce', as in deteriorate, is associated with nominal usage and the verbal and adjectival use are the opposite. *Decline* is mainly nominal, *declining* is adjectival, and *declined* verbal (p. 51). The sense of 'refuse' is verbal and most instances are associated with *declined*.

In another study (Hunston and Francis, 2000: 255–6), the relationship between form and meaning is illustrated by examining the collocates and syntax of the three senses of *reflect*, as presented in *Collins COBUILD English Dictionary* of 1995. One sense relates to light and surfaces (*the sun reflected off the snow-covered mountains, the glass appears to reflect light naturally*). The next is about mirrors (*his image seemed to be reflected many times in the mirror*) and the third is about thinking (*we should all give ourselves time to reflect, I reflected on the child's future, things were very much changed since before the war, he reflected*). Hunston and Francis (2000: 255–6) note that each sense has its own distinct phraseology with distinct collocates (sense 1: *the sun, the glass*; sense 2: *the mirror*; sense 3: *we, I, he*) and different syntax (sense 1: V prep (*reflected off*), V noun (*reflect light*); sense 2: be V-ed (*be reflected*); sense 3: V (*reflect*), V *on* n (*reflect on the child's*), V that (*reflected that*)). In other words, the senses of *reflect* are differentiated by their patterns of collocation and syntax.

On occasion, there can even be different meanings associated with singular and plural forms of a word. Sinclair (2003: 167–72) gives the example of the meanings of singular *eye* versus the meanings of the plural *eyes*. This case is illustrated in Figures 8.4 and 8.5 with a random sample of concordance lines taken from the COBUILD Concordance and Collocations Sampler (www.collins.co.uk/Corpus/CorpusSearch. aspx).

If we study the two concordances, we find that there are two main meanings, each one predominantly associated with one of the forms. One is to do with the 'organ of sight' (e.g., *his fabulous bright blue eyes*) and the other, which has little to do with sight, is figurative being to do with 'monitoring' (e.g., *Under the benevolent eye of this Celtic talisman*), 'critical examination' (*Tibet was no longer much in the public eye*) and 'various points of view' (*These two don't exactly see eye to eye*) (Sinclair, 2003: 170–1). The word form *eyes* is mainly associated with the 'organ of sight', and we can see that this is the case for thirty-two (80 per cent) of the instances of *eyes* (figurative uses of *eyes* are found in lines 2, 4, 18, 21, 25, 26, 30, 34). In the

```
 1 he Field Director keep an eye on its progress, and when our
 2 e been adopted in several eye hospitals. [p] [p] Other stud
 3 s a gleam in his visceral eye. Christian Slater plays Clare
 4 ocusing, individual right-eye focusing to adjust to the use
 5 on thighs and buttocks is eye-watering even to contemplate.
 6 ked. Under the benevolent eye of this Celtic talisman, Nich
 7 dicule them in the public eye AND win a G SHIRT in the proc
 8  admitted that he had his eye on Cromack's figure, but it w
 9  chosen by the discerning eye of leading art critics, inclu
10 writing. [p] The trained eye may find some comparison betw
11 Union does not see quite eye to eye with Jordan on this.
12  doesn't get his batting eye back before August. Both the
13 so he naturally kept his eye on you. When you hadn't come
14 There are three types of eye, the first being the [f] stre
15 r created by the Private Eye satirists in general, and `Mr
16 e John Chapman-Smith, an eye surgeon from New Zealand, and
17 s pleased to discover an eye-witness account of them writt
18 and her father still see eye to eye on immigration. [p] Pro
19 don't exactly see eye to eye. I'm putting them together. T
20 has not sampled a newt's eye, but she has found prescripti
21 amel to pass through the eye of a needle to enter the king
22  ere glued under my left eye and jaw to exaggerate my bags
23 ntroduce free dental and eye checks.[p] Opt-out hospitals a
24 at. [p] The 48-year-old eye patient parked the ageing Mor
25 -3, 6-2. [p] [h] Dallas eye up double; American Football [
26 ed [/sh] [p] Nick's shut-eye sit-in meant he missed his sh
27 pink bow that caught his eye. [p] He chased the kidnapper
28 onger much in the public eye. Although [f] Three Years in
29 Ar-Ex or vaseline in the eye area. When You Wake Up Repea
30 . It looked like a blind eye. Lainey stepped over to it a
31 the pages, and wiped her eye again with the wadded blue ti
32 y. She's pleasing to the eye, runs to the kitchen at the f
33  er voice, a flirtatious eye, and she was manipulative and
34 mply the availability of eye examinations. Fitzgerald has
35 lking, watching from the eye holes of my mask for some bar
36 thing until he and I get eye-to-eye and talk about that. A
37 s finger dexterity, hand-eye coordination, color sense, si
38 ou have to keep an [ZF1] eye on hi [ZF0] eye on him all th
39 No. [ZF1] One of Bart's eye [ZF0] one of Bart's eyes has
40  say it's constantly one eye [F0X] Mm [F03] outside [F0X]
```

Figure 8.4 Sample concordance lines for *eye* from the online Cobuild Concordance and Collocations Sampler

```
 1 ocent people having their eyes gouged out. Children torture
 2 Miller viewed through the eyes of the two women who knew him
 3 d Of Love or Love In Your Eyes he reaches ever lower plateau
 4 estroyed in front of your eyes. You haven't got nothing, you
 5 pale lips with deep, dark eyes. Try Givenchy's new Onyx Pris
 6 opics as well.  Well, our eyes for this view of Brazil - bec
 7 ritz?" [p] The man's cool eyes betrayed nothing, no remorse
 8 ping from her nurse's cap eyes shining: she really was delic
 9 top of his bald head. His eyes were bright, though, and swep
10  his muffler slowly, his eyes fixed on the menu which had b
11    hrist, Stein thought, eyes hurting from too much reading
12   to their mothers. Right eyes denote characteristics inheri
13   picture out through her eyes until she saw it perching on
14 wake, and there were two eyes in there, staring at me. Well,
15  She searched his watery eyes, attempting to find the truth;
16 panting and crossing his eyes to make himself look like an
17 pinched faces, sightless eyes, stumps of limbs and ragged
18 issed without taking his eyes off Marlette. Dennison hurri
19 steer this thing with my eyes closed [p] But Baz chose Cha
20  tie a towel around your eyes and set off.[p] Does that mean
21 autumn, Rousseau has his eyes on breaking it, though he is n
22 his fabulous bright blue eyes. They looked at each other and
23 d Steve Hyett opened his eyes. In a hazy blur he could see h
24 ear a wig. [p] Ol' Blue Eyes sneaked in at the side door on
25 t its business. Such new eyes" exist, fortunately, and they
26 ary. Frannie hadn't laid eyes on her for at least four year
27 He sighed and closed his eyes. Wonder what Gladys engraved
28 ling against a wall, her eyes transfixed with terror. [p] E
29 n of wrinkles around his eyes. He was perhaps only seven or
30 ut she couldn't take her eyes away from Joe. Now," he told
31 cking a bull between the eyes with a two-by-four. In the ar
32 he sighed and closed her eyes. `An" how do I know you ain't
33 en coop. Kate closed her eyes at the expense. The scattered
34 nger be seen because the eyes have moved on. Good readers m
35 ight be possible for his eyes to meet hers. Was he an anima
36 for a Romeo to raise his eyes to. And in the stage floor wa
37  the bed frame. Glaring, eyes fixed upon the stitching of h
38 iving that rope up.  His eyes were big as silver dollars. I
39  look at those sparkling eyes, and you know this spirited p
40 now everyone opens their eyes and [ ZG1] says you know [ ZG0]
```

Figure 8.5 Sample concordance lines for *eyes* from the online Cobuild
        Concordance and Collocations Sampler

case of the singular form *eye*, the picture is different. Sometimes, the meaning of *eye* is to do with the organ of sight (13 instances, 32.5 per cent, in lines 2, 4, 16, 20, 22–4, 29, 31, 34, 35, 37, 39), but most (27 instances, 67.5 per cent) are figurative in meaning.

Corpus-driven and corpus-based approaches

When corpus linguistic studies are reported, there are a number of terms used to describe the approach that has been taken such as 'corpus-based', 'corpus-informed' and 'corpus-driven'. 'Corpus-informed' tends to be used to describe language learning and teaching materials that make use of corpora to provide examples, and is less often used to describe a corpus linguistic study. However, when it is used, it usually describes an approach in line with 'corpus-based', and so here we only review corpus-based and corpus-driven approaches. As we shall see, the two approaches are very different, and so the one that is adopted can significantly influence what a study finds out about language use. These two approaches are discussed most comprehensively by Tognini-Bonelli (2001) who, it should be noted, is a keen advocate of the 'corpus-driven' approach.

Below, in Figure 8.6, the two approaches are expressed as flow charts and we can see that they are diametrically opposed.

The corpus-based approach is 'deductive' because the reasoning works from the more general to the more specific, which is a 'top-down' approach (Tognini-Bonelli, 2001: 10–11). The researcher begins with a theory about a topic of interest and then narrows that down into more specific hypotheses that can be tested using a corpus. The theory is further narrowed down as observations are collected to

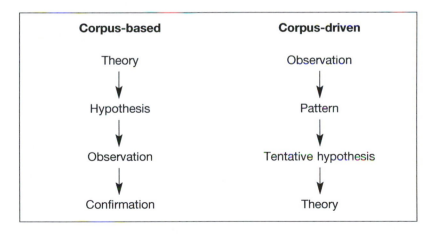

Figure 8.6 Corpus-based and corpus-driven approaches to corpus linguistics

address the hypotheses. Finally, the hypotheses are tested with specific data and the original theory is confirmed (or not) (pp. 10–11).

Conversely, the corpus-driven approach is 'inductive' (Tognini-Bonelli, 2001: 14–18). Inductive reasoning works from specific observations to broader generalisations and theories, and is therefore a bottom-up approach. The researcher begins with specific observations and measures in order to identify patterns and regularities. Once patterns are found, the researcher formulates some tentative hypotheses that can be explored and perhaps developed into some general conclusions or theories (pp. 14–18).

The corpus-driven approach has famously been adopted by Johns (1991a, 1991b) to become a powerful language learning methodology: data-driven learning (DDL). In DDL, the language learner is also a language researcher and, to better learn the language, the learner accesses corpora to explore and make sense of patterns of language use. The approach is captured very succinctly by Johns (1991a: 30): 'research-then-theory'.

A corpus-based approach is a 'a methodology that avails itself of the corpus mainly to expound, test or exemplify theories and descriptions that were formulated before large corpora became available to inform language study' (Tognini-Bonelli, 2001: 65). Thus, a corpus-based study uses a corpus as a resource to validate an existing theory, typically by finding examples in the corpus to support it. The main problem with such an approach is that it greatly reduces the likelihood of finding out new things about language use and hence new theories of language. In fact, Tognini-Bonelli (2001) goes even further and states that the corpus-based approach might be adopted precisely because it will not cast doubt on current language theories and descriptions: 'the potential of corpus evidence is not exploited fully . . . in order not to threaten some existing theoretical positions' (p. 10).

In the corpus-driven approach, 'the corpus is used beyond the selection of examples to support or quantify a pre-existing theoretical category' (Tognini-Bonelli, 2001: 11). In a corpus-driven study, 'the theoretical statement can only be formulated in the presence of corpus evidence and is fully accountable to it' (p. 11).

The differences in approach are clear regarding both the process and the impact of the result, although it should be noted that some researchers (see Rayson, 2008) claim to be able to combine the two approaches even though they would appear to be mutually exclusive. Examples of corpus-driven studies which have resulted in prior theories or descriptions to be rewritten are given below to illustrate the above points.

In a detailed corpus-driven study of *any*, Tognini Bonelli (2001: 15–17) arrives at a new description of the word that adds to the descriptions to be found in traditional grammars. She notes that, traditionally, *any* is contrasted with *some* in terms of the structures that it can occur in – negative sentences (*I haven't any money*), questions (*have you any money*), after *if/whether*, and in expressions of doubt (Thomson and Martinet, 1984: 24; cited in Tognini-Bonelli, 2001: 15). While some of these structures are to be found when a corpus is searched, there is wider variation that suggests the description is lacking. To illustrate her findings, sample concordance lines for *any* (40 out of a total of 15,221) from the HKEC (http://rcpce.engl.polyu. edu.hk/HKEC/) are given in Figure 8.7.

In line with Tognini-Bonelli's (2001: 16–17) findings, the instances of *any* in Figure 8.7 contain 7 (17.5 per cent) instances of *any* in negative sentences (lines 6, 7, 15, 16, 19, 31, 37), no instances of *any* in questions, and no instances of *any* after *if/whether*. What is interesting, and confirms Tognini-Bonelli's (2001) discussion, is that 33 instances of *any* (82.5 per cent) are being used as a determiner in positive sentences. This means that, most of the time, *any* is used in a structure not described in traditional reference works.

In a study by Kennedy (1991) of *between* and *through*, he notes that reference works do not do a good job of explaining the differences between the two words. In order to examine the phraseologies associated with these two words, he adopts a corpus-driven approach. To illustrate his findings, sample concordance lines for *between* and *through* taken from the HKCSE (http://rcpce.engl.polyu.edu.hk/ HKCSE/) are given in Figures 8.8 and 8.9.

It can be seen that *between* is often found after nouns such as difference, differences, differentiation, distinguish, tension, and problem, as well as relationship, co-operation, encounter, negotiation, discourse, conversation and interchange. *Through* is more frequently preceded by verbs such as go, come, pass, follow, think, and look. By identifying the phraseologies of *between* and *through*, Kennedy's (1991) corpus-driven study better identifies key features associated with each word in order to more clearly describe their differences.

Model for the analysis of extended units of meaning

Sinclair's fundamental notion, based on many years of investigation – that we create meaning when we speak and write by the co-selection of words – has been explored throughout this book and underpins much of the work by corpus linguists. Now that we better understand that meaning is created in this way, it follows that language is phraseological in nature. This important conclusion is the basis of Sinclair's (1987) 'idiom principle'.

What is the idiom principle?

According to Sinclair (1991), there are basically two opposing views as to how language is produced. One he terms the 'open-choice

1   Ordinance in respect of **any** activities on the Site; (b) T
2   person at the Meeting or **any** adjournment thereof if you so
3   or holding the meeting or **any** adjournment thereof. 3. Dr. Y
4   reasonably arising from **any** breach or non-compliance by t
5   n 500 mm from any wall of **any** building to provide protection
6   e you usually do not need **any** calibration. 30 sec. nonmoving
7   e side, ATM networks lack **any** commonly-accepted cell managem
8   ent, and compensated for **any** effect of dilution air to the
9   expenditure column Enter **any** expenditure for audio visual
10 le upon allotment, or at **any** fixed date, whether on account
11 suitable for mounting on **any** hard surface and the mounting
12 ogised to the public for **any** inconvenience caused. Senior B
13 ice, full information on **any** individual operation is almost
14 any cracks and edges of **any** inspection openings. The air s
15 rtising notice boards of **any** kind are to be erected on Site
16 oad carrying capacity of **any** member does not cause integrit
17 rate of higher than 4 in **any** 30 minutes) should be paved wi
18 CB certificate issued by **any** NCB and carrying out additiona
19 t and expiry of the CNP, **any** noise levels which may not be
20 of the control valve in **any** of the branches. Hence, instead
21 pecified process; or (c) **any** olefins, derivatives of olefins
22 to make comparisons for **any** one or all these measures in di
23 humidifiers Page 14(b)in **any** other case where the Director i
24 ng should be provided to **any** part of an exit route whether i
25 xternal wall. 11.7 Where **any** part of the external wall comin
26 he platform, the mast or **any** part of the tower working platf
27 h goods or articles.(ii) **Any** person claiming ownership of an
28 nding lecture at home or **any** place through a computer and In
29 Depositing of wastes in **any** place, except with lawful autho
30 l buildings. It includes **any** premises, buildings or activiti
31 , breakdown or failure of **any** process or air pollution contro
32 of the stack, or beneath **any** roof over the storage space. Ou
33 s than 2m/s2 (0.2g). (e) **Any** safety device or electrical tri
34 ring specified times and **any** special noise control measures
35 m or otherwise and with **any** special privileges as to redem
36 the usable floor area of **any** storey above the ground floor
37 had not been notified of **any** substantial shareholders' inte
38 publication and welcome **any** suggestions/views,Please send

Figure 8.7 Sample HKEC concordance lines for *any*

```
1  determine the distance between A and B so B is the known va
2 oint of differentiation between a vowel and a consonant (.)
3 r heat recovery view in between a1: er no er er this er er
4   B: but can maids move between employers here b: oh yes *
5 ee years b: ** mhm  but between five and ten years (.) * th
6 er economic cooperation between Hong Kong and the rest of th
7 a: the the relationship between individual and community (.)
8  low duty that is maybe between maybe eighteen maybe eight p
9 e in lecturer discourse between native and non native Englis
10  some some differences between naturally occurring data and
11 ) er you can say um be between okay between article and nou
12 e for example it is er between one and zero you will obtain
13 Cantonese conversation between other staff))  b: Mister A__
14 t a middle plate in be between P one and P two (.) when the
15 t  show the difference between PE D and N D users in test s
16 the chance * encounter between super infection and b1: ** mm
17 schools to distinguish between the concept of medium of inst
18 sons * that I (.) make between the decisions * that  B: ** m
19 onese acts as a bridge between the foreigners and the local
20  er the health club or between the hotel staff with the clie
21 w there's a difference between the invoice and a delivery s
22 ation problem appeared between the marketing syndicate and o
23 depends on the balance between the need and the resource req
24  recently been tension between the People's Republic and Tai
25 es in response pattern between the previous and present stud
26 re what are we selling between the the seventeenth to the tw
27  * er more interchange between * the two * cultures but do y
28  the i- er negotiation between the two governments you know
29  see okay the function between the two the native one is use
30 na now become problems between the US and Hong Kong for exam
31the the the phase shift between the voltage and the current o
32 s um a huge difference between them B1: er er I mean I I'm s
33 re it's a conversation between them you know  B: alright but
34 ties of the power flow between these three ports and if you
35 .) how does power flow between this input port output port
36  (.) a and e (.) maybe between this one and this one (.) and
37 uence the future trade between United States and US (.) howe
38  arrangement just like between us and Taiwan when b1: ** mhm
39  and they are choosing between us and the Singapore hotels i
40 ng is the relationship between words and concepts (.) but de
```

Figure 8.8 Sample HKCSE concordance lines for *between*

```
 1 d transfer through the through a (inaudible) account in view
 2 s I'm sure you will go through a lot of happy times but I wi
 3 y time during the term through A_ (.) through A_ you can boo
 4 e ICAC and then I stay through B: yeah * yeah a: ** yeah I
 5  to be very popular er through b1: now er KC I think the Fi
 6 ( ) because we went through ( ) been made when there's
 7 wo sons they both went through coeducational * system  a: **
 8  when the reforms come through I think Indonesia's in a simi
 9   B: yeah it's coming through if you just if you just I I'l
10 Kong people have gone through in the last few years they ex
11 pen the door and walk through * (inaudible) we will try to
12 n (.) make them er go through it (.) almost exactly like th
13 it was about half way through last year  b1: probably the m
14 presentation and then through our Q and A question and answ
15 hing er to pay my way through school when I was studying pa
16 be better to say went through several rounds of translation
17 re's a A: ** mm think through sort of there should be a thi
18 d students in general through surveys through erm gaging ex
19 u've   a: ** mhm gone through that * that process the proje
20  Kiel canal that goes through that's where we live  B: betw
21  right because I pass through the (inaudible) K C R station
22 rline we look er * we through the airline to contact him b2:
23 he supply temperature through the control system with the(
24 com  x: *  (.) to get through the course committee of the
25   they say even going through the customs er if you don't
26 is er join is join er through the evaporation er (inaudib
27 e (.) whereas men all through the generations always had
28 U (.) online learning through the Internet and something
29 he talking through my through the interpreter *that I am
30  er   b: I haven't go through the list er I understand th
31 'm just going to flip through the next series of pictures
32 o (.) the storage (.) through the receiving department ok
33  actually er is right through the um primary and secondar
34  to com- um to follow through their learning um process r
35  but er they don't go through this process of shipping tw
36 oun (.) so we've gone through this so I'm not going to go
37 resting when you look through those er the E S P J list p
38 * right   a2: * mhm  through to ours ((Cantonese)) headq
39 with you and then go through with er some of the details
40 don't have this think through you in fact get a lot of fa
```

Figure 8.9 Sample HKCSE concordance lines for *through*

principle' and the other the 'idiom principle'. The open-choice principle is based on a view of language that sees language texts as the product of a very large number of complex choices. At each point in a text where a unit (a word or a phrase or a clause) is completed, a large range of choices opens up and the only restriction on the speaker or writer in terms of choosing the next word in the next unit is whether or not it is grammatical (Sinclair, 1991). In other words, as long as what we say or write is grammatical, we have unrestricted choice at available slots in the unfolding discourse. This is why the open choice principle is sometimes called the 'slot and filler' model of language (p. 109).

The idiom principle is based on a very different view of language. This view argues that words do not appear randomly in a text restricted only by the grammar. Proponents of the idiom principle say that the open-choice principle does not account for the real world restraints on speakers and writers as a discourse unfolds (pp. 110–15).

What are these restraints?

One of the restraints is the language conventions of a particular register or genre (p. 110). When we speak or write, we do so within the context of both a register (e.g., business writing versus conversation) and a genre (e.g., a business email responding to a complaint from a customer versus a conversation among friends). Each register, and each genre within a register, has specific patterns of language use that comprise the set of conventions within which individuals communicate. The similarities and differences between registers and genres have been the subject of many corpus linguistic studies and discourse and genre analysis studies, and some of the findings are described in this chapter and Chapter 5. Much of the time devoted to learning 'business English' or 'legal English', for example, is spent learning and teaching the language patterns associated with these registers and the specific genres within them. The fact that patterns of language are context-dependent means that we are restrained in our language choices and this further supports the basic premise of the idiom principle.

There are a number of semi-preconstructed phrases in English, such as *in terms of*, *of course* and *set eyes on*, which Sinclair argues are not made up of two or three separate choices by the speaker or writer, but are in fact single choices. Such phrases, therefore, are another restraint on us because they are fixed expressions. We all recognise that such expressions are a restriction because of their fixedness, but Sinclair goes much further than this and includes all the phraseology that is not fixed. Here, we need to remember that phraseology consists of patterns of co-selection, and so many phraseologies are not fixed. These forms of phraseology, which include variation, as we have seen in this chapter and Chapter 6, while they are obviously not fixed, still have strong patterns of co-selection that speakers and writers conform to. For example, the co-selection of words (collocation), such as *impending + crisis* and *nagging + doubt* (see Chapter 6), and the co-selection of grammatical choices (colligation), such as *negative structure + budge* (see Chapter 5), are further evidence of the idiom principle at work. Evidence that collocates and colligates are repeatedly co-selected along with the other ingredients of lexical items means that speakers and writers are restrained by collocation and colligation. Similarly, semantic preference is another restraint because lexical items are often associated with a particular semantic environment(s). The ultimate restraint, of course, is the choice of semantic prosody because speakers and writers are restrained by the pragmatic meaning they wish to convey. How that meaning is realised is, in turn, restrained by all of the other restraints mentioned above.

All of these patterns of co-selection can be broken for various reasons – irony, sarcasm, impact on the hearer/reader – all of which may be subsumed under the notion of speaker/writer creativity. When forms of creativity take place which break the patterns of co-selection, we can talk about marked as opposed to unmarked co-selections, where unmarked is what is expected. The fact that we recognise marked co-selections, as opposed to unmarked, can be a source of creativity in language use does not negate the idiom principle. In fact, marked co-selections offer yet more support for the idiom principle because, if there were not unmarked patterns of co-selections, there could be no marked co-selections, thus removing a fertile source of creativity. This is confirmed by Hoey (2005: 176–7), who shows how the title of a famous poem *A grief ago* by Dylan Thomas is marked and, in this case, creative because *ago* is primed to collocate with days, weeks and years, and by choosing the marked co-selection of *ago* and *grief*, the poet achieves his creative goal.

Let us remind ourselves of the five categories of co-selection. There is the obligatory invariable core made up of a word, or words, which is always present in the lexical item and, as such, is evidence of the occurrence of the lexical item in the lists of co-occurring words generated by software such as ConcGram. There is the optional co-selection of words located in the physical text (collocation) and the co-selection of grammatical choices (colligation). Also optional is semantic preference, which is the restriction of instances of a lexical item to a shared semantic feature(s). Finally the most important category, which is obligatory and drives all of the other co-selections: semantic prosody. Semantic prosody is the determiner of the meaning of the whole lexical item and expresses its function (Sinclair, 2004).

Given that there are up to five co-selections to be made by a speaker/writer when a lexical item is produced, which is the first co-selection to be made?

According to Sinclair (2004), words or phrases have particular semantic prosodies that convey the speaker's/writer's attitudinal, pragmatic (context-specific) meaning. A speaker's choice of a particular word or phrase is therefore based on the intention to communicate the associated semantic prosody. The words co-selected by speakers and writers are not independent. If a word is regularly used with other words, and together they create a particular semantic prosody, then this semantic prosody becomes part of the attitudinal and pragmatic meaning.

As Sinclair (2004: 34) states, 'the initial choice of semantic prosody is the functional choice which links meaning to purpose; all subsequent choices within the lexical item relate back to the prosody'. Thus, the process of generating a lexical item is as follows:

1 semantic prosody (+ semantic preference);

2 (+ colligation) (+ collocation);

3 + core.

Corpus-driven studies of the ways in which words are co-selected by speakers and writers have revolutionised our understanding of the full extent and importance of semantic prosodies and underlined the importance of co-selection in creating meaning in context.

One question remains, however. How do we acquire a sense of the marked versus unmarked co-selections in a lexical item?

Hoey (2005), working very much within Sinclair's theoretical framework and extending it 'from the lexical item to the wider text' (Hoey, 2005: 158), offers his theory of lexical priming as an answer to this important question. Hoey argues that patterns of co-selection require that speakers/writers and hearers/readers are primed for (i.e., *prepared for* and *sensitive to*) these co-selections:

> A word is acquired by encounters with it in speech and writing. A word becomes cumulatively loaded with the contexts and co-texts in which they are encountered. Our knowledge of a word includes the fact that it co-occurs with certain other words in certain kinds of context. The same process applies to word sequences built out of these words; these too become loaded with the contexts and co-texts in which they occur.
>
> (Hoey, 2005: 8)

Those who promote the benefits of exposure to, or immersion in, a language to aid language learning, are in effect advocating opportunities for lexical priming to take place. For example, activities such as extensive reading are designed to facilitate the cumulative loading of a word and/or word sequence 'with the contexts and co-texts in which they are encountered' (p. 8).

Hoey argues that when we are exposed to language in use, we are exposed to the related patterns of co-selection comprising lexical items which we then assimilate and use ourselves in similar contexts. According to Hoey (2005: 26–8), every word is primed to occur in association with particular pragmatic functions and these are its pragmatic associations – this is what Sinclair terms semantic prosody. Hoey gives the example of the word *sixty* and argues that this word has a pragmatic association with vagueness and provides examples from a newspaper corpus. Hoey (2005) is unable to confirm a similar association in a spoken corpus, but below are some concordance lines for *sixty* from the HKCSE (http://rcpce.engl.polyu.edu.hk/HKCSE/) (Figure 8.10) which confirm that this pragmatic association (semantic prosody) also holds in spoken discourse.

In the first six lines, all but one instance (line 5) of *sixty* is preceded by an indicator of vagueness (*around, some, over, about*) and when *sixty* is simply part of a larger number (lines 7–10), such as *sixty-six*, it no longer has the association with vagueness. Hoey's (2005) argument is that every time we encounter *sixty*, we also encounter its association with vagueness, and so we are primed to then co-select indicators of vagueness when we use the word.

In addition to Sinclair's (1996) five categories of co-selection, Hoey (2005) adds other patterns of association for which he argues we are primed, and some of these are now described. Co-hyponyms and synonyms differ with respect to their collocations, semantic associations and colligations (pp. 77–9). Hoey gives the examples of the phrases *round the world* and *around the world*. The former collocates with *halfway* and *sail* while the latter with *from* and *people*. The phrase *around the world* is over five times more frequent in his corpus and rarely is meant literally, with 90 per cent of instances meaning 'all over

```
1   should have done around sixty but we only about er forty *
2 pause) I understand some sixty delegates mostly from the Uni
3 e two hundred PC in over sixty different locations for the g
4 l find that um (.) about sixty per cent of subjects are corr
5 tay at their current erm sixty percent (pause) b3: okay I ju
6 tion expenditure by some sixty percent and we have earmarked
7 t now we're only holding sixty-six point three  B1: which on
8 using the wave length of sixty three nano metre radiation of
9 ave their own brands now sixty two percent of our companies
10   nineteen sixty two was sixty eight for men and seventy fiv
```

Figure 8.10 The pragmatic association of *sixty*

the world' (p. 77); whereas *round the world* tends to be used literally and this explains its lower frequency of use. Similarly, when a word is polysemous (i.e., it has more than on meaning), its collocations, semantic associations and colligations convey its meaning in that context of use (p. 87). Hoey (2005) gives the example of *consequence* (meaning result) versus *consequence* (meaning importance) and points out that while the former collocates with *any* the latter does not, and while the later collocates with *of*, the former does not. Also, *consequence* (meaning result) has a pattern of colligation with subject and complement, but *consequence* (meaning importance) does not.

Words are also primed to occur in, or avoid, certain positions within the discourse and these are its textual colligations (pp. 129–33). This type of association is illustrated in Figures 8.11 and 8.12 using samples of concordance lines form the HKCSE (http://rcpce.engl.polyu.edu.hk/HKCSE/). The lines show how the two words *well* and *anyway* tend to be found at the beginning or end of utterances respectively. To help you interpret the lines, it is useful to know that, in the HKCSE, speakers are indicated by a letter (plus number) plus colon.

Of course, both *well* and *anyway* can occur elsewhere in an utterance and this may impact their meaning and/or function. For example, when *anyway* is used at the beginning of an utterance it typically signals a change in topic whereas at the end of an utterance it seems to signal turn completion.

Hoey's (2005) notion of 'lexical priming' fits well with Sinclair's five categories of co-selection. As Hoey states: 'my claim is that priming contextualizes theoretically and psychologically Sinclair's insights about the lexicon' (p. 158). Lexical priming, then, explains the processes by which we learn the patterns of co-selection (i.e. the phraseology) which make up language in use.

```
1 n this six hours  a1: er well according to the concordance I
2       ** ah (pause)  b: well actually * this morning  B:**
3 iven or what  a2: well *  well actually I I I I expect them
4 w I I I * I a: ** why B: well because of the hepatitis scar
5 for me she found him  b: well (.) her office is just next to
6 y pages of the bill  B1: well I agree but most of the bill m
7 use) Secretary Tsang  b: well I am for me it's er er the um
8 ver the twelve years  b: well I mean actually I used to feel
9 hink it is how real  y1: well I think I think it's er also i
10  cope do you agree  b3: well if they can make a very good o
11 at did she do wrong  b: well she er came home very late * a
12   I I will find out  A: well tell me which card it is becau
```

Figure 8.11 Textual colligation: *well*

```
1 ** but you just check it anyway a: mhm mm  B1: cos that's th
2 ould want * some of that anyway a1: ** um ** end ** end of M
3  appropriate one (.) but anyway all you have to bear in mind
4 w whether I will be here anyway ((B and b laugh))b: I think
5 we have * cut a few down anyway b: ** mm  b: mm (.) but thi
6 they own Hong Kong Star anyway b: ah yeah  yeah  * now
7 be right  ((pause)) b:  anyway B: doesn't matter  b: doesn
8 h)) we've a battery sign anyway B: good  b: so I suppose it
9 talk or talk false there anyway b: Si Tung there are stones
10   b: they have to do it anyway B: yeah   b: right thirty p
11 r nothing to talk about anyway B1: mhm  x: but why are the
12 r nothing to talk about anyway B1: mhm  x: but why are the
```

Figure 8.12 Textual colligation: *anyway*

Conclusion

In this last chapter, we have looked at a number of key approaches and theories in corpus linguistics. For corpus linguists, the principled design and collection of naturally occurring texts for their corpora are paramount in order to support their empirical research. The approach taken by corpus linguists in their research is also critical. Should the researcher adopt a top-down corpus-based approach or a bottom-up corpus-driven approach? The decision is not unimportant because it may very well influence what is discovered. The division between form and meaning has been steadily eroded by the plentiful evidence of corpus linguistics to the point where the two aspects are better conceived of as one. Finally, we have reviewed how speakers and writers make five kinds of co-selection when they produce units of meaning (lexical items), and the process of lexical priming explains how we learn these and other patterns of co-selection.

Commentary on selected tasks

The tasks in this book are intended to promote the exploration of corpus linguistics and language learning, to be a source of discussion, and to be a catalyst for further corpus linguistic studies. For those tasks that are based on the study of specific corpora, or the analysis of data provided in the task, this section provides brief commentaries and/or sample analyses to offer both guidance and points for further discussion. Readers' own analyses and discussions will, hopefully, contribute considerably more to those presented here. Tasks that require readers to create or choose their own corpus to work with are not included.

Tasks in Chapter 2

Task 2.4

The potential difficulty is that the corpus of response letters cannot be analysed by a software program directly. It would first need to be manually analysed and classified into three sub-corpora: opening, body and close. Then the sub-corpus of the body of the letters could be examined.

Task 2.5

The spoken academic corpus could be further examined to find out, for example, whether it is the teacher or the student who produces the thanking act more frequently, the context in which they produce the thanking act, particularly to which utterance function the thanking act responds, and so on.

Task 2.6

Quantitative findings such as frequencies and percentages, which can be obtained by searching a corpus for the pronouns *I* and *we*, can provide objective evidence to support statements about the relative importance of these pronouns, compared to, for example, other pronouns in the corpus. Concordance lines for *I* and *we* can also be generated for additional analysis (see later chapters).

Task 2.7

Depending on your interest, and very often and most importantly, whether recording in the organisation is permitted, you would talk to people in the organisation to find out about important specialised genres. The genres could be written or spoken. Once the texts of the genre have been merged together, you could conduct corpus searches to find out word frequencies and other features (see Chapters 5–8).

Tasks in Chapter 3

Task 3.1

Useful corpora might include:

- a cross-section of spoken university English (e.g., lectures, tutorials, presentations by students, supervision meeting);
- a cross-section of written university English (e.g., student's assignments, notes, course handouts, textbooks, articles).

The above corpora could be organised based on genre and also discipline or field of study.

Orientation might be to look for key words by comparing your corpora with general English. You might compare written university English with spoken. Also, genres and disciplines/fields could be compared.

Task 3.2

1 Mode: spoken.

2 Type: lectures, seminars, supervisions, student presentations.

3 Domain: academic.

4 Language: English.

Task 3.3

Specific purpose for compilation: To benefit engineering professionals, academics and students locally and internationally. Also, to learn more about the language of the engineering industry, in particular the study of the patterns of use of specific words and phrases.

Contextualization: Professional engineering settings in which the texts are read, listened to.

Types of text/discourse: For example, transaction proceedings, handbooks, ordinances, media releases and publicity materials.

Subject matter/topic: Engineering.

Variety of English: Hong Kong English.

Task 3.5

The table below illustrates the fact that language use is dynamic because the use of different words and phrases can be seen to increase or decline over time. For example, the word *guy* has become increasingly popular, whereas *Madam* is used less today than before. Similarly, use of the modals *must* and *ought to* are in relative decline:

Word(s)	1920s	1960s	2000s
must	4,052	7,109	1,808
ought to	369	614	178
going to	887	2,284	2,146
guy	112	627	1,164
Madam	16	60	7

Task 3.8

In both the spoken and written components of the BoE, the most frequent words are function (grammatical) words, and the most frequent lexical words are nouns, verbs and adjectives. The function words create frameworks for the lexical words, and the most frequent lexical words tend to be about people and time, involving the most common material and mental processes, and interestingly, the most common modifiers are both positive.

The most frequent words in the spoken sub-corpus of the BoE reflects the higher level of interactivity of spoken language with lots of discourse markers and phatics used by speakers. Also, the shared context and shared experiences of the speakers allows more vague language usage (e.g., *sort* and *thing*) and checking understanding between the participants is one reason for the frequent use of *mean*.

Task 3.10

In lines 1–11, *thing* functions as a proform or vagueness marker. In lines 12–20, *thing* functions to preface a reason, point or new information.

Task 3.11

round as a noun: lines 8, 9, 16, 18
round as an adjective: lines 6, 10, 15, 17
round as a preposition: lines 1–5, 12, 14
round as an adverbial particle: lines 7, 11, 13, 19, 20

Task 3.12

Function 1 – lines 2, 5, 6
Function 2 – lines 1, 3, 8
Function 3 – lines 4, 7, 9, 10

Task 3.13

The co-selections made with *disposable income* tell us whose income it is in this context and how it is calculated. We can see that it is the income of the *public* and of the *population*, and that it is calculated *per capita*. In addition, we can see that disposable income is calculated for different groups in the total population, such as *urban households*.

Task 3.15

Among the top ten, six lexical verbs are common: *says* and *said*, *makes* and *made*, *comes* and *came*, *goes* and *went*, *takes* and *took*, and *looks* and *looked*. Except for the top [VVD] *said* (176,671 instances, versus *says*, 39,352 instances), all the other nine past tense form verbs are two to four times more frequent than the present tense form verbs.

Task 3.16

Focusing use of *physical* is found in lines 2–7, 20.

Task 3.17

Metaphorical use of *fruit* is found in lines 2–4, 6, 7, 11–15, 18–20.

Task 3.18

Lines 1–3: *it* as a pronoun
Lines 4–6: *it*-cleft structure

Task 3.19

Global in these concordance lines is co-selected with, for example, *financial crisis, slowdown, warming, recession, havoc, meltdown, deepening, slowed* and *precipice*. *Global* is further reinforcing these words by expressing the extent of the *crisis, recession*, etc. These co-selections, therefore, create a semantic prosody of a catastrophe of great magnitude.

Task 3.21

In these concordances lines, *I think* is often used as a hedge. There are many reasons why a speaker hedges, for example, because what the speaker says might contradict the previous speaker (see line 1), or the speaker is unsure of the accuracy of what he/she is saying (see line 4), or the speaker gives a reason (see line 15).

Task 3.22

To the left of 'reply', there are often words of appreciation. When used as a noun, 'reply' can be preceded by the pronoun 'your' or adjectives 'favourable', 'prompt' and 'kind'. To the right of 'right', there are often dates or deadlines, urgency ('as soon as possible' and 'at your earliest convenience'). The use and functions associated with 'reply' reflect the nature of business correspondence.

Tasks in Chapter 4

Task 4.1

Examples of some similarities:

* The definite article *the* tops the list of both corpora (although the proportional use is higher in the BNC because it is mostly comprised of written texts and so has more nominal groups requiring the definite article).

* The preposition *to* and the conjunction *and* are also in the top six in both lists.

- Two of the most frequent lexical words in both corpora are *time* and *people*.

Examples of some differences:

- There are some 'words' that are special to spoken language such as the fillers *er*, *um* and *erm*.
- Also, words that are more likely to be used organisationally as discourse markers than for conveying propositional meaning (e.g., <u>*well I don't know*</u> versus *I'm not well*) are found high up in the spoken corpus list (e.g., *so*, *okay*, *now* and *well*). When we write, there are other means of organising the text.
- The word *yes* is not in the BNC list, but it is found in the spoken corpus list along with other manifestations (*yeah*, *mm* and *mhm*). This illustrates the more interactive nature of spoken language.
- Another illustration of the greater interactivity of spoken language is the more frequent use of person pronouns in the spoken corpus. For example, *you* and *I* are in the top six in the spoken corpus.

Task 4.5

The collocates with the highest frequencies in the corpus – *the*, *and*, *a*, *in*, *it*, *was* and *or* – all fit the pattern of downward collocates described by Sinclair (1991), as they are not lexical words. There are then a number of words that, while they are more frequent than *cold*, could be classified as upward collocates, as they tell us something about the semantics of *cold* – *war*, *water*, *air*. Those with a lower frequency – *hot*, *weather*, *winter*, *wet*, *ice*, *wind* and *blooded* – all fit the description of a downward collocate.

Task 4.6

Some examples of collocates of *value*:

- *added* (N+1), *economic* (N+2), *activities* (N+3), *high* (N–1), *add* (N–1)

Some examples of collocates of *committed*:

- *government* (N–2, N–1), *are* (N–1), *is* (N–1), *we* (N–2)

Some examples of collocates of *private*:

- *sector* (N+1), *sectors* (N+1), *hospital* (N+1, N+3), *hospitals* (N–2, N+1, N+2), *promote* (N–1, N–3), *development* (N+2, N–2).

In the cases of the different word forms, *add* and *added* in Figure 4.5 and *sector* and *sectors* in Figure 4.7, there seems to be no great difference in these co-selections in terms of the lexical items they are part of.

Task 4.7

Mostly the 'negative' grammatical category takes the form of *n't* or *not* (e.g., lines 3, 10). At other times it is conveyed in the verb preceding *budge* (e.g., *refused* in line 1) and sometimes by a noun and noun phrase (e.g., *refusal* in line 19 and *vain attempts* in line 9).

Dictionary definitions tend to be something such as 'to move a little', whereas the meaning seems to be 'unwilling or unable to move a little'.

Task 4.8

In Figure 4.10, *care* is preceded at N–1 by a modifier.
In Figure 4.11, *private* is followed at N+1 by a noun.
In Figure 4.12, *hospital* is preceded at N–1 by a determiner and an article.

Task 4.9

Tagging these words (i.e., *burn* and *claim*) would enable them to be more easily studied in contexts where they are a verb or a noun, for example.

Task 4.10

Hong Kong Engineering Corpus (HKEC):
Frequency of *risk* and *management* with a span of 2–281.
Frequency of *risk* and *management* with a span of 5–332.
A span of five words captures instances with substantial variation (e.g., developing *management* systems that minimise the *risk* of unforeseen problems), but also some which are not associated (e.g., financial *management* and the trade-off between *risk* and expected return).

Hong Kong Financial Services Corpus (HKFSC):
Frequency of *risk* and *management* with a span of 2–1,390.
Frequency of *risk* and *management* with a span of 5–1,543.

HKFSC – Annual reports:
Frequency of *risk* and *management* with a span of 2–386.
Frequency of *risk* and *management* with a span of 5–437.

HKFSC – Media releases:
Frequency of *risk* and *management* with a span of 2–38.
Frequency of *risk* and *management* with a span of 5–39.

The phrase *risk* plus *management* is more common in the HKFSC, suggesting that the phrase is register-specific because of the greater need to 'manage risk' in the financial world than in engineering. It can also be seen to be genre-specific in the HKFSC with more instances of the phrase in annual reports than media releases. One of the expectations of an annual report is that it needs to outline how risk is managed in the organisation.

Tasks in Chapter 5

Task 5.3

Expressing relations of time and place.

Task 5.4

1 Assuming common ground.

2 Monitoring the shared versus new knowledge between the speaker and the hearer.

3 Hedging.

4 Assuming common ground.

5 Monitoring the shared versus new knowledge between the speaker and the hearer.

6 Assuming common ground.

Task 5.5

1 *sort of*

2 *and all the rest of it*

3 *and stuff*

4 *and all that sort of thing*

5 *and stuff like that*

6 *a lot of things, a bit of everything.*

Task 5.6

1 *in the first place*

2 *but at the same time*

3 *as a result of*

4 *on the other hand*

5 *in the same way*

6 *as a consequence of.*

Task 5.7

Some examples of turn introduction n-grams:
and then, and this, and I also, and now, and so, and what, alright okay, alright well, alright yes, I know, I mean, I think, I see, no no, right now, so I, so now, so what, so you, yeah well, yeah yeah.

Some examples of turn allocation n-grams:
bye bye, can you, do you, I don't know, in Hong Kong, no idea, thank you, that's it, something like that, things like that, you know, what do you think.

Task 5.9

	HKEC	*HKFSC*	*HKCSE*
carry out	1,511	183	36
carries out	98	35	0
carried out	3,764	468	15

All of the forms are most frequent in the engineering corpus, which suggests that this tells us something regarding the aboutness of engineering texts – engineers spend a lot of their time 'carrying out' procedures and processes. Also, *carried out* is the most common form in the engineering texts and this seems to be because engineers often report on what they have carried out or have to consult rules and regulations as to how things should be carried out (e.g., *Wastewater monitoring was carried out by ET*, and *a fatigue calculation should be carried out*).

Task 5.10

Lines 7 and 18 are not metaphorical. Line 7 refers to the actual colour of the T Ford car and line 18 is a surname.

Task 5.11

Some examples of metaphor-related n-grams:

- *red chip* (refers to major Mainland Chinese companies listed in Hong Kong).

- *red tape* (administrative procedures which are seen as unnecessary and inefficient).

- *green building* (a building which is environmentally friendly).

- *green management* (a management which is environmentally aware and pro-active).

- *speculative attack* (mainly refers to speculation against the Hong Kong dollar).

- *currency attack* (mainly refers to speculation against the Hong Kong dollar).

- *defend the link* (typically involves government and monetary officials reaffirming existing policies with regard to the Hong Kong dollar).

- *defend the Hong Kong dollar* (typically involves government and monetary officials reaffirming existing policies with regard to the Hong Kong dollar).

- *surrender benefits* (the benefits to be had from cashing in a financial product).

- *minimum surrender period* (the minimum period of time a financial product must be owned before it can be cashed in).

Task 5.12

Dictionaries tend to define 'duplication' as simply the act or process of duplicating something. However, examining a corpus suggests that the definition should be expanded to be the act or process of duplicating something which should be avoided if possible (e.g., *the case for R&D agreements is partly that they avoid wasteful duplication of research* and *as items are chosen they are crossed off the list to avoid duplication, and a note will be made of the donor's name*).

Task 5.13

Core – work.

Collocates – *high value added economic activities, add value, high value-added.*

Colligates – to the left of *concern*, the use of present perfect (progressive) and some form of quantifying the extent of concern; to the right of *concern*, present (past) perfect followed by source of concern.

Semantic preference – the provision of services here is in the context of business-related activities.

Semantic prosody – red tape is something unwelcome or unnecessary and needs to removed or cut back because it obstructs competitiveness and the streamlining of procedures.

Task 5.14

Extract 1
Marked usage – *capacity crowd.* Used to describe a relatively small gathering of distinguished guests.

Unmarked usage, confirmed in the BNC, is a large gathering of people typically to watch a sporting event or a large outdoor pop concert (e.g., *A capacity crowd of nearly 6,500, including King Juan Carlos and Queen Sofia, went wild as their 28-year-old world champion went for her own golden bid* and *The match will be all-ticket with an anticipated 25,000 capacity crowd*).

Extract 2
Marked usage – *incessant.* Used to describe the extent to which the discourse particle has been studied and which the writer intends to study once more.

Unmarked usage, confirmed in the BNC, is when incessant collocates with something unpleasant which can't be stopped (e.g., *They fouled their corners and filled the hot room with their smells, and they frightened him with their incessant snarling* and *The nauseating taste of the worm-cakes and the humiliation of the treatment were only outweighed by the sheer relief of being freed from an incessant itching in his backside*).

Extract 3
Marked usage – *compounded by.* Used when good news is supported by more good news.

Unmarked usage, confirmed in the BNC, is when bad news or a bad situation is *compounded by* more bad news or another bad situation (e.g., *These shortcomings are clearly compounded by the difficulty of creating new titles* and *This group's inferior class position is linked to their families' origins as immigrants, and is compounded by poor incomes and racism*).

Scenario
Describing your teacher as elegant is an unmarked compliment confirmed in the BNC (e.g., *She was impressed by how elegant she looked and Ms Fancourt was superb and Ms Coyne would make walking to the bus stop seem a provocative and elegant statement*).

However, describing your teacher as trendy is marked if it is intended as a compliment. The BNC confirms that it is used to describe unconventional people or ideas that are disapproved of, or to describe transient and unattractive fashions (e.g., *Foodie-ism is the logical conclusion of the new Me generation, the I'm-alright-Jacks, the professional ex-carers and the trendy new right* and *They were all in very trendy clothes —; fluorescent shellsuits, gold and silver lame baseball caps*).

Task 5.15

economic/provide – co-occurrences in lines 1–4; meaningfully associated in lines 5–8
additional/provide – meaningfully associated in lines 1–10
development/promote – meaningfully associated in lines 1–13
economic/new – meaningfully associated in lines 4–5; others are co-occurrences
business/Hong Kong – co-occurrences in lines 1–3, 5–6; meaningfully associated in line 4.

Task 5.16

I mean – lines 1, 6, 9
I think – lines 2, 4, 7
so – lines 3, 5, 8
I believe – line 10.

Tasks in Chapter 6

Task 6.4

Literal uses of *attack*: hurt, illness, heart attack, panic attack, violent act.
Metaphorical uses of *attack*: criticize, criticism, ridicule, deal with.
Literal uses of *attack*: Lines 1, 3, 5, 7.
Metaphorical uses of *attack*: Lines 2, 4, 6, 8, 9, 10.

Glossary

aboutness
the words and phrases that differentiate a particular text or corpus by denoting the main contents.

annotation
additional information or codes inserted into a corpus, including tagging and parsing (see also 'automatic tagging' and 'tag').

associated words
words in a concgram that create (part of) a unit of meaning (i.e. a phraseology).

attested
solid evidence, which in corpus linguistics, usually means naturally occurring language.

automatic tagger
software that automatically inserts additional information (a 'tag') into a corpus (e.g. whether a word is a noun or a verb) (see also 'annotation').

bottom-up approach
an approach to language that is driven by evidence from the corpus data to arrive at theory (see also 'corpus-driven' and 'inductive').

canonical meaning
the central meaning of a word or phrase.

colligation
the grammatical company that a word or phrase is associated with; for example, the co-selection of certain word classes or structural patterns to the left and right of the search item.

collocate
a collocate of a word is a word that is co-selected to create an extended unit of meaning (e.g. *happy + new + year* are collocates).

collocation
words collocate when they are co-selected by the speaker or writer and they are not a chance co-occurrence. There are statistical measures to determine the significance of the collocation.

collocational framework
two or more grammatical words that frame sections of text

concgram
two or more words that co-occur irrespective of constituency and positional variation.

concgram configuration
a concgram is made up of words which exhibit variation and can be described in terms of their respective patterns (configurations).

concordance
a list of all the instances of a search item with an amount of co-text either side of the centred search item.

concordance line
a line in a concordance.

constituency variation
occurs when a word or words intervene between associated words (e.g. *work hard*, *work so hard*, *work very very hard*).

co-occurring words
words in a concgram that do not create (part of) a unit of meaning.

core
the invariable word or words in a lexical item, and is one of the obligatory co-selections in a lexical item.

corpora
plural of 'corpus'.

corpus
a specifically designed collection of texts that is machine-readable.

corpus-based
an approach to corpus studies that uses a corpus to confirm an existing theory (see also 'top-down approach).

corpus-driven
an approach to corpus studies that is based on first analysing corpus data and then developing theory (see also 'bottom-up approach').

co-selection
meaning is created by the speaker or writer making multiple choices (i.e. co-selections). These consist of up to five choices: semantic prosody, the core, semantic preference, collocation and colligation.

co-text
the surrounding text that provides information for readers and hearers to interpret meanings.

cultural schemata
an individual's schemata are all her/his previously established patterns of experience, knowledge and belief that can be used to interpret language in context. These can vary across cultures and so some are culture-specific.

data-driven learning
the use of students' own of studies of corpora to enhance their knowledge of the target language.

deductive
(see 'top-down approach').

extended unit of meaning
individual words are not the source of meaning. The speaker or writer makes multiple selections to create meaning and these co-selections mean that meaning creation extends across multiple words.

external criteria
used when deciding what texts, and the size of their representation, to include in a corpus.

general corpus
a large corpus which attempts to represent the general usage of a language through the careful selection of a cross-section of texts.

idiom principle
based on the idea that speakers and writers are restrained in language production by, for example, register, genre and the co-selections which comprise lexical items.

inductive
(see 'bottom-up approach').

internal criteria
used when deciding what to analyse in a corpus.

intertextuality
the ways in which each text, whether spoken or written, is interconnected with others texts.

key word
a word that is found significantly more often in a corpus when compared with another corpus.

keyness
the notion that corpora can be distinguished by their key words; it is a measure of saliency (prominence).

KWIC
Key Word In Context (KWIC), refers to the onscreen display of a concordance in which the search word (node) under examination is centred, with co-text either side of the search word.

language pattern
a recurrent use of language in a corpus.

language variety
in the case of English, there are different varieties of the language; for example, Australian English, Indian English and British English.

learner corpus
a corpus comprised of texts spoken and/or written by learners of the language.

lemma
the canonical form of a word; for example, *GO* is a lemma made up of *go*, *goes*, *going*, *went* and *gone*.

lemmatisation
a way of annotating a corpus so that all the forms of lemma can be found in one search; for example, a search for *get* would also find *gets*, *getting* and *got*.

lexical bundle
a pattern of two or more adjacent words (also known as n-grams, lexical chunks and lexical clusters).

lexical chunk
(see lexical bundle).

lexical cluster
(see lexical bundle).

lexical density
the percentage of words in a text or corpus that are lexical rather than grammatical.

lexical item
consists of up to five categories of co-selections by a speaker or writer, two of which are obligatory (semantic prosody and the core) and three are optional (semantic preference, collocation and colligation).

lexical priming
the process by which we become competent language users through experiencing language patterns.

lexical semantics
studies the meanings of words, and the meaningful relationships between them.

lingua franca
a common language used by individuals to communicate when they have different mother tongues.

local grammar
a grammar that describes the language features of specific language patterns or specific kinds of language use.

machine-readable
can be accessed and searched via computer software.

marked
language use that is not ordinary, usual, expected.

meaning potential
conveys the notion that meaning is not fixed because the same words have the potential to create different meanings in different contexts of situation.

message-oriented element
a term from linear unit grammar (LUG) to describe a chunk of language that is primarily propositional.

mode
the form of communication used; for example, computer mediated or spoken.

move
a text is made up of moves each of which represents a different communicative function.

move structure
the ways in which moves may be organised in a text.

multi-modal corpus
a corpus that contains more than one written text or orthographically transcribed spoken text in order to include other modes of communication such as non-verbal behaviour, the use of images and so on.

multi-word unit
(see 'extended unit of meaning').

n-gram
two or more consecutive words that form an identifiable pattern in a corpus (also known as 'lexical bundles', 'lexical chunks' and 'lexical clusters').

node
the centred search item in a concordance.

normalise
a process to enable direct comparisons to be made easier when comparing datasets of different sizes. The frequencies of one set of findings are adjusted to compensate for the difference.

online corpus
a corpus accessible via the internet.

open-choice principle
the idea that the only restraint in language production is that each choice must be grammatical.

organisational framework
two or more conjunctions, connectors or discourse markers that frame sections of a text.

organisation-oriented element
a term from linear unit grammar (LUG) to describe a chunk of language that functions primarily to organise the text.

orthographic transcription
the transcription of spoken discourse that only includes the words spoken and ignores other features such as intonation and extralinguistic features.

parsing
the process whereby a corpus is annotated for syntactic structures such as noun groups, verb groups and clauses.

part-of-speech tagging
the process of annotating a corpus to enable searches based on grammatical categories such as nouns, modal verbs, and prepositions (see 'tag').

phraseological skeleton
a core component of a phraseological unit that can be added to in order to create a variety of forms.

phraseological tendency
the way in which meanings are created by combinations of associated words.

phraseological variation
many phraseologies are not fixed and can be realised in a variety of forms.

phraseology
the study of the ways in which words combine in patterns of co-selections.

politeness
in pragmatics, politeness consists of strategies employed by participants in spoken and written discourse to best achieve their communicative goals in a particular context while attempting to maintain, or even enhance, their relationship with the hearer or reader.

PoS-gram
two or more grammatical categories, or parts-of-speech (POS), which constitute a language pattern.

positional variation
occurs when associated words combine in different positions relative to one another (e.g. *work hard* versus *hard work*).

prosodically transcribed
spoken textual data transcribed in terms of discourse intonation (e.g. key, termination, prominence and tone).

qualitative approach
a corpus is analysed by, for example, examining individual texts contained within it to provide empirical support for the working hypothesis, principle or rule.

quantitative approach
a corpus is examined for frequency information for words, phrases and other linguistics features.

reference corpus
a corpus designed to be representative of a language in order to provide comprehensive information about the language.

register
a variety of language defined according to its use in social situations (e.g. legal English, engineering English, and medical English).

register-based corpora
corpora that are designed to contain language drawn from specific registers (see 'register').

rhetoric
the effective use of language to achieve a particular purpose.

rhetorical function
the communicative function of a given unit of a discourse.

scaffolding
support strategies provided to learners or speakers to help them achieve a higher level of competence.

semantic preference
the semantic environment in which a lexical item is typically used.

semantic prosody
the attitudinal meaning, often pragmatic, of a lexical item.

skipgram
two or more words, which co-occur in fixed sequence in a corpus, whether or not a limited number of intervening words are found between them (e.g. *a lot of people* and *a lot of different people*).

'slot and filler' model
(see 'open-choice principle').

span
the number of words either side of a search item to set the parameters when searching for co-occurrences of words.

specialised corpus
a corpus designed to contain a collection of texts of a specific type and communicative purposes.

speech act
a chunk of language defined by its specific function (e.g. request, offer, confirm).

sub-corpus
texts in a corpus that can be grouped together based on specified criteria and machine-readable.

tagging
procedures carried out to add a code to each word in a corpus such as parts of speech.

token
each word in a corpus irrespective of whether or not it is repeated.

top-down approach
a methodology based on deductive reasoning that aims to test or exemplify theories and descriptions. (See also 'deductive' and 'corpus-based').

type
each distinct word in a corpus (a frequency count of types does not include repeats of each distinct word – see also 'token').

type/token ratio
the proportions of distinct words and total number of words in a corpus.

unmarked
language use that is ordinary, usual, expected.

utterance final
language use that is found at the end of an utterance.

utterance initial
language use that is found at the beginning of an utterance.

utterance medial
language use that is found in the middle of an utterance.

Further reading

The following is a suggested list of additional reading that you might like to consult. The references below do not appear in the main text. The brief comment after each reference is intended for guidance only.

Books

Adolphs, S. (2011) *Multi-modal spoken corpus analysis*. London: Routledge.
This book offers the most up-to-date account of a burgeoning new field – multi-modal corpus (and discourse) analysis.

Bondi, M. and Scott, M. (eds) (2010) *Keyness in texts*. Amsterdam: John Benjamins.
This excellent collection of papers provides the latest insights into how keyness can be determined and the implications of such studies for our understanding of language use.

de Klerk, V. (2011) *Corpus linguistics and world Englishes: An analysis of Xhosa English*. London: Continuum.
The corpus linguistic analysis of varieties of English has increased in popularity and this book is a very good example of how different Englishes can be compared.

Farr, F. (2011) *The discourse of teaching practice feedback: A corpus-based investigation of spoken and written modes*. New York: Routledge.
The study aims to investigate the salient aspects responsible for making teaching practice feedback both effective and affective.

Flowerdew, L. (2008) *Corpus-based analyses of the problem-solution pattern. A phraseological approach*. Amsterdam: John Benjamins.
Illustrates how corpus linguistics can be used to analyse the rhetorical structures of texts.

Frankenberg-Garcia, A., Flowerdew, L. and Aston, G. (eds) (2011) *New trends in corpora and language learning*. London: Continuum.
All the latest applications of corpus linguistics in language learning and teaching are covered in this thought-provoking collection of papers.

Hunston, S. (2010) *Corpus approaches to evaluation. Phraseology and evaluative language*. New York: Routledge.
This book applies a set of corpus investigation techniques to the study of evaluation, or stance, or affect, in naturally occurring discourse.

Knight, D. (2011) *Language, corpus and gesture: A multimodal corpus approach*. London: Continuum.
How should we tackle the difficulties of capturing all of the multi-layered features of multi-modal discourse in a corpus? This book describes a range of options in a reader-friendly style.

Mahlberg, M. (2011) *Corpus stylistics and Dickens's fiction*. London: Routledge.
This book demonstrates how corpus linguistics can provide us with exciting new insights into stylistics, and literary studies generally.

McEnery, T. and Xiao, R. (2010) *Corpus-based contrastive studies of English and Chinese*. New York: Routledge.
The corpus studies in this book comprise cross-linguistic contrast of major grammatical categories in English and Chinese, two of the most important yet different world languages.

Murphy, B. (2010) *Corpus and sociolinguistics. Investigating age and gender in female talk*. Amsterdam: John Benjamins.
This book shows how corpus linguistics can complement more traditional sociolinguistic studies to offer new insights into female talk across generational divides.

Philip, G. (2011) *Colouring meaning. Collocation and connotation in figurative language*. Amsterdam: John Benjamins.
This fascinating study makes use of corpora to examine figurative language use with respect to colour, and the variety of forms such language can take.

Quaglio, P. (2009) *Television dialogue. The sitcom 'Friends' vs. natural conversation*. Amsterdam: John Benjamins.
An inherently interesting study thanks to its choice of data, which provides lots of examples of how to conduct a comparative study using corpora.

Journal articles

The following is a list of key papers that have been published on issues relating to corpus linguistics in the past few years:

Biber, D. (2006) 'Stance in spoken and written university registers', *Journal of English for Academic Purposes*, 5: 97–116; *International Journal of Corpus Linguistics*, 14/3: 275–311.
The study compares and contrasts the use of a wide range of lexico-grammatical features used for the expression of stance in spoken and written university registers.

Cheng, W. and Lam, P. (2010) 'Media discourses in Hong Kong: Change in representation of human rights', *Text & Talk*, 30/5: 507–27.
Through analysing the extended units of meaning of lexical items, the study examines the portrayal of human rights in Hong Kong in articles in a leading local English newspaper before and after the handover 1997.

Fischer-Starke, B. (2009) 'Keywords and frequent phrases of Jane Austen's Pride and Prejudice: A corpus-stylistic analysis', *International Journal of Corpus Linguistics*, 14/4: 492–523.
Through the analyses of keywords and most frequent phrases, the corpus stylistic study uncovers literary meanings of fiction texts that are left undetected by the intuitive analyses of literary criticism.

Groom, N. (2005) 'Pattern and meaning across genres and disciplines: An exploratory study', *Journal of English for Academic Purposes*, 4: 257–77.
The corpus study compares the introductory *it* patterns with that-clause and to-clause complementation to find out how they are realised in two genres and two disciplines.

Hyland, K. (2008) 'As can be seen: Lexical bundles and disciplinary variation'. *English for Specific Purposes*, 27: 4–21.
This study compares the forms, structures and functions of 4-word bundles in a corpus of academic writing in four disciplines in terms of disciplinary variations in their frequencies and preferred uses.

Lam, P. (2009) 'The making of a BNC customised spoken corpus for comparative purposes', *Corpora*, 4/2: 167–88.
The process of building a tailor-made spoken corpus out of the BNC is described and the practical issues involved in selecting specific texts from the BNC spoken sub-section are discussed.

Morley, J. (2006) 'Lexical cohesion and rhetorical structure', *International Journal of Corpus Linguistics*, 11/3: 265–82.
A corpus of newspaper texts is examined to explore the rhetorical structure of phrases in the thematic position in terms of how the phrases trigger evaluation in the form of counter arguments.

Römer, U. (2009) 'The inseparability of lexis and grammar: Corpus linguistic perspectives', *Annual Review of Cognitive Linguistics*, 7, 141–63.
The study explores the use of a selected lexical-grammatical patterns, such as the introductory *it* pattern in corpora of expert and apprentice academic writing.

Vefali, G.M. and Erdentug, F. (2010) 'The coordinate structures in a corpus of New Age talks: "man and woman"/"woman and man"', *Text & Talk*, 30/4: 465–84.
The study examines the coordinate structures 'man and woman' and 'woman and man' in a specialised corpus of gender-related talk to better understand gender construal.

Wong, M.L.Y. (2010) 'Expressions of gratitude by Hong Kong speakers of English: Research from the International Corpus of English in Hong Kong (ICE-HK)', *Journal of Pragmatics*, 42/5: 1243–57.
The main findings in this study are that the Hong Kong speakers of English do not employ a wide variety of thanking strategies compared to other groups of speakers discussed in other studies because Chinese may be too reserved to express their gratitude openly and explicitly.

References

Aarts, J. and Granger, S. (1998) 'Tag sequences in learner corpora: A key to interlanguage grammar and discourse', in S. Granger (ed.), *Learner English on computer*. Boston, MA: Addison Wesley, pp. 132–41.

Adolphs, S. (2008) *Corpus and context: Investigating pragmatic functions in spoken discourse*. Amsterdam: John Benjamins.

Ahmad, K. (2005) 'Terminology in text', Tuscan Word Centre Workshop. Siena, Italy. June 2005.

Aijmer, K. (1986) 'Discourse variation and hedging', in J. Aarts and W. Meijsm (eds), *Corpus linguistics II. New studies in the analysis and exploitation of computer corpora*. Amsterdam: Rodopi, pp. 1–18.

Aijmer, K. (1996) *Conversational routines in English: Convention and creativity*. London: Longman.

Allen, C.M. (2005) *A local grammar of cause and effect: A corpus-driven study*. Unpublished Ph.D Thesis. Birmingham: University of Birmingham.

Allen, J. and Core, M. (1997) Draft of DAMSL: Dialog Act Markup in Several Layers, www.cs.rochester.edu/research/cisd/resources/damsl/.

Anthony, L. (2006) *Concordancing with AntConc – An Introduction to Tools and Techniques in Corpus Linguistics – Proceedings of the JACET 45th Annual Convention*, pp. 218–19.

Askehave, I. and Swales, J.M. (2001) 'Genre identification and communicative purpose: A problem and a possible solution', *Applied Linguistics*, 22/2: 195–212.

Baker, P., Hardie, A. and McEnery, T. (2006) *A glossary of corpus linguistics*. Edinburgh: Edinburgh University Press.

Barlow, G.M. (2008) *ParaConc and parallel corpora in contrastive and translation studies*. Houston, TX: Athelstan, p. 110.

Barnbrook, G. (1996) *Language and computers*. Edinburgh: Edinburgh University Press.

Barnbrook, G. (2002) *Defining language: A local grammar of definition sentences*. Amsterdam: John Benjamins.

Barnbrook, G. and Sinclair, J. McH. (2001) 'Specialised corpus, local and functional grammars', in M. Ghadessy, A. Henry and R.L. Roseberry (eds), *Small corpus studies and ELT*. Amsterdam: John Benjamins, pp. 237–76.

Bhatia, V.K. (1993) *Analysing genre: Language use in professional settings*. London: Longman.

Biber, D. (1988) *Variation across speech and writing*. Cambridge: Cambridge University Press.

Biber, D. (1995) *Dimensions of register variation: A cross-linguistic comparison*. Cambridge: Cambridge University Press.

Biber, D. (2006) *University language: A corpus-based study of spoken and written registers*. Amsterdam: John Benjamins.

Biber, D. (2009) 'A corpus-driven approach to formulaic language in English: Multi-word patterns in speech and writing', *International Journal of Corpus Linguistics*, 14/3: 275–311.

Biber, D. (2010) 'What can a corpus tell us about registers and genres?' in A. O'Keeffe and M. McCarthy (eds), *The Routledge handbook of corpus linguistics*. Abingdon: Routledge, pp. 241–54.

Biber, D., Connor, U. and Upton, T. (2007) *Discourse on the move: Using corpus analysis to describe discourse structure*, Amsterdam: John Benjamins.

Biber, D., Conrad, S. and Reppen, R. (1998) *Corpus linguistics: Investigating language structure and use*. Cambridge: Cambridge University Press.

Biber, D., Johansson, S., Leech, G., Conrad, S. and Finegan, E. (1999) *Longman grammar of spoken and written English*. Harlow: Longman.

Bondi, M. and Scott, M. (2010) *Keyness in text*. Amsterdam: John Benjamins.

Bowker, L. and Pearson, J. (2002) *Working with specialized language: A practical guide to using corpora*. London/New York: Routledge.

Brazil, D. (1997) *The communicative role of intonation in English*. Cambridge: Cambridge University Press.

Brown, P. and Levinson, S. (1978) 'Universals in language usage: Politeness phenomena', in E.N. Goody (ed.), *Questions and politeness: Strategies in social interaction*. Cambridge/New York: Cambridge University Press, pp. 56–311.

Brown, P. and Levinson, S. (1987) *Politeness: Some universals in language usage*. Cambridge: Cambridge University Press.

Butler, C. (1985) *Statistics in linguistics*. Blackwell: Oxford.

Cameron, L. (2010) 'The discourse dynamics framework for metaphor', in L. Cameron and R. Malsen (eds), *Metaphor analysis: Research in applied linguistics, social sciences and the humanities*. London: Equinox, pp. 77–97.

Carletta, J.C., Isard, A., Isard, S., Kowtko, J., Doherty-Sneddon, G. and Anderson, A. (1997) 'The reliability of a dialogue structure coding scheme', *Computational Linguistics*, 23/1: 13–31.

Carter, R. and McCarthy, M. (2006) *Cambridge grammar of English*. Cambridge: Cambridge University Press.

Carter, R., Hughes, R. and McCarthy, M. (2000) *Exploring grammar in context*. Cambridge: Cambridge University Press.

Chafe, W. (1982) 'Integration and involvement in speaking and writing, and oral literature', in D. Tannen (ed.), *Spoken and written language: Exploring orality and literacy*. Norwood, NJ: Ablex, pp. 35–53.

Channel, J. (2000) 'Corpus-based analysis of evaluative lexis', in S. Hunston and G. Thompson (eds), *Evaluation in text: Authorial stance and the construction of discourse*. Oxford: Oxford University Press, pp. 38–55.

Cheng, W. (2006) 'Describing the extended meanings of lexical cohesion in a corpus of SARS spoken discourse', in J. Flowerdew and M. Mahlberg (eds), *Special Issue of International Journal of Corpus Linguistics: Corpus Linguistics and Lexical Cohesion*, 11/3: 325–44.

Cheng, W. (2007) '"Sorry to interrupt, but . . .": Pedagogical implications of a spoken corpus', in M.C. Campoy-Cubillo and M.J. Luzon (eds), *Spoken corpora in applied linguistics*. Bern: Peter Lang, pp. 199–216.

Cheng, W. and Mok, E. (2008) 'Discourse processes and products: Land surveyors in Hong Kong', *English for Specific Purposes*, 27/1: 57–73.

Cheng, W. and Warren, M. (2005) '// → *well I have a DIFferent //* ↓ *THINking you know //*: A corpus-driven study of disagreement in Hong Kong business discourse', in F. Bargiela-Chiappini and M. Gotti (eds), *Asian Business Discourse(s)*. Frankfurt: Peter Lang, pp. 241–70.

Cheng, W. and Warren, M. (2006) 'I would say be very careful of . . .: Opine markers in an intercultural business corpus of spoken English', in J. Bamford and M. Bondi (eds), *Managing interaction in professional discourse. Intercultural and interdiscoursal perspectives*. Rome: Officina Edizioni, pp. 46–58.

Cheng, W. and Warren, M. (2007) 'Checking understandings in an intercultural corpus of spoken English', in A. O'Keefe and S. Walsh (eds), *Corpus-based studies of language awareness. Special issue of Language Awareness*, 16/3: 190–207.

Cheng, W., Greaves, C. and Warren, M. (2006) 'From n-gram to skipgram to concgram', *International Journal of Corpus Linguistics*, 11/4: 411–33.

Cheng, W., Greaves, C. and Warren, M. (2008) *A corpus-driven study of discourse intonation*. Amsterdam/Philadelphia, PA: John Benjamins.

Cheng, W., Warren, M. and Xu, X. (2003) 'The language learner as language researcher: Putting corpus linguistics on the timetable', *System*, 31/2: 173–86.

Cheng, W., Greaves, C., Sinclair, J. McH. and Warren, M. (2009) 'Uncovering the extent of the phraseological tendency: Towards a systematic analysis of concgrams', *Applied Linguistics*, 30/2: 236–52.

Cobuild, C. (2006) *Collins COBUILD advanced learner's English dictionary*. Glasgow: HarperCollins.

Conrad, S. (2010) 'What can a corpus tell us about grammar?' in A. O'Keeffe and M. McCarthy (eds), *The Routledge handbook of corpus linguistics*. Abingdon: Routledge, pp. 227–40.

Coulthard, M. and Johnson, A. (2007) *An introduction to forensic linguistics: Language in evidence*. London/New York: Routledge.

Crystal, D. (1992) *A dictionary of linguistics and phonetics* (3rd edition). Oxford: Blackwell.

Devitt, A.J. (1991) 'Intertextuality in tax accounting: Generic, referential, and functional', in C. Bazerman and J. Paradis (eds), *Textual dynamics of the professions: Historical and contemporary studies of writing in professional settings*. Madison, WI: University of Wisconsin Press, pp. 336–57.

Fairclough, N. (1995) *Critical discourse analysis*. London: Longman.

Fairclough, N. (2001) *Language and power* (2nd revised edition). London: Longman.

Firth, J.R. (1957) *Papers in linguistics 1934–51*. London: Oxford University Press.

Flowerdew, L. (2001) 'The exploitation of small learner corpora', in M. Ghadessy, A. Henry and R.L. Roseberry (eds), *Small corpus studies and ELT*. Amsterdam: John Benjamins, pp. 363–79.

Flowerdew, L. (2004) 'The argument for using English specialised corpora to understand academic and professional language', in U. Connor and T. Upton (eds), *Discourse in the professions: Perspectives from corpus linguistics*. Amsterdam: John Benjamins, pp. 11–33.

Francis, G. (1993) 'A corpus-driven approach to grammar – principles, methods and examples', in M. Baker, G. Francis and E. Tognini-Bonelli (eds), *Text and technology*. Amsterdam: John Benjamins, pp. 137–56.

Friginal, E. (2009) *The language of outsourced call centers: A corpus-based study of cross-cultural interaction*. Amsterdam: John Benjamins.

Fromkin, V., Rodman, R. and Hyams, N. (2011) *An introduction to language* (9th edition). Florence, KY: Wadsworth, Cengage Learning.

Granath, S. (2009) 'Who benefits from learning how to use corpora ?' in K. Aijmer (ed.), *Corpora and language teaching*. Amsterdam: John Benjamins, pp. 47–66.

Granger, S. (ed.) (1998) *Learner English on computer*. London: Longman.

Granger, S. (2009) International Corpus of Learner English – ICLE, Available from: http://cecl.fltr.ucl.ac.be/Cecl-Projects/Icle/icle.htm (last accessed: 27 September 2010).

Granger, S. and Rayson, P. (1998) 'Automatic profiling of learner texts', in S. Granger (ed.), *Learner English on computer*. London/New York: Longman, pp. 119–31.

Granger, S., Dagneaux, E., Meunier, F. and Paquot, M. (2009) *International corpus of learner English, version 2*. Louvain-la-Neuve: Presses Universitaires de Louvain.

Greaves, C. (2009) *ConcGram: A phraseological search engine*. Amsterdam: John Benjamins.

Greaves, C. and Warren, M. (2010a) 'Taking corpus linguistics mainstream: Corpora as a resource for professionals'. Paper presented at Interpreting Corpora: IVACS Annual International Symposium. Leeds University, UK.

Greaves, C. and Warren, M. (2010b) 'What can a corpus tell us about multi-word units?' in A. O'Keeffe and M. McCarthy (eds), *The Routledge handbook of corpus linguistics*. London: Routledge, pp. 212–26.

Greenbaum, S. (ed.) (1996) *Comparing English worldwide: The International Corpus of English*. Oxford: Clarendon Press.

Gries, S. Th. (2010) 'Corpus linguistics and theoretical linguistics: A love-hate relationship? Not necessarily . . .' *International Journal of Corpus Linguistics*, 15/3: 327–43.

Gross, M. (1993) 'Local grammars and their representation by finite automata', in M. Hoey (ed.), *Data, description, discourse*. London: HarperCollins, pp. 26–38.

Grundy, P. (2000) *Doing pragmatics* (1st edition). London: Edward Arnold.

Gu, Y. (2006) 'Multimodal text analysis: A corpus linguistic approach to situated discourse', *Text & Talk*, 26/2: 127–67.

Halliday, M.A.K. (1985) *Spoken and written language*. Oxford: Oxford University Press.

Halliday, M.A.K. (1987) 'Spoken and written modes of meaning', in R. Horowitz and S.J. Samuels (eds), *Comprehending oral and written language*. San Diego, CA: Academic Press, pp. 55–87.

Halliday, M.A.K. (1989) *Spoken and written language.* Oxford: Oxford University Press.

Halliday, M.A.K. (1993) 'Towards a language-based theory of learning', *Linguistics and Education,* 5: 93–116.

Halliday, M.A.K. and Hasan, R. (1989) *Language, context, and text: Aspects of language in a social-semiotic perspective.* Oxford: Oxford University Press.

Halliday, M.A.K. and Matthiessen, C. (2004) *An introduction to functional grammar* (3rd revised edition). London: Edward Arnold.

Harwood, N. (2005) '"Nowhere has anyone attempted . . . In this article I aim to do just that": A corpus-based study of self-promotional *I* and *we* in academic writing across four disciplines', *Journal of Pragmatics,* 37: 1207–31.

Herriman, J. and Aronsson, M.B. (2009) 'Themes in Swedish advanced learners' writing in English', in K. Aijmer (ed.), *Corpora and language teaching.* Amsterdam: John Benjamins, pp. 101–20.

Hillier, H. (2004) *Analysing real texts: Research studies in modern English language.* Basingstoke: Palgrave Macmillan.

Hoey, M. (2005) *Lexical priming: A new theory of language.* London: Routledge.

Hunston, S. (2002) *Corpora in applied linguistics.* Cambridge: Cambridge University Press.

Hunston, S. (2010) *Corpus approaches to evaluation: Phraseology and evaluative language.* London: Routledge.

Hunston, S. and Francis, G. (2000) *Pattern grammar: A corpus-driven approach to the lexical grammar of English.* Amsterdam: John Benjamins.

Hunston, S. and Sinclair, J. McH. (2000) 'A local grammar of evaluatiom', in S. Hunston and G. Thompson (eds), *Evaluation in text: Authorial stance and the construction of discourse.* Oxford: Oxford University Press, pp. 74–101.

Hyland, K. (1998) *Hedging in scientific research articles.* Amsterdam: John Benjamins.

Hyland, K. (2008) 'As can be seen: Lexical bundles and disciplinary variation', *English for Specific Purposes,* 27/1: 4–21.

Jackson, H. (2007) *Key terms in linguistics.* London: Continuum.

Johns, T. (1991a) 'Should you be persuaded: Two examples of data driven learning', in T. Johns and P. King (eds), *Classroom concordancing, ELR Journal.* University of Birmingham, pp. 1–16.

Johns, T. (1991b) 'Contexts: The background, development and trialling of a concordance-based CALL program', in A. Wichmann, S. Fligelstone, T. McEnery and G. Knowles (eds), *Teaching and language corpora.* Harlow: Addison Wesley Longman, pp. 100–15.

Johns, T. (2002) 'Data-driven learning: The perpetual challenge', in B. Kettemann and G. Marko (eds), *Teaching and learning by doing corpus analysis.* Amsterdam: Rodopi, pp. 107–17.

Kennedy, G. (1991) 'Between and through: The company they keep and the functions they serve', in K. Aijmer and B. Altenberg (eds), *English corpus linguistics: Studies in honour of Jan Svartvik.* London: Longman, pp. 95–110.

Kilgarriff, A. and Grefenstette, G. (2003) 'Web as corpus: Introduction' *Special Issue. Computational Linguistics,* 29/3: 333–47.

Knight, D., Evans, D., Carter, R. and Adolphs, S. (2009) 'HeadTalk, HandTalk and the corpus: Towards a framework for multi-modal, multi-media corpus development', *Corpora*, 4/1: 1–32.

Knight, D., Tennent, P., Adolphs, S. and Carter, R. (2010) 'Developing heterogeneous corpora using the Digital Replay System (DRS)', *Proceedings of the LREC 2010 (Language Resources Evaluation Conference) Workshop on Multimodal Corpora: Advances in capturing, coding and analyzing multimodality*, May 2010, Giessen, Germany, pp. 16–21.

Koester, A. (2010) 'Building small specialized corpora', in A. O'Keeffe and M. McCarthy (eds), *The Routledge handbook of corpus linguistics*. Abingdon: Routledge, pp. 66–79.

Lam, P. (2009) 'Discourse particles in corpus data and textbooks: The case of well', *Applied Linguistics*, 31/2: 260–81.

Lee, D.Y.W. (2010) 'What corpora are available?' in A. O'Keeffe and M. McCarthy (eds), *The Routledge handbook of corpus linguistics*. Abingdon: Routledge, pp. 107–21.

Leech, G. (2005) 'Politeness: Is there an East–West divide?' *Journal of Foreign Languages, Shanghai*, 6: 3–31.

Leech, G. (2007) 'The changing of linguistic change: Insights from standard corpora over a period of 60 years', *ICAME 28*, 23–27 May 2007, Stratford-upon-Avon, UK.

Leech, G. and Eyes, E. (1997) 'Syntactic annotation: Treebanks', in R. Garside, G. Leech and A. McEnery (eds), *Corpus annotation: Linguistic information from computer text corpora*. London: Longman, pp. 34–52.

Leech, G. and Weisser, M. (2003) 'Pragmatics and dialogue', in R. Mitkov (ed.), *The Oxford handbook of computational linguistics*. Oxford: Oxford University Press, pp. 136–56.

Leech, G., Rayson, P. and Wilson, A. (2001) *Word frequencies in written and spoken English: Based on the British National Corpus*. London: Longman.

Leech, G., Hundt, M., Mair, C. and Smith, N. (2009) *Change in contemporary English: A grammatical study*. Cambridge: Cambridge University Press.

Li, L. and MacGregor, L. (2009) 'Colour metaphors in business discourse', in V.K. Bhatia, W. Cheng, B. Du-Babcock and J. Lung (eds), *Language for professional communication: Research, practice and training*. Hong Kong: City University of Hong Kong and The Hong Kong Polytechnic University, pp. 11–24, www.engl.polyu.edu.hk/rcpce/documents/Language ForProfessionalCommunication.pdf.

Li, L. and Zhong, X. (2008) 'Food and Cooking Metaphors in Business Discourse: A Contrastive Study'. Paper presented at Partnerships in Action: Research, Practice and Training, Inaugural Conference of the Asia Pacific-Rim LSP & Professional Communication Association, 8–10 December 2008, City University of Hong Kong and The Hong Kong Polytechnic University.

Li, Y.Y. and Warren, M. (2008) '"in … of": What are collocational frameworks and should we be teaching them?' Paper presented at the Fourth International Conference on Teaching English at Tertiary Level, Department of Foreign Languages Tsinghua University, Beijing, China and Department of English, The Hong Kong Polytechnic University, 11–12 October 2008, Hong Kong.

Louw, B. (1993) 'Irony in the text or insincerity in the writer? The diagnostic potential of semantic prosodies', in M. Baker, G. Francis and E. Tognini-Bonelli (eds), *Text and technology*. Amsterdam: Benjamins, pp. 157–76.

McCarthy, M. (1998a) *Spoken language and applied linguistics*. Cambridge: Cambridge University Press.

McCarthy, M. (2003) 'Talking back: "Small" interactional response tokens in everyday conversation', in J. Coupland (ed.), *Research on language in social interaction. Special issue on small talk*, 36/1: 33–63.

McEnery, T. and Wilson, A. (2001) *Corpus linguistics: An introduction*. Edinburgh: Edinburgh University Press.

McEnery, T., Xiao, R. and Tono, Y. (2006) *Corpus-based language studies: An advanced resource book*. London: Routledge.

Mollin, S. (2009) '"I entirely understand" is a Blairism. The methodology of identifying idiolectal collocations', *International Journal of Corpus Linguistics*, 14/3: 367–92.

Moon, R. (1998) *Fixed expressions and idioms in English*. Oxford: Clarendon Press.

Moon, R. (2010) 'What can a corpus tell us about lexis?' in A. O'Keeffe and M. McCarthy (eds), *The Routledge handbook of corpus linguistics*, Abingdon: Routledge, pp. 197–211.

Mukherjee, J. (2009) 'The lexicogrammar of present-day Indian English: Corpus-based perspectives on structural nativisation', in U. Römer and R. Schulze (eds), *Exploring the lexis-grammar interface*. Amsterdam: John Benjamins, pp. 117–35.

Oakes, M.P. (1998) 'Statistics for corpus linguistics', *International Journal of Applied Linguistics*, 10/2: 269–74.

O'Donnell, M.B., Scott, M. and Mahlberg, M. (2008) 'Exploring text-initial concgrams in a newspaper corpus'. Paper presented at the 7th International Conference of the American Association of Corpus Linguistics, Brigham Young University, Provo, Utah, USA, 12–15 March 2008.

O'Keeffe, A., McCarthy, M. (eds) (2010) *The Routledge handbook of corpus linguistics*. London/New York: Routledge.

O'Keeffe, A., McCarthy, M. and Carter, R.A. (2007) *From corpus to classroom*. Cambridge: Cambridge University Press.

Ooi, V.B.Y. (2008) Lexis of electronic gaming on the Web: A Sinclairian approach, *International Journal of Lexicography*, 21/3, 311–23.

Petrovic, S., Osborne, M. and Lavrenko, V. (2010) 'Streaming first story detection with application to Twitter', *Human Language Technologies: The 2010 Annual Conference of the North American Chapter of the ACL (NAACL)*, pp. 181–9.

Philip, G. (2008) 'Reassessing the canon: 'fixed phrases' in general reference corpora', in S. Granger and F. Meunier (eds), *Phraseology: An inter-disciplinary perspective*. Amsterdam: John Benjamins, pp. 95–108.

Phillips, M. (1989) *Lexical structure of text [discourse analysis monographs 12]*. Birmingham: English Language Research, University of Birmingham.

Quaglio, P. (2009) *Television dialogue: The sitcom Friends vs. natural conversation*. Amsterdam: John Benjamins.

Quirk, R., Greenbaum, S., Leech, G. and Svartvik, J. (1985) *A comprehensive grammar of the English language*. London/New York: Longman.

Rayson, P. (2008). 'From key words to key semantic domains'. *International Journal of Corpus Linguistics*, 13/4: 519–49.

Rayson, P. (2009) 'Wmatrix: A web-based corpus processing environment', Computing Department, Lancaster University. http://ucrel.lancs.ac.uk/wmatrix/.

Reinhard, F. and Swales, J. (2003) 'Among or between?' MICASE Kibbitzer 2, 21 July 2003, http://micase.elicorpora.info/files/0000/0045/Kibbitzer_2-Among_or_Between.pdf.

Renouf, A. and Banerjee, J. (2007) 'Lexical repulsion between sense-related pairs', *International Journal of Corpus Linguistics*, 12/3: 415–44.

Renouf, A. and Sinclair, J. McH. (1991) 'Collocational frameworks in English', in K. Ajimer and B. Altenberg (eds), *English corpus linguistics. Studies in honour of Jan Svartvik*. Harlow: Longman, pp. 128–43.

Rühlemann, C. (2010) 'What can a corpus tell us about pragmatics?' in A. O'Keeffe and M. McCarthy (eds), *The Routledge handbook of corpus linguistics*. London/New York: Routledge, pp. 288–301.

Sacks, H. (1984) 'Notes on methodology', in J.M. Atkinson, and J. Heritage (eds), *Structures of social action: Studies in conversation analysis*. Cambridge: Cambridge University Press, pp. 2–27.

Sacks, H., Schegloff, E. and Jefferson, G. (1974) 'A simplest systematics for the organization of turn-taking for conversation', *Language*, 50: 696–735.

Schofield, N., Green, C. and Creed, F. (2008) 'Communication skills of health-care professionals working in oncology – can they be improved?' *European Journal of Oncology Nursing*, 12: 4–13.

Scott, M. (2004) *Oxford Wordsmith Tools version 4*. Oxford: Oxford University Press.

Scott, M. (2008) *WordSmith Tools version 5*. Liverpool: Lexical Analysis Software.

Scott, M. and Tribble, C. (2006) *Textual patterns: Key words and corpus analysis in language education*. Amsterdam: John Benjamins.

Sebba, M. (1997) *Contact languages: Pidgins and creoles*. London: Palgrave Macmillan.

Sinclair, J. McH. (1987) 'Collocation: A progress report', in R. Steele and T. Threadgold (eds), *Language topics: Essays in honour of Michael Halliday, II*, Amsterdam: John Benjamins, pp. 319–31. Reprinted in J. McH. Sinclair (1991) *Corpus, concordance, collocation*. Oxford: Oxford University Press, pp. 109–21.

Sinclair, J. McH. (1991) *Corpus, concordance, collocation*. Oxford: Oxford University Press.

Sinclair, J. McH. (1994) *Trust the text: Language, corpus and discourse*. London: Routledge.

Sinclair, J. McH. (1996) 'The search for units of meaning', *Textus*, 9/1: 75–106.

Sinclair, J. McH. (1998) 'The lexical item', in E. Weigand (ed.), *Contrastive lexical semantics*. Amsterdam: John Benjamins, pp. 1–24.

Sinclair, J. McH. (2001) 'Preface', in M. Ghadessy, A. Henry and R.L. Roseberry (eds), *Small corpus studies and ELT*. Amsterdam: John Benjamins, pp. vii–xv.

Sinclair, J. McH. (2003) *Reading concordances*. London: Longman.

Sinclair, J. McH. (2004) 'Introduction', in J.M. Sinclair (ed.), *How to use corpora in language teaching*, Amsterdam/Philadelphia, PA: John Benjamins, pp. 1–13.

Sinclair, J. McH. (2005a) 'Corpus and text: Basic principles', in M. Wynne (ed.), *Developing linguistic corpora: A guide to good practice*. Oxford: Oxbow Books, pp. 1–16, http://ahds.ac.uk/linguistic-corpora/.

Sinclair, J. McH. (2005b) 'Appendix to Chapter One: How to make a corpus. Basic principles', in M. Wynne (ed.), *Developing linguistic corpora: A guide to good practice*. Oxford: Arts and Humanities Data Service, pp. 98–103.

Sinclair, J. McH. (2007a) 'Data-derived multilingual lexicons', in T. Wolfgang (ed.), *Text corpora and multilingual lexicography*. Amsterdam: John Benjamins, pp. 69–81.

Sinclair, J. McH. (2007b) 'Defining the definiendom' – new (manuscript), Tuscan Word Centre, Italy.

Sinclair, J. McH. (2008) 'The phrase, the whole phrase and nothing but the phrase', in S. Granger and and F. Meunier (eds), *Phraseology*. Amsterdam: John Benjamins, pp. 407–10.

Sinclair, J. McH. and Mauranen, A. (2006) *Linear unit grammar: Integrating speech and writing*. Amsterdam: John Benjamins.

Sinclair, J. McH. and Renouf, A. (1988) 'A lexical syllabus for language learning', in R. Carter and M. McCarthy (eds), *Vocabulary and language teaching*. Harlow: Longman, pp. 140–58.

Sinclair, J. McH., Jones, S. and Daley, R. (1970) *English lexical studies*. Report to the Office of Scientific and Technical Information, UK.

Sinclair, J. McH., Jones, S. and Daley, R. (2004) *English collocation studies: The OSTI Report*. London/New York: Continuum.

Stenström, A-B. (1994). *An introduction to spoken interaction*. London: Longman.

Stiles, W.B. (1992) *Describing talk: A taxonomy of verbal response modes*. Newbury Park, CA: Sage.

Stolcke, A., Ries, K., Coccaro, N., Shriberg, E., Bates, R., Jurafsky, D., Taylor, P., Martin, R., Ess-Dykema, C. Van and Meteer, M. (2000) 'Dialogue act modeling for automatic tagging and recognition of conversational speech', *Computational Linguistics*, 26/3: 339–73.

Stubbs, M. (1995) 'Collocations and semantic profiles: On the cause of the trouble with quantitative studies', *Functions of Language*, 2/1: 23–55.

Stubbs, M. (1996) *Text and corpus analysis: Computer-assisted studies of language and culture*. Cambridge, MA: Blackwell.

Stubbs, M. (2002) *Words and phrases: Corpus studies of lexical semantics*. Oxford: Blackwell.

Svartvik, J. (ed.) (1990) *The London Corpus of Spoken English: Description and research*. Lund Studies in English 82. Lund: Lund University Press.

Swales, J. (2001) 'Metatalk in American academic talk: The cases of "point" and "thing"', *Journal of English Linguistics*, 29: 34–54.

Swales, J. (2004) *Research genres: Exploration and applications*. Cambridge: Cambridge University Press.

Teubert, W. and Krishnamurthy, R. (2007) 'General introduction', in W. Teubert and R. Krishnamurthy (eds), *Corpus linguistics: Critical concepts in linguistics*. London/New York: Routledge, pp. 1–37.

Thomas, J. (1995) *Meaning in interaction: An introduction to pragmatics*. London/New York: Longman.

Thomson, A.J. and Martinet, A.V. (1984) *A practical English grammar*. Oxford: Oxford University Press.

Thornbury, S. (2010) 'What can a corpus tell us about discourse?' in A. O'Keeffe and M. McCarthy (eds), *The Routledge handbook of corpus linguistics*. London: Routledge, pp. 270–87.

Tognini-Bonelli, E. (2001) *Corpus linguistics at work*. Amsterdam/Philadelphia, PA: John Benjamins.

Tribble, C. (2000) 'Genres, keywords, teaching: Towards a pedagogic account of the language of project proposals', in L. Burnard and T. McEnery (eds), *Rethinking language pedagogy from a corpus*. Frankfurt: Peter Lang, pp. 75–90.

Tribble, C. and Jones, G. (1990) *Concordances in the classroom: A resource book for teachers*. London: Longman.

Trudgill, P. (1996) 'Series editor's preface', in M. Stubbs, *Text and corpus analysis: Computer-assisted studies of language and culture*. Oxford/Cambridge, MA: Blackwell, p. xi.

van Dijk, T. (2007) 'Comments on context and conversation', in N. Fairclough, G. Cortese and P. Ardizzone (eds), *Discourse and contemporary social change*. Bern: Lang, pp. 281–316.

Warren, M. (2009) 'The phraseology of intertextuality in English for professional communication', *Language Value*, 1/1: 1–16.

Warren, M. (2010) 'Online corpora for specific purposes', *ICAME Journal*, 34: 170–88.

Warren, M. (2011) 'Realisations of intertextuality, interdiscursivity and hybridisation in the discourses of professionals', in G. Garzone and M. Gotti (eds), *Discourse, communication and the enterprise genres and trends*. Frankfurt: Peter Lang, pp. 91–110.

Wilson, A. and Thomas, J. (1997) 'Semantic annotation', in R. Garside, G. Leech and G. McEnery (eds), *Corpus annotation. Linguistic information from computer text corpora*. London/New York: Longman, pp. 53–65.

Wodak, R. (2008) 'The glocalization of politics in television: Fiction or reality?' *European Journal of Cultural Studies*, 13/1: 43–62.

Zipf, G.K. (1935) *The psycho-biology of language*. Boston, MA: Houghton Mifflin.

Index

Words and phrases used as examples or in exercises are given in italics. Text within Tasks is indexed where useful and/or where a corpus web address is given.